T0377179

Participatory Archaeology and Heritage Studies

Participatory Archaeology and Heritage Studies: Perspectives from Africa provides new ways to look at and think about the practice of community archaeology and heritage studies across the globe. Long hidden from view, African experiences and experiments with participatory archaeology and heritage studies have poignant lessons to convey about local initiatives, local needs, and local perspectives among communities as diverse as an Islamic community on the edge of an ancient city in Sudan to multiethnic rural villages near rock art sites in South Africa. Straddling both heritage studies and archaeological practice, this volume incorporates a range of settings, from practical experiments with sustainable pottery kilns in Kenya, to an elite palace and its hidden traditional heritage in Northwestern Tanzania, to ancestral knowledge about heritage landscapes in rural Ethiopia. The genesis of participatory practices in Africa are traced back to the 1950s, with examples of how this legacy has played out over six decades—setting the scene for a deeply rooted practice now gaining widespread acceptance.

The chapters in this book were originally published in the *Journal of Community Archaeology and Heritage.*

Peter R. Schmidt has studied and conducted archaeological, ethnographic, and heritage research in Africa for more than five decades. He is the author of twelve books about African archaeology, technology, history, and heritage as well as numerous journal articles and book chapters.

Participatory Archaeology and Heritage Studies

Perspectives from Africa

Edited by
Peter R. Schmidt

Routledge
Taylor & Francis Group

LONDON AND NEW YORK

First published 2018
by Routledge
2 Park Square, Milton Park, Abingdon, Oxon, OX14 4RN, UK

and by Routledge
711 Third Avenue, New York, NY 10017, USA

Routledge is an imprint of the Taylor & Francis Group, an informa business

British Library Cataloguing-in-Publication Data
A catalogue record for this book is available from the British Library

ISBN13: 978-1-138-49663-7

Typeset in Myriad Pro
by codeMantra

Publisher's Note
The publisher accepts responsibility for any inconsistencies that may have arisen
during the conversion of this book from journal articles to book chapters, namely
the possible inclusion of journal terminology.

Disclaimer
Every effort has been made to contact copyright holders for their permission to
reprint material in this book. The publishers would be grateful to hear from any
copyright holder who is not here acknowledged and will undertake to rectify any
errors or omissions in future editions of this book.

Contents

CONTENTS

Citation Information

The chapters in this book were originally published in various special issues of *Journal of Community Archaeology & Heritage*. When citing this material, please use the original page numbering for each article, as follows:

Chapter 1

Rediscovering Community Archaeology in Africa and Reframing its Practice
Peter R. Schmidt
Journal of Community Archaeology & Heritage, volume 1, issue 1 (2014) pp. 37–55

Chapter 2

Archaeology and the local community in Africa: A retrospective
Merrick Posnansky
Journal of Community Archaeology & Heritage, volume 4, issue 2 (2017) pp. 77–84

Chapter 3

Seniority through ancestral landscapes: Community archaeology in the highlands of southern Ethiopia
Kathryn Weedman Arthur, Yohannes Ethiopia Tocha, Matthew C. Curtis, Bizuayehu Lakew and John W. Arthur
Journal of Community Archaeology & Heritage, volume 4, issue 2 (2017) pp. 101–114

Chapter 4

Community archaeology and heritage in coastal and Western Kenya
Chapurukha M. Kusimba
Journal of Community Archaeology & Heritage, volume 4, issue 3 (2017) pp. 218–228

Chapter 5

Contests between heritage and history in Tanganyika/Tanzania: Insights arising from community-based heritage research
Peter R. Schmidt
Journal of Community Archaeology & Heritage, volume 4, issue 2 (2017) pp. 85–100

Chapter 6

Chapter 7

Chapter 8

For any permission-related enquiries please visit:
http://www.tandfonline.com/page/help/permissions

Notes on Contributors

John W. Arthur is an Associate Professor of Anthropology at the University of South Florida, St. Petersburg, USA. He has been working in Ethiopia since 1995 focusing on issues related to ceramic ethno-archaeology, caste, and development of food production.

Kathryn Weedman Arthur is an Associate Professor of Anthropology at the University of South Florida, St. Petersburg, USA. She has been working with Gamo communities in Ethiopia over the last 20 years focusing on issues related to women, craft specialists, and heritage.

Rebecca Bradshaw submitted her PhD at the School of Oriental and African Studies, University of London, UK, in which she examines the political and economic impact of archaeology in Sudan. She is currently working as community engagement officer for UCL Qatar in Sudan.

Matthew C. Curtis is an Anthropologist specializing in the Holocene Archaeology of Eastern Africa, with a particular focus on the Archaeology of complex societies in Ethiopia and Eritrea. He is the founder of Eastern African Archaeology Online, a cultural heritage information and advocacy website, and teaches Anthropology and African studies for UCLA Extension, Ventura College, College of the Canyons, and the Osher Lifelong Learning Institute at California State University, Channel Islands, Camarillo, USA.

Jane Humphris is Head of UCL Qatar Research in Sudan. She holds a PhD in African Archaeometallurgy and an MA in African Archaeology from UCL, London, UK and a BA in Ancient History and Archaeology from the University of Manchester, UK. Jane's research in Sudan focuses mainly on ancient iron production associated with the Kingdom of Kush. Alongside the research, she runs a community engagement and capacity building program, which involves meetings, interviews, and lectures, as well as training Sudanese students.

Susan Osireditse Keitumetse works for the University of Botswana's Okavango Research Institute in Maun, Botswana, as a research scholar in cultural heritage tourism.

Chapurukha M. Kusimba is a Professor of Anthropology in the Department of Anthropology at American University, Washington DC, USA. His research focuses on the roles of economy and technology in transforming culture and ecology.

Bizuayehu Lakew earned an MA in Anthropology from Addis Ababa University, Ethiopia, and has committed decades of service with the Southern Nations, Nationality, and Peoples Region Bureau of Culture and Information in Awassa, Ethiopia.

Nthabiseng Mokoena is a PhD Candidate with the University of Cape Town, South Africa. She currently serves on the council of the Association of Southern African Professional Archaeologists (ASAPA) as the SADC Officer. She is also serving on the Southern African Archaeological Student Council. Her research interests include heritage and rock art management, community archaeology, and the past and present meaning of heritage sites in Africa.

Michelle Genevieve Pampiri is an Early Childhood Teacher at Raising Education Within Africa.

Merrick Posnansky is the Doyen of African archaeology. He started his career in African archaeology during the mid-1950s in Kenya and Uganda. He has influenced several generations of researchers while teaching at Makerere University in Uganda, the University of Ghana, Legon, and UCLA.

Peter R. Schmidt has studied and conducted archaeological, ethnographic, and heritage research in Africa for more than five decades. He is the author of twelve books about African archaeology, technology, history, and heritage as well as numerous journal articles and book chapters. He is Professor of Anthropology at the University of Florida, USA, and Extraordinary Professor of Anthropology and Archaeology at the University of Pretoria, South Africa.

Yohannes Ethiopia Tocha earned a BA in Sociology and Anthropology from Arba Minch University, Ethiopia, and is currently working for CVM-Ethiopia Italian Development/ Volunteering Organization.

Preface

Participatory Archaeology and Heritage Studies: Perspectives from Africa

Carol McDavid and Suzie Thomas

The papers for this edited volume were originally published in the *Journal of Community Archaeology & Heritage* (JCAH) across several issues. Most of the chapters were originally part of a special series, 'African Perspectives on Community Engagements', which appeared in Volume 4, Issues 2 and 3 and was guest edited by this volume's editor, Peter R. Schmidt. The goal of the special series was to shine a light on the richness and diversity of community archaeology and heritage approaches across sub-Saharan Africa. In addition to the papers from the special series, there are two additional pieces with a similar goal—an article by Susan Keitumetse and Michelle Pampiri (from Volume 3, Issue 2) and an overview article by Peter Schmidt (from Volume 1, Issue 1). Together, this collection forms an important contribution to broader discussions about the practice, history, and impact of community archaeology and heritage as they are emerging from the continent of Africa (see Schmidt and Pikirayi 2016).

It is clear from this volume that community-based and community-focused approaches in Africa are not necessarily new—some, for example, are rooted in modes of practice heretofore classified as 'archaeological ethnography' or simply 'ethnography'. Here, however, community practice is situated more critically, especially with respect to the explicit rejection of colonialist mindsets and practices. These chapters come from a diverse group of scholars in terms of experience and nationality as well as geographic and temporal focus. All illustrate themes that often emerge in JCAH: that 'community' is a slippery term, that context-dependent approaches are essential, and that intersectionality is essential to understanding how archaeologists and communities can both identify and work toward common goals.

These chapters also demonstrate our journal's aim to relate contemporary academic ethics to academic writing. We believe that academic writing, particularly when it concerns the complex relationships between professionals and 'the public', should be not only understandable but also useful to both. By 'the public', we refer to those who emerge in professional writing as amateurs, avocationals, collaborators, 'co-creators' (Bollwerk and Connolly 2015; Simon 2010), community members, 'ethical clients' (Mack and Blakey 2004), and volunteers. JCAH wants to open academic conversations about community heritage and archaeology to these people and groups, and we see this mandate as part of a larger ethical aim to find new ways to decolonize academic discourse (McDavid and Thomas 2018).

Finally, we want to recognize the Taylor & Francis Special Issues as Books (SPIBs) program, which enables peer-reviewed journal content to reach larger audiences than it would otherwise. Therefore, we thank our colleagues at Taylor & Francis, the contributing authors, and especially Peter Schmidt for bringing this volume together so well. We hope it will be the first of many such volumes deriving from research first presented within the pages of the *Journal of Community Archaeology & Heritage*.

References

Bollwerk, Elizabeth, and Robert Connolly. 2015. "Special Issue on Co-Creation: Co-Creation and Public Archaeology." *Advances in Archaeological Practice* 3 (3):178–187.

Mack, Mark E., and Michael L. Blakey. 2004. "The New York African Burial Ground Project: Past Biases, Current Dilemmas, and Future Research Opportunities." *Historical Archaeology* 38 (1):10–17.

McDavid, Carol and Suzie Thomas. 2018. "Editorial." *Journal of Community Archaeology and Heritage* 5 (1):1–3.

McGimsey, Charles. 1972. *Public Archaeology*. London: Seminar Press.

Schmidt, Peter R., and Innocent Pikirayi, eds. 2016. *Community Archaeology and Heritage in Africa: Decolonizing Practice*. New York, NY: Routledge.

Simon, Nina. 2010. *The Participatory Museum*. Santa Cruz: Museum 2.0.

Smith, Laurajane. 2006. *The Uses of Heritage*. Oxford: Routledge.

Introduction: Intersectionality at work in participatory approaches in African archaeology and heritage studies

Peter R. Schmidt

This book purposely addresses participatory methods in archaeological and heritage research and management. Participation as used here focuses on community initiatives to study local archaeological problems and heritage management issues as well as professional assessments of the readiness of various communities to engage with archaeological inquiries and heritage studies in a manner that constitutes genuine involvement in developing and executing research and management plans. It is instructive that only one significant book on community approaches specifically elevates participatory approaches—Sonya Atalay's (2012) *Community-Based Archaeology: Research with, by, and for Indigenous and Local Communities*. Atalay draws inspiration from public health's long legacy of community participation to articulate principles appropriate for the practice of archaeology. She implicitly sets off participatory approaches from many other treatments in community archaeology that fall under the public archaeology rubric, a very broad grouping that includes outreach programs, inclusion of pupils/students/ community members in excavations, and programs that disseminate research results from such efforts to a broad public—not just academic audiences. Public archaeology in all its guises has been an important thrust in archaeological practice for some decades now, but rarely does it address long-term community needs as well as the thorough incorporation of community participants in deciding what kinds of inquiries have relevance to the historical and heritage needs of local community members, regardless of their makeup (e.g., a religious community, a community of interest, a neighborhood, a kinship network, etc.).

Short-term research projects that incorporate community members on research teams belong to a different genre, as they often lack deep engagement with formulating research designs and full inclusion in all decision-making. Common to these forms of public participation are oversight and governance of excavations and heritage mapping and other heritage studies by professionals, an exercise of power by those with advanced training. In most such cases, the initiative to include non-professionals in excavations or heritage studies may be motivated by diverse motives—a desire for free labor, compelling social and economic needs to include local people, and the need for public appreciation of the research being conducted. These are bona fide concerns but not participatory in the most central of considerations—power sharing, the acceptance of mutuality, and the needs of community members in meeting their long-term goals.

Long-term goals are perhaps best met when there is a synthesis of local knowledge with knowledge held by professional archaeologists and heritage managers—a condition that arises out of the intersection of values from diverse partners. To arrive at a synthesis requires patient listening, a readiness to change and accommodate, and a willingness to arrive at the best pragmatic solutions.

Ndoro and Chirikure (2018) argue in *Managing Heritage in Africa, Who Cares?* that the challenge before the study and management of heritage in Africa is the adoption of an adaptive approach that incorporates both best Western and best indigenous practices. I prefer to conceptualize this process as synthesis—a combination of elements to form a whole—rather than "adaptive", which carries considerable evolutionary baggage. When intersectionality—the intertwining and interlocking of elements— leads to synthesis, then a pragmatic pathway is mapped for the future (see Mrozowski 2013). Such results are precisely what is presented recently in a collection of essays (Schmidt and Pikirayi 2016) that illustrate how intersectionality (Crenshaw 1995) occurs in different African settings.[1] Yet, attempts in community archaeology and heritage to incorporate indigenous practices and values—long marginalized and erased by colonial archaeology and historical preservation philosophies—often elicit characterizations as unscientific (Pikirayi and Schmidt 2016; Ndlovu 2016), or they are overlooked because they sometimes engage elite settings with exclusionary ritual practices (Chirikure, Ndoro, and Deacon 2018). Even with such caveats in mind, and with recognition that indigenous management practices may be efficacious, best local practices will remain obscured until such time that archaeologists and heritage researchers open themselves to genuine local participation. Intersectionality is seen at work in Innocent Pikirayi's (2016) interactions with Zimbabwe farmers, revealing how education can impede success in archaeological inquiry. Coming to understand that farmers held invaluable knowledge of soils and landscape intersected with Pikirayi's conventional surveys to lead him to important site discoveries as well an appreciation for indigenous landscape knowledge.

Intersectionality is also vividly illustrated in Patrick Abungu's (2016) analyses of the Shimoni slave site on the Kenya coast. Confronted with local narratives held by a stigmatized ethnic group that denies the site was used to house enslaved people, Abungu and his collaborators worked under the concept of multi-vocality in archaeological thinking to accommodate alternative narratives during site tours—intersectionality in action.

While we may recognize the value of best indigenous practices within their local contexts (see Jopela 2018 and Asombang 2018), such principles are context-specific and often limited by elite and restricted institutions responsible for conservation. In the case of Bafut, Cameroon (Asombang 2018), conservation efforts are overseen by the *Fon* (King) who is now limited in his capacity to marshal resources in the postcolonial period. Without direct engagement—day to day searches for solutions to preservation and development problems (Schmidt 2017a)—professionals will be unable to understand critical gender, ethnic (group identity), and class influences that influence which indigenous principles might be used to effect a more viable approach to heritage study and preservation—the step that requires long-term engagement and learning, followed by practice. Only under these conditions of engagement can best local practices be expressed, recognized as meaningful, and incorporated into research and management programs.

Ndoro and Chirikure (2018: 209) observe: "There is a need to develop a culture of research in conservation in Africa by Africans and not to always rely on solutions and guidelines from outside which may not take the context into consideration." I imagine that they are not advocating the diminishment of outside researchers devoted to finding and developing avenues of intersectionality but support initiatives that bring together best practices from Africa and the West offer hope for pragmatic approaches sensitive to the diversity of the quickly changing cultures of Africa today. Indeed, we cannot arrive at such conditions if criteria and guidelines are imposed from the outside by individual researchers or international institutions, no matter how well meaning.

This book takes that pragmatic step, addressing this challenge by illustrating how such engagements lead to intersectionality. All the examples are drawn from Africa and reflect degrees of engagement that are sensitive to indigenous ways of seeing and believing. Outsiders in such settings bring valuable intersectionality, drawing on diverse backgrounds and a broad range of theoretical standards. Such richness in perspective that engaged outside researchers bring must not be lost under a prescription that external guidelines be avoided.

To make the jump from recognized best indigenous practices to daily practice in archaeological inquiry and heritage management there needs to be readiness to engage with and learn from communities who still value and implement heritage preservation and utilization. This cannot be done by concocting research agendas in the academy, museum, or government institution and then implementing them amongst communities without understanding how local groups define and value their heritage as well as what they consider to be necessary and legitimate research into their pasts. These top-down approaches run the risk of reifying colonial practices and alienating communities from their heritage—a long legacy on the continent now experiencing decolonization through a number of indigenous/professional initiatives (Pikirayi and Schmidt 2016). Even when archaeologists and heritage managers attempt to engage local sensibilities, they may be constrained by requirements imposed by outside funding agencies or academic notions of how to do it correctly, using checklists. For example, the prescriptions proffered by Moser et al. (2002) about inclusion of local communities in research are in fact a top-down set of criteria arising from a project that was academy-centered from its inception. Its genesis illustrates the flaw of other such prescriptions, failing to start with questions that count for the community, and not accounting for participation in problem formulation and local needs in the first instance.

If local initiative and local goals are not incorporated from the inception of engagement, then 'participation' is often consigned a back seat: consultation about a preformed research agenda, consultation with token participation by some key community members to make it appear inclusive, and participation without consideration for capacity building. The issue of capacity building is central to building a synthetic practice. It is a two-way avenue that includes the technical and theoretical training of local participants and the education of professional heritage managers and archaeologists in the viability of local preservation and utilitarian principles. It is not enough to hire laborers, use local research assistants, and contribute to community well-being by economic infusions. These do not add up to participatory approaches. They are closer to what we may recognize as patronage, not true mutuality. If we accept the principle that local participants have the capacity to learn archaeological practices as well as any university student, then we have taken a significant step toward equalizing power and realizing a practice that is relevant to contemporary and future community needs.

The chapters in this book take on this fundamental issue: how do we translate the principles of best indigenous definitions of heritage and heritage management practices into our practice as archaeologists and heritage managers conscious of meeting the future needs of African cultures? There is no definitive answer, as Ndoro and Chirikure (2018) observe. Rather, it is experimental, trying to set aside our normal authoritarian practices as PI, Professor, Director, Curator, or whatever other role we are accustomed to playing, and take the back seat—practicing 'archaeologies of listening' and learning from the knowledge held by local communities (Kehoe and Schmidt 2017). This entails the practice of epistemic humility—the shedding of power and authority and their replacement with a receptivity to new ways of learning, different ontologies, and efficacious local means of preservation and vitalization of the past (Schmidt and Kehoe forthcoming). In Africa this started, ironically, with several colonial archaeologists—Merrick Posnansky and Thurston Shaw, both of whom were sensitive to the needs of local communities and went to lengths to privilege local knowledge (Schmidt 2014, this volume).

Part I: Legacies of Long-Term Community Engagement

The chapters in Part I of this book are a natural outcome of the influence of Professor Merrick Posnansky on African archaeology and heritage. Peter Schmidt's chapter (2014, this volume) digs into the deeper history of participatory approaches in African archaeology and heritage studies. We learn that Thurston Shaw's (1970) excavations at Igbo-Ukwu in Nigeria employed visionary inclusion of community members as participating investigators/owners. Shaw accompanied his inclusionary practice with a pragmatic view that the results of the Igbo-Ukwu findings should be shared with a wide Nigerian public—marking one of the first attempts to practice a public archaeology with dissemination of results in accessible language. On the eastern side of the continent, Posnansky was prescient in his belief that local narratives were critical for understanding the context of heritage sites in Uganda. Posnansky's chapter (2017, this volume) captures the verve and commitment he brought to the inclusion of local African residents in the museum programs that he supervised as well as research that he initiated in rural areas of Uganda and later in Ghana. His integration of oral traditions into archaeological narratives marked a new departure for African archaeology. It privileged local views of history while also examining material and archival evidence. Posnansky went on to inspire Schmidt and his peer group to be mindful of what indigenous voices could add to the fabric of history. As a university teacher with similar disposition, Schmidt shared such views with students, among them Kathy Weedman Arthur, John Arthur, and Matthew Curtis—coauthors with Ethiopian counterparts of the chapter focused on Ethiopia (2017, this volume). Thus, three intellectual generations of community archaeology are represented here, a legacy that speaks to the long-term engagement that Africanists have had with African communities.

Posnansky also shares his background in English archaeology and extramural engagements with local people, a perspective that he took with him to Uganda with brilliant results that challenged conventional practices some 60 years ago. It was Schmidt's good fortune to study with him at Makerere University in Kampala, Uganda in the mid-1960s, visiting many sites that had rich oral traditions associated with them. His methods were very much ethnographic, digging into local beliefs and practices to gain more diverse and powerful insights into the African past. Given his influence on others' practice as well as teaching, it is a natural outcome that long-term ethnographic inquiry—with guidance from local participants—is a perspective taken in research among the Haya in far Northwest Tanzania as well as those in this volume who examine sacred space and belief systems among the Gamo of Ethiopia.

The richness of these studies arises from the knowledge systems of those among whom we work and study, for we become students of local history. By becoming participants in local culture, we can hope to gain an appreciation of what heritage means to local people. We rub shoulders with them as they live their heritage in sacred places and daily activities, listening to their discourse about what they mean by heritage, coming to an awareness of points of intersectionality. Part of Schmidt's two chapters (2014, this volume; 2017a, this volume) bring intersectionality to the fore with a discussion of one of the earliest community initiatives in archaeological inquiry (also see Schmidt 2017c), when elders guided him to the Kaiija shrine tree in Katuruka village and insisted that he excavate at the place where iron smiths were said to have forged iron for a legendary iron tower. This locally directed inquiry led to the discovery of iron working of great antiquity—resulting in a coalescence of local knowledge and archaeological inquiry, an intersectionality leading to a better pathway by which indigenous knowledge was linked to archaeological inquiry. The longer-term upshot of this engagement was the adoption of the archaeological findings into heritage discourse, with community members representing the antiquity of their village by calling it the "Olduvai of the Iron Age"—underwriting pride in local heritage.

Part II: Applications

The second part of this book illustrates how the practice of participatory community approaches leads to insights that go beyond drawing on indigenous knowledge to benefit communities. By listening to and learning from local discourse, it is possible to find points of intersectionality that translate to better heritage preservation and conservation as well as economic advantages. The chapter by Kathryn Weedman Arthur et al. (2017, this volume) illustrates vividly how trust is built over the long term between outside scholars and local heritage keepers. Working for 20 years among the Boreda, a Gamo group in Ethiopia, Arthur patiently and with epistemic humility listened to local needs about heritage preservation as expressed by Boreda elders. The intersectionality between locally articulated needs for heritage preservation and parallel Western values arises in part because of the recognition by the elders that knowledge of their sacred landscapes is quickly disappearing both from memory and from the landscapes because of changing farming practices.

Rather than impose values on the Boreda elders, Arthur and her collaborators asked a simple yet profoundly important question: "what do you wish us to prepare and accomplish with all the histories we were collecting?" (Arthur et al. 2017: 101, this volume). The answer was equally direct—the elders wanted their heritage locales recorded in writing for posterity, recognizing that without such documentation their knowledge was destined to be forgotten. Out of this intersectionality arose a synthetic model for archaeological and ethnographic recording of ancient sacred heritage sites. This study captures a rapidly changing Africa, with informed local heritage managers and preservationists prepared to use whatever methods are appropriate to maintain the vitality of their heritage knowledge—a fine example of how intersectionality leads to pragmatic pathways.

Yet, the pathway to such intersectionality was bumpy amongst the Boreda, with descendants of the elders taking up ownership of one of the most important ancestral sites, Ochollo Mulato. Because of political and cultural changes, farming by the sons of the elders had seriously modified the site, creating questions about future preservation and participatory study. By careful listening to local needs and by carefully explaining the intersectionality of interests, a political solution was found to protect the site. The rich narratives of Boreda elders about the ritual activities carried out at the site entangle it with a thick intangible heritage fabric. The level of detail and particular knowledge that intersect with archaeological evidence illustrate how the practice of epistemic humility in the face of such knowledge reveals pragmatic alternatives for heritage study and preservation.

The chapter by Chapurukha Kusimba adds dimensions to our understanding of community archaeology in Africa. Kusimba's initial focus is a 'community of interest'—the community of archaeologists engaged in the study of the Eastern African past. Using an ethical lens, Kusimba explores best practices and their compromise by archaeologists who specifically re-excavated—in the exact loci—sites researched by a prominent Tanzanian archaeologist, without consulting and collaborating with this well-established professional. Kusimba's point is powerful: good community engagement begins at home—in our professional 'neighborhoods', social and professional societies—not just with communities in far off places. This blemish on Eastern African archaeology is a potent lesson of the consequences of failing to engage one's own immediate community and using 'scientific' justifications for ethically questionable practices. Kusimba then focuses on issues of social justice in his immediate study communities. He relates how, after showing solidarity with his Swahili neighbors and coresidents who suffered deprivations at the hands of land-grabbing Kenyan elites, he was vilified for his community allegiances. His subtext is that confronting both colonial and neocolonial practices by using principles of community engagement sometimes comes with significant costs.

Kusimba then turns to immediate, more familiar communities in his final example of community engagement, this time speaking to the economic well-being of neighbors through collaborative initiatives. After realizing from his direct experience with farming near Mt. Elgon that deforestation is a severe local problem exacerbated by quickly growing populations, Kusimba worked with local female potters to keep vital this culturally and economically important activity. His study first established that ceramic production was the only surviving traditional craft and was still viable. Kusimba then worked with a wide variety of local stakeholders in Bungoma County in Western Kenya to produce a fuel-efficient kiln for firing traditional ceramics. Impressed by the experimental results of this collaboration, local political authorities quickly endorsed the propagation of similar kilns as a significant conservation activity for both forests and swamp grass. Helping neighbors help themselves is a mostly unrecognized form of collaborative heritage work, but Kusimba convincingly illustrates how intersectionality is central to a community-participatory approach.

Peter Schmidt's chapter (2017b, this volume) on the contests between historical representations and heritage practices of the Kings of Kihanja Kingdom and Kanazi Palace of Northwest Tanzania centers our attention on the problems that infuse elite group management of heritage sites. Chirikure et al. (2018) observe that when heritage conservation is held by ritual groups that are exclusionary, then points of intersectionality are limited. Schmidt argues that the use of long-term ethnographic studies of elite ritual practices offers significant alternative views about what happened to indigenous religious systems during colonialism. Realizing the disabilities that come with exclusively elite practices, he and his counterparts engaged in a broad inquiry that incorporated all walks of life, including those who held views at odds with the royal clan. By examining ritual practices at Kanazi Palace, he unveils how exclusive heritage practices helped to preserve critical heritage knowledge that was otherwise suppressed by Christianity and colonial representations. The study of contests between colonial, class-influenced, historical representations about Kanazi Palace and deeply embedded, hidden heritage practices shows how intersectionality may lead us, even in elite settings, toward synthetic, pragmatic approaches in heritage studies and archaeology (Schmidt 2017b, this volume). Elite perspectives are balanced by non-royal testimonies and contradict colonial missionary accounts—based on rumor—about royal traditional religious practices. Embedded within the palace compound are heritage practices that invite intersectionality—practices that complement Western preservation philosophies that when taken together ensure the future of the palace as a vital medium for heritage conservation. Such intersectionality leads to syntheses, opening pragmatic avenues for heritage preservation and conservation. Once revealed, such practices offer hope for conservation of ancillary heritage values—intersectionality in action.

Part III: Assessment and Management Issues

The three chapters in Part III of this book address a significant need in participatory community engagements. Nthabiseng Mokoena's chapter explores the significant potential that heritage practitioners in Southern Africa have for understanding *community* attitudes toward and practice of heritage meanings and needs vis-a-vis rock art sites, as opposed to authorized heritage view on such sites. Located along the foothills of the Maloti Drakensberg Mountains in the Eastern Cape of South Africa, the Matatiele community and its Mehloding Community Trust wanted to understand community views about a proposed heritage center earlier proposed by rock art researchers. The Trust asked Mokoena to research, collaborate with, and assist the ethnically diverse Matatiele communities to gain this understanding. This led to important understandings that went beyond the heritage center to reveal indigenous heritage values as well as new heritage management strategies for rock art, a fine example of pragmatic results arising out of intersectionality.

Mokoena's interviews with residents led her to understand that rock art sites have a variety of heritage meanings, foremost of which is their association with sacred practices. Using community meetings and outreach, she came to understand that the sacred aspects of rock art sites (as places of healing, communication with ancestors, and initiation centers) dominated local perspectives over economic uses (e.g., herding locales). Local discussions affirmed that heritage management and tourism plans must privilege these places as sacred sites, regardless of official regulations. Searching for intersectionality, Mokoena provides a pragmatic management agenda that arises from the communities' views, too long ignored in many regions of Africa. Her recognition that heritage preservation entails the continuation of sacred rituals in rock art sites (even when such rituals lead to activities that change the rock art) is critical to our growing understanding that heritage is much more than the tangible art and must encompass the processes by which rock art is created, used, and perpetuated. Mokoena demonstrates that intersectionality incorporates recognition that indigenous views are critical for ethical best practices in any future management plan.

After several years of archaeological inquiry in and around Meroe in Sudan, Jane Humphris and Rebecca Bradshaw came to an awareness that a strong colonial tradition in archaeological research marginalized local communities. Not satisfied to work in this tradition and seeking a remedy, they shifted their focus to analyzing how archaeology has been, and could be, practiced in specific villages. In an explicit attempt to decolonize their practice, they explored local ideas about and reactions to the practice of archaeology in and around ancient Meroe, Sudan, from a different perspective. Long known in the West as a center of Kushitic civilization as well as one of the great iron production centers of Africa, Meroe has been the focus of numerous archaeological investigations over the last two centuries, controlled and conducted by Western investigators. Their project, based at University College London (UCL) Qatar, incorporates a significant number of Sudanese professionals and addresses capacity building among Sudanese students and local peoples. Local villagers have long participated as laborers with little idea about the wider significance of their tasks or knowledge about research goals. Humphris and Bradshaw found themselves facing a long legacy of 'distancing' from local people, which caused them concern in light of efforts to decolonize archaeological practice.

To learn what local people think about and know about archaeology, Humphris and Bradshaw examined attitudes in several local villages in the Royal City of Meroe zone. They used anonymous questionnaires to understand the 'social fabric' surrounding Meroe archaeology and found significant community diversity, with a wide variety of identities and experiences with archaeology. In this respect, their setting resembles the multiethnic circumstances experienced by Mokoena, the result being significant diversity of responses to outsiders' questions about heritage and archaeology.

A distinctive part of their research program, however, was to learn how the UCL Qatar investigators could successfully mount a community archaeology program in such culturally complex settings. Focusing on six villages, their team used a mixed set of methods, drawing on ethnographic principles to build trust and familiarity with communities, while employing quantitative methods to reveal how (or whether) attitudes and experiences intersect. Among the more interesting findings is that local knowledge about Meroe's role in Kushitic civilization is basic and not well developed. This is one of the legacies of colonial archaeology—a surrounding population mostly uninformed about professional findings, despite often being 'engaged with' archaeology as laborers, an observation also made by Atalay (2012) about communities that provided laborers at the Neolithic site of Çatalhöyük, Turkey. Perhaps most importantly, the village studies revealed that people—some 44 percent—considered archaeology to be economically and educationally important, observations that led Humphris and Bradshaw to design more appropriate future community projects with local expectations in mind—a pragmatic outcome that arises out of multiple points of intersection.

The chapter by Susan Keitumetse and Michelle Pampiri (2016, this volume) provides an assessment of dormant community attitudes toward their heritage locales, an initiative taken by the investigators for better development planning in Maun, Botswana. Working at the behest of community needs, the authors show how community interests and needs unfolded beyond the applied academic goals of the project. Their study falls within the orbit of a diagnostic assessment/inventory of both the environment and intangible heritage on the Maun landscape. Concerned with the impact of tourism development on local heritage, the authors used questionnaires informed by follow-up interviews. With local assistance, the researchers were able to revive dormant heritage knowledge and map heritage landscapes. Though conceived as a top-down project and implemented by drawing on elite and subsequently non-elite knowledge to enhance better development planning, the project's most important contribution is the transformation of 'semi-participants' into fully engaged and contributing participants. Proving that pragmatic avenues open at unexpected moments, the Maun project generated perhaps its most important contributions *after the completion of the project*—when former "semi-participants" began to contact the researchers with suggestions for additional inquiry and documentation: "Keitumetse still receives phone calls from participants to discuss the research. Their enthusiasm gave birth to a need to develop archival storage for Maun village cultural heritage of both published and nonpublished formats for use in various activities" (Keitumetse and Pampiri 2016: 111). At that point, the local heritage keepers took control by identifying community needs that intersected with heritage management and development planning. Keitumetse and Pampiri illustrate short-term engagements remain a common thrust in community archaeology and heritage studies; however, in their study of heritage values in Maun they provide the building blocks for future, community-initiated research—launch points for a more engaged participation during later stages of implementation.

We should not assume that a community will welcome or understand a participatory community archaeology or heritage project. Instead, we make careful inquiries to determine if such an assumption will work, and then learn how to tailor a project to fit *mutually agreed* research protocols along with local expectations and needs. Such pragmatic outcomes underwrite the search for intersectionality and promise hope that participatory principles in our community engagements will lead to solutions that decolonize the discipline and offer positive pathways for Africa and other regions in the study and management of heritage, be it physical sites or intangible values and their expressions.

References

Abungu, Patrick O. 2016. "Heritage, Memories, and Community Development: The case of Shimoni slave caves heritage site, Kenya." In *Community Archaeology and Heritage in Africa: Decolonizing Practice*, edited by Peter R. Schmidt and Innocent Pikirayi, 91–111. New York, NY: Routledge.

Asombang, Raymond N. 2018. "Traditional Methods of Conservation a Case Study of Bafut" In *Managing Heritage in Africa: Who Cares?*, edited by Webber Ndoro, Shadreck Chirikure, and Janette Deacon, 62–72. New York, NY and London: Routledge.

Arthur, Kathryn Weedman, Yohannes E. Tocha, Matthew C. Curtis, Bizuayehu Lakew, and John W. Arthur. 2017. "Seniority Through Ancestral Landscapes: Community Archaeology in the Highlands of Southern Ethiopia." *Journal of Community Archaeology & Heritage* 4 (2):101–114.

Atalay, Sonya. 2012. *Community-Based Archaeology: Research with, by, and for Indigenous and Local Communities.* Berkeley, CA: University of California Press.

Chirikure, Shadreck, Webber Ndoro, and Janette Deacon. 2018. "Approaches and Trends in African Heritage Management and Conservation." In *Managing Heritage in Africa: Who Cares?*, edited by Webber Ndoro, Shadreck Chirikure, and Janette Deacon, 13–26. New York, NY and London: Routledge,

Crenshaw, Kimberlé. 1995. "Mapping the Margins: Intersectionality, Identity Politics, and Violence Against Women of Color." In *Critical Race Theory: The Key Writings that Formed the Movement*, edited by Kimberlé Crenshaw, Neil Gotanda, Gary Peller, and Kendall Thomas, 357–383. New York, NY: New Press.

Humphris, Jane, and Rebecca Bradshaw. 2017. "Understanding 'The Community' before Community Archaeology: A Case Study from Sudan." *Journal of Community Archaeology and Heritage* 4 (3):203–217.

Jopelo, Albino. 2018. "Reorienting Heritage Management in Southern Africa: Lessons from Traditional Custodianship of Rock Art Sites in Central Mozambique." In *Managing Heritage in Africa: Who Cares?*, edited by Webber Ndoro, Shadreck Chirikure, and Janette Deacon, 51–62. New York, NY and London: Routledge.

Kehoe, Alice, and Peter R. Schmidt. 2017. "Introduction: Expanding Our Knowledge by Listening." *The SAA Record* 17 (4):15–19.

Keitumetse, Susan O., and Michelle G. Pampiri. 2016. "Community Cultural Identity in Nature-Tourism Gateway Areas: Maun Village, Okavango Delta World Heritage Site, Botswana." *Journal of Community Archaeology & Heritage* 3 (2):99–117

Kusimba, Chapurukha M. 2017. "Community Archaeology and Heritage in Coastal and Western Kenya." *Journal of Community Archaeology and Heritage* 4 (3):218–228.

Mokoena, Nthabiseng. 2017. "Community Involvement and Heritage Management in Rural South Africa." *Journal of Community Archaeology and Heritage* 4 (3):189–202.

Moser, Stephanie, Darren Glazier, James E. Phillips, Lamya Nasser el Nemr, Mohammed Saleh Mousa, Rascha Nasr Aiesh, Susan Richardson, Andrew Conner, and Michael Seymour. 2002. "Transforming Archaeology Through Practice: Strategies for Collaborative Archaeology and the Community Archaeology Project at Quseir, Egypt." *World Archaeology* 34:220–248.

Mrozowski, Stephen A. 2013. "The Tyranny of Prehistory and the Search for a Deeper History." In *The Death of Prehistory*, edited by Peter R. Schmidt and Stephen A. Mrozowski, 220–240. Oxford and New York, NY: Oxford University Press.

Ndlovu, Ndukuyakhe. 2016. "Old Archaeology Camouflaged as New and Inclusive? South African Community Archaeology in the Twenty-First Century." In *Community Archaeology and Heritage in Africa: Decolonizing Practice*, edited by Peter R. Schmidt and Innocent Pikirayi, 136–153. New York, NY and London: Routledge.

Ndoro, Webber, and Shadreck Chirikure. 2018. "Caring Matters: The Future of Managing Heritage in Africa." In *Managing Heritage in Africa, Who Cares?*, edited by Webber Ndoro, Shadreck Chirikure, and Janette Deacon, 200–209. New York, NY and London: Routledge.

Ndoro, Webber, Shadreck Chirikure, and Janette Deacon, eds. 2018. *Managing Heritage in Africa, Who Cares?*. New York, NY and London: Routledge.

Pikirayi, Innocent. 2016. "Archaeology, Local Knowledge, and Tradition: The Quest for Relevant Approaches to the Study and Use of the Past in Southern Africa." In *Community Archaeology and Heritage in Africa: Decolonizing Practice*, edited by Peter R. Schmidt and Innocent Pikirayi, 112–135. New York, NY and London: Routledge.

Pikirayi, Innocent, and Peter R. Schmidt, eds. 2016. "Introduction: Community Archaeology and Heritage in Africa: Decolonizing Practice." In *Community Archaeology and Heritage in Africa: Decolonizing Practice*, 1–20. New York, NY and London: Routledge.

Posnansky, Merrick. 2017. "Archaeology and the Local Community in Africa: A Retrospective." *Journal of Community Archaeology and Heritage* 4 (2):77–84.

Schmidt, Peter R. 2014a. "Rediscovering Community Archaeology in Africa and Reframing Its Practice." *Journal of Community Archaeology and Heritage* 1 (1):38–56.

Schmidt, Peter R. 2014b. "Hardcore Ethnography: Interrogating the Intersection of Disease, Human Rights, and Heritage." *Heritage and Society* 7:170–188.

Schmidt, Peter R. 2017a. *Community-Based Heritage in Africa: Unveiling Local Research and Development Initiatives.* New York, NY and London: Routledge.

Schmidt, Peter R. 2017b. "Contests between Heritage and History in Tanganyika/Tanzania: Insights Arising from Community-Based Heritage Research." *Journal of Community Archaeology and Heritage* 4 (2):85–100.

Schmidt, Peter R. 2017c. "Listening and Waiting, Excavating Later." *SAA Record* 17 (4):36–37.

Schmidt, Peter R., and Alice B. Kehoe, eds. Forthcoming. *Archaeologies of Listening.* Gainesville, FL: University Press of Florida.

Shaw, Thurston. 1970. *Igbo-Ukwu: An Account of Archaeological Discoveries in Eastern Nigeria.* London: Faber Institute for African Studies.

Note

1 Intersectionality is a concept used in critical race theory and feminist theory for assessments of identity (see Crenshaw 1995). It diminishes the idea that identity be considered as a collection of separate elements and instead posits that the elements are interwoven, interlocking parts of a whole. When we speak of intersectionality in heritage, it is not one element from an indigenous context juxtaposed to an element in Western practice. Rather, both are viewed as parts of a heritage world with intersectionality focusing on elements that are linked in practice and philosophy, with some elements interlocking with others that previously have been submerged through colonialism, racism, gender, and other forces. The same principles apply to archaeology, with Western practices interwoven with indigenous practices, but with indigenous practices all too often oppressed or erased because of race, gender, ethnicity, or scientific prejudice.

Rediscovering Community Archaeology in Africa and Reframing its Practice

Peter R. Schmidt

Community archaeology and heritage work have a long history in Africa, a history embedded in the practice of ethnoarchaeology, studies of indigenous knowledge systems, and the collaborative study of oral traditions and other intangible heritage. This paper reviews some of the intellectual legacies that foreground community approaches today in Africa. Whilst top-down approaches have tended to characterize many projects in recent history, the requirements of outside development agencies often force archaeologists into collaborative compliance that communities are not ready to embrace or where histories of land alienation complicate best efforts to engage communities. An alternative community approach arising from a grassroots initiative in Northwest Tanzania is discussed to illustrate how collaboration may lead to mutual research and heritage development that contribute new knowledge to African history and archaeology and improve community well-being.

Reflection and rediscovery

Thirty years ago I shared with a mostly American audience some common practices in African archaeology that privileged local needs and sensibilities — one of the first explicit recognitions of a collaborative approach in the practice of archaeology in Africa, namely:

> One of the most critical issues facing archaeology in Africa (and North America) today is the need to perform research on problems that are significant to the historical self-identity of living peoples, particularly those descended from the prehistoric and historic populations we study. As anthropologists we cannot continue to perpetuate Western paradigms that militate against local historical sensibilities. This is particularly true of the practice of archaeology in the colonized world; it is even more poignantly relevant in Africa because of the colonial history of the West on that continent. (Schmidt 1983, 63)

My point in citing this passage is to refocus attention on research that emphasizes local historical identity as a key benefit to emerge from collaborative research amongst archaeologists, heritage workers, and communities in Africa. This perspective has been an integral part of African archaeology for decades, although it was not named or consciously recognized as community archaeology. Rather, it was a holistic anthropological inquiry using archives, archaeology, and oral testimonies — the latter depending on the participation if not the initiative of African peoples who engage heritage studies and archaeology. Following a full review of the ethnohistorical and ethnoarchaeological research carried out in Africa up to 1983, I concluded in the same *American Antiquity* essay that,

> [...] ethnoarchaeology and historical archaeology in Africa have pioneered perspectives that are sensitive to history, symbolic systems, and the historical sensibilities of local peoples. This further suggests that *when cultures in Africa participate in the interpretation of their own past*, we can begin to build a self-enriching tradition of archaeology free from the domination of Western paradigms and appropriate to the African setting. (emphasis mine; Schmidt 1983, 75)

This insight into archaeological practice in Africa was not self-consciously intended to complement what we would now call community archaeology, but it certainly anticipated by several decades the importance of integrating local historical knowledge, namely: 'Bringing this knowledge to the foreground and acknowledging ethnohistoric data as central for including Indigenous views in interpretations are both aspects of a decolonizing archaeology practice' (Atalay 2006a, 275). Long an unrecognized if not a subaltern practice in African settings, we may now openly acknowledge its place in the lineage of thought related to what has become known as community practices. There are a variety of ways in which these perspectives are represented in the literature, including public and participatory archaeology rubrics. Here I consider both archaeology and heritage together as community actions in Africa, because in my research in Northwest Tanzania (Kagera Region) heritage sites are the focus of collaborative research that often have archaeological components, with their archaeological dimension seen by some people as an integral part of their heritage.

My very first step as a young archaeologist was to collect oral traditions and oral histories about the Haya people in Northwest Tanzania for a full year before I put a spade or trowel in the ground, building a collaborative approach that privileged the way that the Haya thought about and related their histories. I was a neophyte in the midst of a sophisticated system of oral record keeping that depended on rigorous transmission of oral accounts and sacred places that acted as mnemonics — parts of the sacred and political landscape such as shrines, burial places, and royal palace locations (Schmidt 1978, 2006).

Forty-four years ago, this participatory community approach fit well with local cultural sensibilities and was in keeping with my apprenticeship to the most knowledgeable keepers of oral accounts, allowing me to reach a deeper understanding of Haya history (Schmidt 1978). These relationships led, organically, to more detailed collaborations and dynamic planning and strategizing over potential sites where archaeological investigations were considered as a possible form of joint inquiry.

More than five decades later, such approaches are appropriately being heralded in settings around the globe as the future of archaeology — a collaborative or public archaeology that incorporates the participation and initiative of communities for their benefit. This trend, specifically called Community Archaeology and Community Heritage, are much needed perspectives that balance the scientific objectives of archaeology driven by professionals and brings a new, local perspective to bear on what constitutes heritage at a local level. The most positive attributes out of this increasingly popular agenda is a focus that continues the goals followed more than five decades ago in Africa — a privileging of local needs, foremost of which is to overcome representations of local history that arose out of colonialism.

Decolonization

Decolonization of archaeological practice looms very large in community archaeology and heritage work because it addresses issues of power and control of archaeology — who initiates archaeological research or heritage work, who sets the research and interpretative agendas, and who controls the dissemination of results (see Atalay 2006a, 2006b; Schmidt and Patterson 1995; Smith and Wobst 2005). The last issue may be one of the most difficult to address. It was the focus of our introduction to *Making Alternative Histories* (Schmidt and Patterson 1995), where we argued that specialized esoteric language of archaeological reports alienated people whose history was being studied, and that it drove a significant wedge between archaeologists and the communities in which they worked — a theme reiterated recently by Chirikure and Pwiti (2008) in their review of African community experiments. Participatory approaches have grown in popularity over the last two decades around the globe and in Africa (e.g. Abu-Khafajah 2010; Atalay 2012; Colwell-Chanthaphonh and Ferguson 2008; Cooke 2010; Dowdall and Parrish 2001; Marshall 2009; McDavid 2002; Murimbika and Moyo 2008; Silliman 2008), but archaeological practice that unites rather than separates archaeologists and local people in the field has been much slower to follow the academic rhetoric underwriting such views. In spite of the multiple resolutions and codes of ethics, such as those implemented by the World Archaeological Congress insisting that communities must be brought into the process of archaeological planning, execution, and writing, we have far to travel to deliver the goods.

Sonya Atalay (2006b, 2012), one of the most effective advocates amongst the community of Native American archaeologists, writes compellingly about the need for archaeology to develop new methodologies and new theoretical approaches based on community initiatives in archaeology and heritage work (see Kuwansisiwma 2008). This perspective resonates with initiatives taken by communities in Kagera, Tanzania — engagements that are a relatively infrequent genre of community participation, yet that hold great promise in the valourization and revitalization of histories shredded through colonialism, globalization, and trauma. When archae-ologists try to implement ideas, Atalay is quick to note that it is a slippery slope when archaeologists try to implement *their* ideas of fulsome community engagement based on reciprocity and mutual benefits. She strongly believes, as do I, that community engagement is the way of the future in archaeology and that archaeologist-driven projects not accounting for the needs of the community are practices that retain colonial legacies of non-consultation and separation of 'subject peoples' to the directives and desires of a science often practiced in the interest of imperial interests, whether the early twentieth-century colonial state or the postcolonial state. Lest we forget, Bruce Trigger (1980) made similar points in his seminar article on science and history in Native American settings.

A slippery slope enters the picture when archaeologists, well-intended and earnest to apply such a philosophy, try to put it into practice and find that some communities have no interest in the archaeology of their past nor in heritage work in their midst. Or, they may find that the communities where they would like to establish collaborative programmes mistrust archaeologists, manipulate them to their economic advantage, or provide only token forms of collaboration. Each of these scenarios — only a small sampling of what one might expect — present soul-searching challenges and sometime impossible difficulties. Basically they speak to the issue of what happens when outside agendas for participatory approaches are presented to a community, rather than what happens when a community comes to life with its own agenda. The direction from which the initiative flows will often influence success and engagement.

Atalay's (2012) recent review of her attempts to engage very different genres of communities provides some useful insights into some of the difficulties and successes that emerge in community-oriented research. Her review provides a device through which insights into top-down and bottom-up collaborations can be applied to Africa and other world regions. She starts with how she tried to interest communities around Çatalhöyük, Turkey, in archaeological research. She admits that her initiative — and her refreshing honesty in describing it as her initiative rather than the communities' initiative — did not elicit positive reactions. No one in these five communities initially saw any benefit in archaeological research. It was only after an extensive and complex educational campaign that local people slowly began to see ways that they could participate.

Despite its best intentions, the Çatalhöyük experiment started with top-down practice whilst it espoused participatory engagement. This is not an anomaly. In fact it is the common template for projects that want community engagement. It was not the community that came to Hodder, Atalay, or other archaeologists engaged in research. People in the villages from which labourers were drawn did not seek ways to engage archaeology. It was archaeologists affiliated with the project after it had been up and running for years who took initiatives to the villagers, engaging in extensive efforts at education about archaeology. Some of these top-down initiatives led to positive results. This is a powerful case study because it illustrates how much hard work is in store for archaeologists who recognize the importance of participatory archaeology benefiting descendants and local people but where such communities display little or no interest in archaeological inquiry. Most archaeologists working in rural areas of Africa, Asia, or the Americas can expect similar disinterest on the part of local people unfamiliar with archaeology, unless we modify our approach to work with communities in developing training and other educational perspectives before projects are launched. To engage with communities in this manner before launching projects presents some stiff challenges of the sort that Atalay shares.

Her study sets out a stark prescription for extensive preparatory work. It also causes us to ask — how might the Çatalhöyük project have avoided the disengagement of nearby communities over the long term? One answer, I believe, lies in capacity building before a project begins or at least from the very beginning of projects; that is, training local people how and *why* archaeology is conducted and what kinds of questions are appropriate. It also means working together with those associated with the project in whatever role they play — labourer, technician, manager — about how *they* interpret the research results — be they archaeological finds or heritage management plans. This should be a prelude to more complex interactions and on-site training that privilege the intelligence and potential contributions of the labour force.

An important part of any collaborative project is the exercise of a reflexivity that questions privileging scientific goals over local participation, and examines the degree to which we are willing to accept that intelligent people will respond enthusiastically to skilled training if they are invested with trust. I find that local farmers are much more skilled in many archaeological tasks than advanced archaeology students. They quickly recognize changes in soil colour and texture, recognizing odd features such as micro-inclusions of clay, and practice an archaeology that has much finer motor-control of tools than most university students and even some professional archaeologists. I sometimes pair university students with locally trained archaeologists, with the latter acting as trainers. We must also ask if mental restraints in our thinking — no matter how reasonably justified — are a form of denial, a way of exclusion that seeks comfort in expeditious research results over the more demanding but ultimately more satisfying task of inclusion and full training, not just in sieving, flotation, sorting — all tasks that require lower levels of training. Given that most rural folk are better equipped to deal with the basics of archaeology than are university students, then why are they not included from the beginning and invested with trust to increase their confidence and sense of ownership?

Investing trust in local collaborators — an African legacy

A recent initiative taken in Kagera Region during 2008 by the leadership of Katuruka village (Schmidt 2010) to restore, preserve, and reclaim their heritage cannot be explained by formal training in archaeology at university level or the presence and active involvement of a developed infrastructure, such as an active Non-Governmental Organization (NGO) dedicated to cultural heritage and preservation. Rather, such spirited awareness may be traced back to the extensive participation of Katuruka residents in the archaeology of heritage sites within their community between 1969 and 1984 and their clear awareness that archaeological goals were linked to the oral traditions told about sites. The original research programme effected several decades earlier was guided and jointly designed by elders, building on and complementing local values and needs — now part of the legacy of local engagement. Through this period, several of those who were talented in archaeological inquiry went on to lead excavations and supervise major regional surveys, clearly understanding the goals and helping to design the day-to-day methods that were appropriate to the local circumstances as well as finding sites of major importance (Schmidt and Childs 1985). Memories of these engagements and the significance of the archaeology previously conducted in the community by community members lived on through time to create informed knowledge ready for additional development.

The methods that were developed with Haya collaborators and communities during the 1969–84 period were later taken into the university classroom, laboratory, and field schools when the formal teaching of archaeology was launched in Tanzania in 1985 (Schmidt 2005). Amongst the innovations introduced into the instructional programme at the University of Dar es Salaam (UDSM) was the idea, soon formalized as a requirement, that students design their field school research project. The faculty felt that it was critical that students, as the most important stakeholders, take ownership of the research programme in which training occurred. Initially the intake of students was so small that all could participate as a group, but soon students were required to present individual proposals, the best designed of which would be chosen for collective treatment leading to field school research.

There were detractors who said, 'How can you expect naive students without any significant prior experience to design research projects?' Our response was simple: that we were not looking for precise and theoretically informed projects — those would come through instruction and growing confidence through time. Rather, we were looking for innovative ideas that drew on local histories and ideas about the past where archaeology could contribute. We encouraged our students to think out of the box, asking them to move beyond established, colonial, and normative research ideas that could be challenged by research in new regions and sites. Once a basic research idea was accepted and discussed at length, then students were asked to design a research strategy that would be used to obtain information that they needed to test their ideas. The next step was implementation, close guidance, and modifications as the research strategies were applied in the field. Constant discussion about the adequacy or inadequacy of strategies and tactics built a sense of empowerment and ownership in students, who by their second year were eager to test their ideas in a new setting. This approach stands in stark contrast to most western field schools, where students are plugged into faculty-determined agendas to perform rote tasks that often help advanced academics achieve their goals.

Within the Tanzanian setting, then, capacity building unfolded in two dimensions: 1) with local people in the field, stakeholders and collaborators who assimilated and engaged archaeological research as trusted associates; and 2) with students a decade later, given freedom to exercise their informed but creative imaginations and to take ownership of research ideas and results. The two are irrevocably linked, the first setting the scene for the development of the second. I recently learned from a Senior Lecturer of Archaeology at the UDSM that this training practice was still drawn upon occasionally despite much larger enrolments and, moreover, that the staff considered it a centrepiece of their former training programme. I suspect that the investment of trust in students is one reason that the UDSM now has one of the most productive archaeological research teams in the African continent today and produces more MA and PhDs than any other institution. This history also helps to explain why the scene was set for an enthusiastic initiative for heritage preservation and development in Katuruka in 2008, with an emphasis on the emotional qualities of interanimation

(Basso 1996) that occur in the presence of ancient places and sacred shrines. The elders understood that archaeology and heritage were significant to the health of their community. They envisioned that if heritage work focused on a well-known archaeological site with a high level of significance, then they would follow an expeditious route to realize heritage development goals that were brewing for years. It was serendipity that I happened upon the scene in 2008, when my reappearance after more than two decades away crystalized these long held views into rapidly formulated plans (see Schmidt 2010).

Heckenburger (2008) describes the development of a similar process in Amazonia, where initially he worked alone but by the 1990s trained his local collaborators as fully qualified archaeologists who understood archaeological principles and wanted to put them to work for the benefit of their community. Since then his collaborators have co-published professional papers about the archaeology they helped to perform in their communities. Elsewhere in Brazil these principles were translated into university pedagogy for field schools.

Paying respect to our ancestors and others

Given the growing interest in community and participatory archaeology over the last decade, it is easy to forget the ground-breaking work in community approaches of archaeologists over the last half century. One early example of community engagement is Thurstan Shaw's investigations at Igbo Ukwu in southeastern Nigeria in the mid-1960s. As a colonial era archaeologist, Shaw did not justify the Igbo Ukwu excavations in the language of postcolonial theory, as decolonization through community archaeology, but he did involve himself in several activities that have since become hallmarks for community and public archaeology elsewhere. First, the Igbo Ukwu excavations of a royal burial and associated shrines occurred as the result of an invitation to Shaw on the part of local administrative authorities in 1958, based on a report about discoveries in the community. From the beginning, the excavations were not part of Shaw's research agenda. His reputation as someone who worked easily within Nigerian cultural settings paved the way for his engagement with the community, along with his personal ties to people in the community. Igbo . Ukwu is distinctive for Shaw's integration of the community into the project from the very beginning, along with a wide array of other stakeholders, including the local chief, district officer, police, land owners, and Federal officials. This was partly by necessity to deal with difficult and mercurial negotiations for permission to excavate sites under multiple ownership as well as threats of looting. The village setting of the excavation meant intimate daily contact with the members of the community, many of whom participated as trained labourers in the excavations conducted in the yards of several land owners who also provided guidance in finding sites and performed rituals to propitiate the ancestors.

The clearest and most significant contributions that Shaw made to public and community archaeology were his diverse publications about the site. He followed academic expectations by publishing a comprehensive two volume report (Shaw 1970), but perhaps more importantly he also published an accessible book written in plain English that appealed to a wide audience (Shaw 1977; see Schmidt 1983). In other words, he demystified archaeology for Nigerians, making it easy to understand whilst simultaneously featuring a spectacular shrine with very early and remarkable bronze objects. Through this approach he created an identity with the mission of archaeology amongst a large Nigerian audience. This is an enduring legacy, public/community archaeology at its best, very early in its practice in Africa.

The real milestone in community archaeology in Africa is Merrick Posnansky's investigations at Begho in Northwest Ghana (Posnansky 1979, 2004, 2009, 2010). Starting in 1970, this project first investigated the impact of trade in a medieval to modern era (1200–1900) town in Northwest Ghana organized into different quarters attributed by oral traditions to different ethnic-linguistic groups. The archaeology conducted at Begho from 1970 to 1979 demonstrated that different artisanal skills were represented over time, including ivory carving, as well as iron, textile, and brass production that were linked with Saharan trade. Beyond the substantive contributions that long-term archaeology at Begho made to African archaeology and history, Posnansky's research at Begho brought community archaeology into the spotlight (2004). Parallel to his conventional archaeological investigations, Posnansky developed a long-term ethnoarchaeological study that deeply involved the local community over a period of 28 years until 1998. Initially the research agendas were collaborative with Ghanaian researchers but over time the residents in the community — from multiple walks of life — were brought into the research as critical participants in the research. As Posnansky (2004, 34; emphasis mine) describes:

> During all this time we have worked closely with different sectors of the local community, with the chief and his elders, amongst whom I have the honor to sit as the Ahohohene, literally 'Chief of the Foreigners,' who include the Dagarti laborers, the schoolteachers as well as people who may have come from villages only a few kilometers away. We have consulted with the town development committee and with various political committees, which have changed their names over the years in reflection of the prevailing political ideology such as the local committee for the Defense of Revolution in the 1980s. *These bodies have assisted us* with the data to assess population, numbers of inhabited houses, education statistics, festival observance, rubbish disposal, etc. This local help, together with our periodic visits, enables us to have a better control over basic data than the two official census exercises that have taken place since we started our surveys.

Posnansky's longitudinal study focuses on processes of change, including population change, the expansion of the physical village, and changing farming practices amongst others. The gaps in visits by researchers to the contemporary village of Hani made the participation of the community members critical to this long-term study. Success in documenting change depended on devoted engagement by community members over a long period of time, a gradual process in which community archaeology and research expertise flowered. This marks the Begho/Hani project as one the best illustrations of community archaeology at work in Africa, long hidden from recognition because of its early implementation and because it was not represented using the tropes of more recent community archaeology.

What insights develop out of top-down Africa?

When we look at the current literature about community archaeology in Africa today, we are struck by the scarcity of substantive examples that illustrate the recognition of these earlier principles at work in African practice. An overview by Chirikure and Pwiti (2008) takes a global perspective by examining community archaeology in other parts of the world and relating them to conditions in southern Africa. Chirikure *et al.* (2010) discuss the same case studies using a heritage management trope. These are useful exercises, for they show a paucity of archaeological practice and heritage work with community participation in a significant region of Africa. These studies mostly examine southern African cases. Southern Africa is a large region with a long history of heritage work and is therefore a field of inquiry that is deservedly important for the continent. In either case — archaeology or heritage management — there is little evidence presented of communities that fabricated and participated in the activities, or took initiatives or contributed to and were integrated into development and research agendas. Africa appears to have fewer recent cases illustrating active initiatives and engagements by communities. This illusion results from two trajectories: 1) quality projects that are not widely reported (e.g. Keitumetse 2002; Mayor 2013; Muringaniza 1998; Ndlovu 2005; Negussie and Wondimu 2012); 2) significant projects that are in their incipient stages or recently reported (e.g. Abungu 2012; Apoh 2013; Pikirayi 2011); and 3) an emphasis on projects that previously encountered problems — poorly demonstrating the viability of community engagement.

A central theme that emerges in the southern African overviews is that participatory approaches are about 'giving power to the local communities in all aspects of heritage, including research and management' (Chirikure *et al.* 2010, 31). This is an important principle that incorporates ideas of social justice, but it also reveals a fundamental problem in heritage work as it is currently being conceptualized in contemporary Africa. The notion that power must be *given* to the local communities assumes a higher agency — someone or some entity *with the power and* sufficiently enlightened to bestow power on communities. In other words, agency lies outside the communities.

Under this way of thinking, communities are bestowed power, a top-down approach that runs the risk of dependency, and creates a separation between communities and those who decide which local actors have the greatest potential to be 'empowered'. This is not unique to African archaeology or heritage work; it is an issue that infuses much of the development discourse today, with an abundance of rhetoric about empowering communities by those who set the ideological agenda and hold the purse strings, usually outside of archaeology and heritage studies and management.

Chirikure and Pwiti provide some important insights into the top-down approach that has informed so much of Africa. They examine case studies where community participation has been implemented, and it is important to understand that implementation comes from agents *outside* the communities. Herein lies the most vexing problem of community archaeology and heritage work in Africa — outside imposition of participatory frameworks. They also make the excellent point that heritage professionals, when reporting on participatory aspects of heritage work, have been required to downplay failures, as they often represent institutions funded to implement such programmes. Sadly, when heritage work has a required participatory component compelled by another, usually foreign institution, it is virtually inevitable that such a top-down action will result in frustrations and failures. What then, can be done to overcome the imposition of participatory frameworks from outside the communities and to *engender enfranchisement within* local communities to take initiatives? I will return to this key question in the final part of this essay.

Perhaps the most instructive case study is Old Bulawayo, the first capital site of King Lobengula just outside of contemporary Bulawayo, Zimbabwe (Muringaniza 1998). Intended as an educational and tourism theme park, the royal compound was reconstructed at the initiative of the National Museum and Monuments of Zimbabwe (NMMZ) in partnership with archaeologists and the community using documentary, oral, and archaeological evidence. The descendant community lived on the site and was described as having equal decision-making powers with archaeologists and the NMMZ, the two other primary agents and those responsible for initiating the project (Gilbert Pwiti, personal communication 2013), though are told that it was a local initiative (Chirikure and Pwiti 2008). They describe the ground rules of the project (2008, 473): 'The most important feature of the Old Bulawayo Project, when compared with other archaeological projects in the world, was that local communities and in particular the Khumalo people could veto decisions made by the archaeologists.' One is moved to ask if one partner having veto power over other partners overwhelms the idea of collaboration, where discussion and negotiation should prevail. This leaves the impression that arbitrary decisions may occur.

This case study successfully isolates an important dilemma that influences many heritage projects where there are differing perspectives amongst key partners in collaborative work. At Old Bulawayo differing views on the orientation of the door of one house led to the local view prevailing over archaeological knowledge. The building was reconstructed according to this perspective, but as discussions continued, the local partners admitted that they were incorrect. There is no certain blueprint to handle such differing perspectives, except to continue discussions until a consensus is reached based on full review of the evidence. In fact, multivocal views were not achieved; the authors appropriately acknowledge that a plaque *should be mounted* to explain the discrepancy between the reconstruction and the archaeological evidence. At the heart of this dilemma are different views on authenticity and the role of science in heritage work — unresolved idealizations held by different partners.

There is a clear need to overcome a significant dependency on top-down approaches, for inevitably they are taken with good intentions but without the extensive preparatory work that is required to develop a true sense of ownership in projects at the community level. There are few examples of grassroots initiatives. In light of this history, the Katuruka initiative and other grassroots initiatives in Kagera Region of Tanzania help to unveil the circumstances in which it may be possible to aid, assist, and work alongside communities with positive visions but that lack the skills and means to realize their goals.

If, as heritage workers and archaeologists, we come to find that no one in a 'community' identifies with a heritage property or that local people display a disinterest in archaeology or heritage work, or when conflicting economic, political, and social conflicts dissipate a unified perspective, then 'community' may indeed become ephemeral, lacking concreteness, as Chirikure and colleagues (2008, 2010) point out at the Khami World Heritage Site in Zimbabwe. To unlock understanding of where community is situated and how it is defined requires close observation of the source of community initiatives. Are they coming from the top, from archaeologists or heritage managers *to* the community, or are they emanating *from* the grassroots? I want to speak to these questions using Katuruka village, where a grassroots initiative by community members has led to new perspectives on what heritage means locally and how such local understandings figure into reconfigurations of identity in a globalized world.

An indigenous approach in Northwestern Tanzania

Elders in Katuruka village of Northwestern Tanzania took me aside during a social visit in 2008 to insist that I should return to their community to help them reclaim their history (Schmidt 2010), an insistence that came with conditions and explicit caveats. They had witnessed the degradation of their community's respect for the past, respect for traditional religion and other social institutions, and respect for elders by youth. The crisis of respect in Haya life has been long developing because of incremental devaluation linked to colonialism, Christianity, and globalization (Schmidt 2012). Christianity in particular has deeply denigrated principles of respect at multiple social levels because traditional authorities responsible for enforcement of ethical codes, well-being, and peace were demonized by Christian churches.

Since 2008 I have worked to assist Katuruka villagers in their research into oral traditions and to help them develop a major royal capital site and ancient shrine as a heritage destination for limited domestic and foreign tourism. I employ a discourse-based approach that captures what people say in their daily discourse about reclaiming their intangible heritage as they restore their ancient sacred and historical places. Out of such analysis comes a better understanding of *when* local heritage concepts emerge, how they are socially acted out, and when and under what conditions ethical values are articulated in making heritage and human rights claims (Schmidt 2012). In Northwest Tanzania, local heritage work puts ethical principles to work within heritage activities that incorporate embodied actions. I focus on the discourse of heritage workers in multiple settings in two Tanzanian villages, with the goal to understand how people make heritage claims in their daily lives through conversations and in more public, rhetorical pronouncements about heritage. I find that social practices of ethical theories unfold in *specific* settings (Meskell and Van Damme 2008), as during the revitalization of heritage places of deep meaning and the recovery and preservation of oral traditions in Katuruka.

One of the most potent changes introduced by Christianity amongst the Haya is in *senses of place*, where powerful emotions and social memories well up when places of meaning are encountered along the paths and in the homesteads — places where kingdom, clan, lineage, and family histories are encapsulated on the landscape. Christian teachings explicitly identified ancient shrines and other religious places as the devil's residences, a view that continues to threaten places with centuries of meaning once embodied through oral recitations and ritual performances. Under such conditions, sacred shrines such as Kaiija — a sacred shrine tree that we informally call the Tree of Iron — began to fade from consciousness.

Symbolically and ritually associated with iron working and dating to 2500 years ago, Kaiija — the place of the forge — was celebrated as the central place of reproductive power, a key trope derived from iron production and linked to political legitimacy in the region. Many genres of texts led us to the ancient Kaiija shrine, now celebrated in the archaeological literature as an extraordinary axis mundi for the Eastern Bantu reproductive and productive worlds (Schmidt 1978, 2006, 2010). This and other sacred places associated with past kings and key religious leaders and ancestors were given the official blessing of neglect in 1963 when the new independence government abolished chiefs and kings. No longer were subsidies from government available for kings to maintain shrines so critical to the integrity of the kingdoms. This would be fatal for Kaiija's upkeep and the social memory attached to it. Without a ritual official to conduct the new moon rituals, no animating social action occurred at the shrine.

Without regular rituals, local tribute, and royal support to maintain the primary shine and all its ancillary shrines, little vitality resided in these once evocative and potent places after the 1960s. People began to look upon shrine trees as undermining their economic interests, with the shade from the huge canopies inhibiting the growth and ripening of banana plantings. Residing since childhood near the shade cast by Kaiija, one Timothy Njuma (a fictitious name) decided to remove Kaiija in the late 1990s, failing to heed warnings about probable punishment and dying from a terrible ordeal meted out by the ancestors to those disrespecting this heritage. He did the unthinkable. By pounding iron spikes into Kaiija, covered with salt, he killed the huge shrine tree and paid the price for such evil-doing: he went mad and could be heard raving in his locked room for months before he finally died.

No one would discuss this cultural travesty in 2008 when I revisited the village, save one quick mention within the first minute of my arrival. It took nearly two years before people felt comfortable discussing a history that took away their identities, erased their spiritual senses of place, and besmirched the memory of a neighbour and kinsman. This and many other erasures of ancestors from the landscape ushered in a disquieting sense of dread and loss further exacerbated by the HIV/AIDS epidemic that was sweeping through their villages at the same time (e.g. Ndeki *et al.* 1992; Rugalema 1999).

The significant reduction in the numbers of elderly males because of HIV/AIDS opened fresh opportunities for elderly women to rise into positions of leadership by organizing aid societies — replacing traditional clan responsibilities — for funeral expenses and other assistance.

When village elders decided in 2008 that they would form a committee to address heritage issues, they articulated their desires during that first meeting around a sense of loss accelerated during the HIV/AIDS crisis (Schmidt 2010). Its social effects were then obvious everywhere: overgrown fields where prosperous farms were abandoned, collapsed houses, multiple grandchildren living with a single grandmother, the death of complete households, and a huge number of youth and few remaining elders. A repeated reference in heritage discourse was the need to educate people about the antiquity of their villages and to use the archaeological evidence from 1970 excavations to teach the youth and others about the history of technological innovation that marked their ancient history.

Other key issues also took centre stage: 1) talk about creating a heritage tourism site was clearly lodged in a larger discourse about tourism and heritage within the region; 2) a desire to reclaim their heritage, which they articulate as oral traditions, respect for the ancestors, and learning about sacred places; 3) detailed discussions about researching and documenting living oral traditions today, with the aim to create a permanent archive for future educational goals. Quite vehemently, they insisted that heritage thinking focus on economic well-being, such as how idle youth could gain employment as tour guides and simultaneously become teachers of the past: '*Perhaps if we restore these shrines and the palace, with a museum inside, we could attract tourists to visit this important place. Our young people could be employed to take them around the site and we could train them in the oral traditions that were once told here*' (Schmidt 2008–2011 field notes).

When I returned in 2009 at the behest of the villagers, my mission was to understand local ways of constructing heritage — how people thought about and talked about heritage. I was more concerned with how heritage ethics were put into action and made vital through daily embodied practice. I wanted to understand the reasons that people give for wanting to reclaim a heritage, the emotions they express when engaged in reclaiming their relationships with the ancestors, how they struggle to talk about how their ethical codes of yesteryear were erased by the Christian church, what they fear from the diminishment of respect and prosperity, and why they want to reclaim economic security through their recuperation of past heritage institutions and practices. I also wanted to understand how Katuruka residents think and feel when they build traditional houses to serve as shrines, and thus embrace ritually potent, spiritually elevated, and historically meaningful places belonging to lost ancestors.

Following Keith Basso (1996), I call this practice the revitalization of interanimation or *re-interanimation* — knowledge that comes alive, with emotion, in the presence of places of spiritual and emotional meaning. As participants in the village embarked upon their daily tasks, they made new pasts by cutting and weaving elephant grass, by fetching building poles, and by cutting thatch for shrines. As they worked they reviewed and explored why they were acting out their ideas about social practices tabooed by churches that saw traditional houses as the abodes of the Bacwezi spirits. They also openly discussed why they were embracing heritage values distinctive to their historical past as well as inserting archaeology into their heritage discourse, now accepted as an important part of heritage in their contemporary world. My role in this mutual research is to wrap together and present to other audiences these diverse threads of discourse and the daily practice of heritage values that mark the contingent historical contributions that the Haya make to heritage discourse more broadly.

Heritage tropes

Haya elders reframed their claims to a past through heritage tropes of their own making. The elders saw that with the valourization of heritage, economic security would come hand in hand with education into indigenous knowledge. They discussed and strongly argued on behalf of: 1) restoring sacred places — seeing this as heritage work; 2) creating a local museum that memorialized the antiquity and significance of the history of iron production in the area, including the archaeology about it; 3) developing a heritage tourism site with multiple implications, including the building of a sense of self-worth and well-being in the community; and 4) instilling a sense of pride and identity in the community about the significance of local history.

They rapidly designed and set out a programme that could be acted on daily to recuperate respect for the past. Such daily practice took multiple forms and led to a high degree of heritage consciousness within certain sectors of the community. Amongst the first actions were: 1) restoration and revitalization of a sacred shrine belonging to Mugasha, the god of the waters and storms; 2) a village organized census to determine the effects of HIV-AIDS on the community; and 3) identification of all keepers of oral traditions and oral history.

HIV/AIDS and social disruption

The results of village censuses confirmed initial impressions about the absence of elderly males. The severity of HIV/AIDS over the previous 25 years was stunning. Nearly half of the older generation of males — those over 65 years — were lost since 1978, when there were 97 males for every 100 females over 65 years of age. By the 1988 census this proportion dropped to 54:100, recovering a little 15 years later because of intervention programmes to 58:100 in 2003, but returning to 54:100 at the time of the village census. This is enormous demographic change. Since elderly males were once the keepers of oral traditions and knowledgeable about landscape histories, a severe rupture in the chair of transmission at this scale is devastating to the integrity and vitality of oral testimonies and helps explain another reason for the steady erosion of sacred places on the cultural landscape. After the completion of the village censuses, several members of the committee gathered together to compile a list of expert keepers of history. I was surprised by the appearance of women's names, filling about half the list — not experts in oral traditions but in oral histories about social relations in the community. In the past, women were not recognized as experts in a field of knowledge dominated by males, but with the loss of so many male keepers of history, women are now recognized for their abilities to remember social histories.

With the initiation of interviews for oral traditions and histories, I removed myself as outside expert, diminishing some of the anthropologist's place of power (see Rizvi 2006). Interviews were conducted by village elders, who were free to explore whatever subjects appeared to be germane to the knowledge of those with whom they spoke. The results of these interviews provided some very significant findings. Some women, because of naturally good memories and confidence gained as single heads of households, brought forth important subaltern histories. Their testimonies are vivid, as when an 86-year-old woman complained: '*I can be sick here and die. Even my brother did not come once when I summoned him. No one will bring you food these days. I am on my own, I plant my own plot without help*' (Katuruka Interviews 2009–2011).

Subaltern women's history

Elderly women command an intimate knowledge of social interactions in the community and clear historical reminiscences about their neighbours and kin. Now elevated to history keepers, their newly recognized expertise reflects their deep knowledge of people and events they have witnessed in their life-times. After long interviews with two women, we came to understand that a woman named Njeru lived in the former royal palace of King Rugomora (*c.* 1650–1675), where Kaiija tree is located, between 1900 and 1963 (the latter date marks the abolition of kings and chiefs in Tanzania and is approximate for Njeru's departure). Njeru cared for the regalia of the dead king and also maintained the burial estate of King Rugomora. She married the dead king in 1900 as a virgin, conducted the monthly new moon ceremonies (ritual renewals) in the shadow of Kaiija shrine on behalf of the ancient kingdom over which Rugomora once ruled, was given the same respect and tribute as a king, and could deeply influence the welfare and well-being of her neighbours who widely admired her beauty and respected her. As historical narratives about this important historical figure were unveiled, so too did an awareness develop amongst women that they had much to add to local history and to the heritage project. These narratives, never before recorded, deeply enrich the texture of the history of the royal compound and mark this local initiative into collaborative research as distinctive in subaltern studies.

These new female participants in Katuruka's heritage work now to advise the project on an interpretative trail that includes Njeru's place of royal residence as well as her menstrual house. Thus, heritage work in Katuruka has come to insert women of importance into heritage claims, along with their appearance in historical narratives. A heritage that valourizes important historical women is now emerging. It is claimed by contemporary elderly women, who enacted it through their daily practice by embracing and caring about heritage in the community.

As subaltern histories rose to the surface of local inquiry, so too did the insistence that the committee keep to its original agenda to create a museum that would commemorate the technological history and antiquity of Katuruka, drawing deeply on archaeological histories. The elders' goal to build a small museum was realized in 2010 with the construction of a traditional *omushonge* house in the exact location where oral traditions held that King Rugomora held consultations with his advisors and his spirit mediums. Known as Buchwankwanzi, this house was later used by Njeru to curate the royal regalia. It was precisely in this place that the 1970 excavations recovered many artefacts and features suggestive of intense ritual activities as well as deep time connections to Early Iron Age activities. The construction of Buchwankwanzi was a daily activity that ran for nearly a month, with visits from scores of villagers, most of whom never witnessed the construction of a traditional house.

Re-interanimation reprised

The heritage interventions pertaining to these shrines mark their *re-interanimation*, a phenomenon that includes the recursive quality of places and their relationships to human actors. As Basso (1996, 55) observes: 'As places animate the feelings and ideas of persons who attend to them, these same ideas animate the places on which attention has been bestowed.' Such participatory heritage work in Katuruka is considered by some as liberation from the strictures of Christianity enforced for more than a century. The willing participation of villagers in the shrine and Buchwankwanzi revitalizations is a clear declaration that even devout Christians no longer accept the idea that they must not participate in senses of place.

Motivations for these *re-interanimations* are linked to the rise of disenchantment over what people see as the failure of the Christian church to mediate the HIV/AIDS epidemic. The church is closely identified with western medicine, having introduced it to rural and urban communities. Western medicine and the church provided no relief from the ravages of the disease, leading many people to question, as they witness the moral decline of their villages, if they and their direct ancestors erred in accepting the precepts of the church. Discourses about Jesus as alien to Haya cosmology are increasingly common, with sometimes biting commentary mixed with frustration and bitterness, a profound depth of disenchantment as Haya Christians measure their present against their pasts as they work and talk in the place where spirit mediums once gathered in the service of their king.

Revitalized knowledge and heritage

In early 2011, the committee began to take new directions. Discussions with visitors showed that both local and foreign guests *'wanted to see more things, such as furnaces — not just look at a place in a field where there were once furnaces'*. The committee requested excavations to expose ancient iron smelting furnaces so visitors could visually experience the 2000-year-old technology, *'to make the ancient remains clearer and more obvious'* (Schmidt 2008–2011 field notes). This desire to bring archaeology into the heritage talk and planning writes archaeology into a plan to concretize history. Archaeology organized by the committee became a focus of the project in the summer of 2011 when test excavations uncovered remains of 2000-year-old furnaces. As these were unveiled, villagers gathered by the scores at the excavations to participate in the discoveries.

Working together with trained archaeologists from the village, we observed several positive participatory developments: 1) village citizens mobilized to assist with the construction of exhibit shelters and the relocation of a major, traditional road, readily signing over rights of way; and 2) local secondary school students visiting Katuruka responded with great enthusiasm and excitement to the tour exhibits. This last development points to the project's capacity to satisfy the right to an education that incorporates local histories that value senses of place. The absence of local history in the secondary or primary curricula is a target that the project and regional and district authorities are taking on in 2013, with Katuruka heritage as the educational medium. Students visit these potent places and begin to develop their own senses of place through repeated visits. This experiential learning is accompanied by a dedicated website with academic resources, curricula, videos, and other images as well as teacher resources (www.tanzaniaheritage.org). The people of Katuruka, through their own distinctive wisdom, devised a community solution to a long-standing human rights issue in Tanzania — a hegemonic nationalist history that has helped to erase local heritage.

As Haya villagers engage in therapeutic heritage work (Meskell and Scheermeyer 2008) through the recuperation of oral traditions and histories and as they begin to daily engage in their *re-interanimation* of places, their senses of sacred places are being restored incrementally. Their ethical practice incorporates the recovery of interpersonal respect as well as respect for places of meaning that were once dominant in their moral lives. And, their initiative and determination to reclaim and remake a heritage severely eroded by change over the last 120 years marks this community as distinctive in the annals of African archaeology and heritage work. That they incorporated collaborative research — oral traditions, oral histories, and archaeology — into their development agenda speaks to a vision arising from familiarity with these genres of heritage from both indigenous culture and lived experience.

Acknowledgements

Thanks to Fulbright-Hay for support of a year's ethnographic research and to the University of Florida for release time and financial support. Assistance for heritage development was generously provided by the US Embassy, Dar es Salaam TANAPA (Tanzania National Parks Association), and the College of Liberal Arts and Sciences, University of Florida. My deepest appreciation goes to many friends and collaborators in Katuruka and Nkimbo villages in Kagera Region and to Charles Mafwimbo of the Kagera Regional government for his unfailing support. This research was conducted under permit from the Tanzania Commission on Science and Technology and the Antiquities Division, Ministry of Natural Resources and Tourism. This article is dedicated to the memory of Benjamin Shegesha, the leader of the Katuruka movement to revitalize the community's heritage.

References

Abungu, Patrick. 2012. World Heritage and Local Communities: The case of the 'Rabai *kaya* Conservation Community Project', Kenya. Nairobi: The National Museums of Kenya, 2012.

Abu-Khafajah, Shatha. 2010. "Meaning-Making and Cultural Heritage in Jordan: The Local Community, the Contexts and the Archaeological Sites in Khreibt al-Suq." *International Journal of Heritage Studies* 16(1–2):123–39.

Apoh, Wazi. 2013. "Archaeology and Heritage Development: Repackaging German/British Colonial Relics and Residues in Kpando, Ghana." In *Germany and Its West African Colonies: Excavations of German Colonialism in Post-Colonial Times*, edited by W. Apoh, and B. Lundt, 29–55. Berlin and Zurich: Lit Verlag.

Atalay, Sonya. 2006a. "Decolonizing Archaeology." *American Indian Quarterly* 30(2–4):269–79.

Atalay, Sonya. 2006b. "Archaeology as Decolonizing Practice." *American Indian Quarterly* 30(3–4):280–310.

Atalay, Sonya. 2012. *Community-Based Archaeology: Research with, by, and for Indigenous and Local Communities*. Berkeley: University of California Press.

Basso, Keith H. 1996. "Wisdom Sits in Places: Notes on a Western Apache Landscape." In *Senses and Place*, edited by Stephen Feld, and Keith H. Basso, 53–90. Santa Fe, NM: SAR Press.

Chirikure, Shadreck, and Gilbert Pwiti. 2008. "Community Involvement in Archaeology and Cultural Heritage Management: An Assessment from Case Studies in Southern Africa and Elsewhere." *Current Anthropology* 49(3):467–85.

Chirikure, Shadreck, Munyaradzi Manyanga, Webber Ndoro, and Gilbert Pwiti. 2010. "Unfulfilled Promises? Heritage Management and Community Participation at Some of Africa's Cultural Heritage Sites." *International Journal of Heritage Studies* 16(1–2):30–44.

Colwell-Chanthaphonh, Chip, and T. J. Ferguson, eds. 2008. *Collaboration in Archaeological Practice: Engaging Descendant Communities*. Lanham, MD: AltaMira Press.

Cooke, Elizabeth. 2010. "The Politics of Community Heritage: Motivations, Authority and Control." *International Journal of Heritage Studies* 16(1–2):16–29.

Dowdall, Katherine. M., and Otis Parrish. 2001. "A Meaningful Disturbance of the Earth." *Journal of Social Archaeology* 3(1):99–133.

Heckenberger, Michael. 2008. "Entering the Agora: Archaeology, Conservation, and Indigenous Peoples in the Amazon." In *Collaboration in Archaeological Practice: Engaging Descendant Communities*, edited by C. Colwell-Chanthaphonh, and T. J. Ferguson, 243–72. Lanham, MD: AltaMira Press.

Katuruka Interviews. 2009–2011. Interviews on deposit in the archives of the Katuruka Preservation and Conservation Association, Katuruka, Bukoba, Tanzania.

Keitumetse, Susan O. 2002. "Living and Archaeological Sites in Botswana: Value and Perception in Cultural Heritage Management." MA Thesis, University of Cambridge.

Kuwansisiwma, Leigh J. 2008. "Collaboration Means Equality, Respect, and Reciprocity: A Conversation about Archaeology and the Hopi Tribe." In *Collaboration in Archaeological Practice: Engaging Descendant Communities*, edited by C. Colwell-Chanthaphonh, and T. J. Ferguson, 151–70. Lanham, MD: AltaMira Press.

McDavid, Carol. 2002. "Archaeologies that Hurt: Descendants that Matter: A Pragmatic Approach to Collaboration in the Public Interpretation of African-American Archaeology." *World Archaeology* 34(2):303–14.

Marshall, Yvonne. 2009. "Community Archaeology: What is Community Archaeology?" In *Oxford Handbook of Archaeology*, edited by Barry Cunliffe, Christopher Gosden, and Rosemary A. Joyce, 1078–102. Oxford: Oxford University Press.

Mayor, Anne. 2013. *Préservation du patrimoine culturel en Pays dogon (Commune rurale de Dimbal, Mali): Rapport Final*. Geneva: University of Geneva.

Meskell, Lynn, and Colette Scheermeyer. 2008. "Heritage as Therapy: Set Pieces From the New South Africa." *Journal of Material Culture* 13:153–73.

Meskell, Lynn, and Lynette S. M. Van Damme. 2008. "Heritage Ethics and Descendant Communities." In *Collaboration in Archaeological Practice: Engaging Descendant Communities*, edited by C. Colwell-Chanthaphonh, and T. J. Ferguson, 131–50. Lanham, MD: AltaMira Press.

Murimbika, McEdward, and Bhekinkosi Moyo. 2008. "Archaeology and Donor Aid in the 'Developing World': The Case for Local Heritage in Zimbabwe." In *Managing Archaeological Resources: Global Contexts, National Programs, Local Actions*, edited by Francis P. McMamanon, Andrew Stout, and Jodi A. Barnes, 87–106. Walnut Creek, CA: Left Coast Press.

Muringaniza, J. 1998. "Community Participation in Archaeological Heritage Management in Zimbabwe: The Case of Old Bulawayo." MPhil thesis, University of Cambridge.

Ndeki, S. S., Knut-Inge Klepp, and G. R. Mliga. 1992. "AIDS Knowledge and Risk Behavior Among Primary School Children in Arusha and Kagera Regions." *Tanzania International Conference on AIDS* 8:220 (abstract no. PuD 9129).

Ndlovu, Nukuyakhe. 2005. "Incorporating Indigenous Management in Rock Art Sites in KwaZulu-Natal." MA thesis, Rhodes University.

Negussie, Elene, and Gatu A. Wondimu. 2012. "Managing World Heritage Sites as a Tool for Development in Ethiopia: The Need for Sustainable Tourism in Lalibela." In *Community Development through World Heritage*, edited by M.-T. Albert, M. Richon, M. J. Viñals, and A. Witcomb, 93–99. World Heritage Papers no. 31. Paris: UNESCO.

Pikirayi, Innocent. 2011. *Tradition, Archaeological Heritage Protection and Communities in the Limpopo Province of South Africa*. Addis Ababa, Ethiopia: Organisation for Social Science Research in Eastern and Southern Africa.

Posnansky, Merrick. 1979. "Excavations at Begho, Ghana, 1979." *Nyame Akuma* 15:23–27.

Posnansky, Merrick. 1987. "Prelude to Akan Civilization." In *Golden Stool Studies of the Asante Center and Periphery*, edited by E. Schildkrout, Vol. 65, Part 1. New York: Anthropological Papers of the American Museum of Natural History.

Posnansky, Merrick. 2004. "Processes of Change: A Longitudinal Ethnoarchaeological Study of a Ghanaian Village: Hani 1970–90." *African Archaeological Review* 21(1):31–47.

Posnansky, Merrick. 2009. "Hani." In *Africa and Archaeology: Empowering an Expatriate Life*, 176–203. London: Radcliffe Press.

Posnansky, Merrick. 2010. *Reflections on Begho and Hani: 1970–1998*. Encino, CA.

Rizvi, Uzma. 2006. "Decolonizing Methodologies as Strategies of Practice: Operationalizing the Postcolonial Critique in the Archaeology of Rahasthan." In *Archaeology and the Postcolonial Critique*, edited by M. Leibmann and U. Rizvi, 109–40. Lanham, MD: AltaMira Press.

Rugalema, Gabriel. 1999. "It is Not Only the Loss of Labour: HIV/AIDS, Loss of Household Assets and Household Livelihood in Bukoba District, Tanzania." In *AIDS and African Smallholder Agriculture*, edited by Gladys Mutangadura, Helen Jackson, and Duduzile Mukurazita. Harare, Zimbabwe: Southern African AIDS Information Dissemination Service.

Schmidt, Peter R. 1978. *Historical Archaeology: A Structural Approach in and African Culture*. Westport, CT: Greenwood Press.

Schmidt, Peter R. 1983. "An Alternative to a Strictly Materialist Perspective: A Review of Historical Archaeology, Ethnoarchaeology, and Symbolic Approaches in African Archaeology." *American Antiquity* 48(1):62–81.

Schmidt, Peter R. 2005. "Teaching Revolutionary Archaeology: African Experiments in History Making and Heritage Management." *Archaeologies* 1(2):46–59.

Schmidt, Peter R. 2006. *Historical Archaeology in Africa: Representation, Social Memory, and Oral Traditions*. Lanham, MD: AltaMira Press.

Schmidt, Peter R. 2008–2011. Field Notes. Archived in personal holdings, University of Florida, Gainesville, Florida.

Schmidt, Peter R. 2010. "Trauma and Social Memory in Northwestern Tanzania: Organic, Spontaneous Community Collaboration." *Journal of Social Archaeology* 10(2):255–79.

Schmidt, Peter R. 2012. "Hardcore Ethnography: Interrogating the Intersection of Disease, Poverty, Social Collapse, Human Rights, and Heritage." Paper presented at the conference on Heritage and Human Rights, Stanford University, 13–14 April 2012.

Schmidt, Peter R., and S. Terry Childs. 1985. "Innovation and Industry during the Early Iron Age in East Africa: KM2 and KM3 Sites in Northwest Tanzania." *African Archaeological Review* 3:53–96.

Schmidt, Peter R., and Thomas Patterson. 1995. "From Constructing to Making Alternative Histories." In *Making Alternative Histories*, edited by P. Schmidt and T. Patterson. Santa Fe, NM: SAR Press.

Shaw, Thurston. 1970. *Igbo-Ukwu: An Account of Archaeological Discoveries in Eastern Nigeria*. London: Faber for Institute of African Studies.

Shaw, Thurston. 1977. *Unearthing Igbo-Ukwu: Archaeological Discoveries in Eastern Nigeria*. Ibadan and New York: Oxford University Press.

Silliman, Stephen. 2008. *Collaborating at the Trowel's Edge: Teaching and Learning in Indigenous Archaeology*. Tucson: Amerind Studies in Archaeology. University of Arizona Press.

Smith, Claire, and Martin Wobst. 2005. *Indigenous Archaeologies: Decolonizing Theory and Practice*. New York: Routledge.

Trigger, B. 1980. "Archaeology and the Image of the American Indian." *American Antiquity* 45:662–76.

Archaeology and the local community in Africa: A retrospective

Merrick Posnansky

One of my abiding principles in research has been to involve the community as much as possible. History is not the preserve of the investigator but it represents the identity and integrity of the people most involved whose ancestors we disturb. The descendants of those ancestors have the most vital stake in our work. We spent a great deal of time listening to those descendants. We normally worked though the chief and his elders but we also tried to spend as much time exploring the lives of the people, visiting them on their farms and learning about their fantastic knowledge of the environment, especially of plants. For many years we conducted questionnaires to discover changes in their lives. We had closeness to the land where we were working – the researchers wanted to find out about the ancestors, the villagers hoped to achieve pride in their past and prosperity for their children.

Though Africa has witnessed a greater share of adventure archaeology in which sites are dug because of their prestige and often in avoidance of local involvement ('interference' as regarded by the non-indigenous archaeologist), it has been impossible to exclude the impact of the local community. Resident and descendant communities have only slowly come into play as archaeology becomes integrated into the educational system and the development of museums and monuments services. The consequent attempt to understand communities outside the major urban centres has led to folk museums and finally the development of integrated research programmes.

Archaeology developed differently in colonial Africa from archaeology in Britain and France, the metropolitan centres of Imperial and later colonial power. In Britain, in particular, archaeology in the 19th century grew from the grass roots of community involvement. Many regional archaeological societies, most often on a county framework, developed thriving local clubs and societies that had an interest in local history and archaeology. Several societies built up respectable libraries and organized regular programmes of talks to cater for their groups. The membership of many societies, often composed of loyal Anglican churchgoers, were mainly interested in their old local churches, abandoned monastic sites and medieval art and architecture, though not exclusively, since an interest in Roman archaeology was also cultivated. Many of the societies produced transactions that allowed their members to describe the antiquities of the areas in which they lived. Several groups organized excavations of their recognized antiquities. As archaeology developed in the 20th century, several societies provided funds or support for young professionally trained archaeologists to work on their sites where society members could also participate. As a graduate researcher in the English Midlands in the 1950s, I was greatly assisted by such societies as the Thoroton Society in Nottingham, the Derbyshire Archaeological Society, the Northamptonshire Natural History Society and Field Club, and the Leicestershire Archaeological Society. My earliest papers were all published in the pages of their well-edited scholarly journals. One of the ambitions of the more scholarly members who wrote for their local journals was to be eventually elected as Fellows of the distinguished national Society of Antiquaries of London that began in the 17th century.

Many of the county societies regarded themselves as custodians of their local past. These societies were regarded as somewhat exclusive and arcane and, like many societies Britain in the first half of the 20th century, required known existing members to introduce prospective members often imposing an admission fee. The societies were continuing an antiquarian tradition that had started in the 18th century. By the end of the 19th century, rather more plebeian interests were being generated by such organizations as the Workers' Educational Association based in larger urban centres rather than in county towns. The WEA introduced classes on England's past and following the Second World War they expanded their scope and were often integrated into schemes run in association with University Extra Mural programmes. Many of the most renowned Africanist archaeologists, like John Alexander, Thurstan Shaw and I taught in Extra Mural Programmes. In the period from 1945 to1980, many of the adult students of such educational programmes, many of whom were schoolteachers, spread a wider knowledge of archaeology and provided a ready audience for the growing numbers of programmes devoted to archaeology by such media outlets as the BBC. New non-county archaeological clubs were started, many of which excavated important prehistoric sites, as opposed to church and monastic ruins. In many ways archaeology became democratized.

In Africa many of the traditions of Europe were continued including the terminology for 'cultures' and finds (Posnansky 1982). Archaeology was initially the preserve of white Europeans who had received their training in Europe. The interest in African archaeology did not have the same grass root origins as had the growth of European archaeology but was a singular interest of largely government officials or museum personnel looking at a strange landscape in which they had no roots. There were several levels of separation of researchers from what they were studying. Much of the archaeology was relatively small scale, often initiated from museums in the capital city, museums that were often Natural Science or oriented to colonial history. Though some locals were employed as labourers on excavations, there was little continuity of interest and the few publications produced were often printed overseas with little information in the local English language press and none in the sparser vernacular outlets. Except for museum displays, the local impact of discoveries was minimal until the post-World War II period when there was a growing demand for school curricula to reflect up to date research. Dr L.S.B. Leakey trained field assistants, but they were trained for the specific job they had to do rather than acquiring a broader knowledge of Africa's past. The work of pioneering archaeologists rarely impinged on the prevailing educational systems. Regional colonial administrators, such as District Commissioners, were informed about research to be undertaken in their areas, but far less care was taken to involve the African 'traditional' hierarchy, though some researchers like Louis Leakey built up networks of informants who kept local chiefs involved.

Virtually all excavations conducted in Africa before the late 1950s involved African labour but that did not imply the help of the community. All it meant was that a call was made for labour by the European District Commissioner or a member of his staff. The foreign team normally lived away from the labour crew so there was little social interaction. The workers on the site, normally men, were not necessarily from the exact area where the dig took place. Community involvement under these conditions meant that the director of the excavation approached the chief or residents of the area and requested help. The mission objectives were carefully laid out and the labourers had a commitment to their community to keep them informed of developments; and, the director of research had a commitment to keep the chief and his elders informed about the work. On many earlier excavations there was no feed-back to the community and very often the local community knew very little about what was happening. There was often little follow-up by the District Commissioner's office to the director of the mission.

The situation began to change in the 1950s and 1960s. In Northern Rhodesia J. Desmond Clark began a yearly Winter School that introduced students to both African archaeology and the basic techniques of discovery. The students, however, many from the Union of South Africa, were largely white and mostly archaeology students from the University of Cape Town. In Kenya the first field school to accept high school students was conducted at Lanet in 1957 and directed by myself. Unfortunately, at that time the schoolchildren involved were all Europeans. At Bweyorore in Uganda, in 1959, the first Ugandan field school was conducted by the Uganda Museum for African students from Makerere University College and was attended by several University teachers. These schools provided instruction in basic recording methods, field survey and the preliminary analysis, conservation and interpretation of finds. The big advance of these projects over previous archaeology in Africa was that the students provided the labour and the whole group lived and ate together. The field school ultimately laid the groundwork for introducing archaeology into University curricula.

A common misconception in the 1950s was that Africa had a restricted past and that the rich heritage of the Stone Age with its spectacular lacustrine and cave sequences and rock art was somehow not connected with the 20th-century descendants whom the colonialists 'discovered' in darkest Africa. The few exceptions to the cultural deprivation that the colonialists described were found on the fringes of that impoverished world such as the Swahili towns of the East African Coast or the Islamic states of the Sahelian belt of the Western Sudan. These developed societies were regarded as the outliers of an Islamic world that had impinged on Africa only within the past millennium. Because of these misconceptions, the new post-Independence generation of African students regarded archaeology as only dealing with stones and bones, a prejudice that persisted into the 1970s. The earliest generation of African students was more attracted to history, with its indigenous states, royal dynasties and links with the contemporary scene, rather than to the ancient pre-colonial history of Africa.

African museums had a great impact. They provided a glimpse of the pre-colonial past, sometimes mistakenly referred to as traditional Africa. There was in fact no single traditional Africa; traditions refer to the passage of ideas, processes, technologies and behaviour through time from generation to generation. In the early days of Independence, there was a desire and effort to snatch back and restore what had been lost during colonialism and the very fast process of urbanism that brought large rural populations into urban areas. Traditions were lost, technologies evolved, and much was changed in fields like music and the performance and religious arts. Some traditions were recaptured, others improved upon - the effort was made and society enriched. Museums in the period from the 1950s to the 1970s placed an emphasis on the ethnographic differences that had created the rich new national panoplies. In Niger, Zambia, and Tanzania folk villages were created to demonstrate the cultures of those societies that had not been previously displayed fully in museums. Different crafts were re-enacted in the open-air museums such as leather and metal working to give visitors an idea about pre-Industrial technology. Many more states planned folk museums or craft villages, like Togo, in their development plans but the economic depression of the 1980s resulted in their abandonment. The great advantage of folk museums was that they tried to recreate village life or at least the tangible aspects of various activities to enrich the cultural awareness of the new urban masses and particularly urban schoolchildren whose educational aspirations and opportunities had been enhanced with Independence.

Somalia came late into the surge to make its past relevant. Its original colonial museum, in a large 19th century Zanzibar-style stone building in Mogadishu, had important collections of geology, numismatics, and Arabic culture reminiscent of the Swahili coast and the material culture relevant to such a population. The collections certainly did not adequately reflect all the people of Somalia. This museum and its collections were largely destroyed in the wars that broke out in the 1990s. In some ways its loss was not universally mourned, as it was largely a colonial edifice with collections deemed important to the restricted vision of the colonial powers. In contrast, the Museum at Hargeisa, the capital of Somaliland, built as a people's museum in the 1970s with inspiration from North Korea and China, was more reflective of Somalia's diverse cultures, particularly its dominant pastoral sector. The museum itself was a circular building with an interior circular courtyard where activities could take place. The broader community with a grass roots enthusiasm provided its collections. Its premises were used for activities that promoted local culture. Sadly, with the internecine Somali wars the Museum quickly went into decline but its creation pointed the way to how a community can contribute to provide collections that are reflective of their own ways of life. The emphasis in the Hargeisa Museum was not on well-worn specimens but on contemporary material actually used by the people whose story was being told. The object *itself* was less important than its purpose and the processes that had produced it. The intangible aspects of history portrayed by the object had replaced the previous idea that the object should be regarded as art or reflective of a past culture. This is an idea that is well represented in the scholarship of Sada Mire (Mire 2007).

In the Uganda Museum, where I worked from 1958 to 1962, rather than bring the village life to the central museum in the capital, we were more interested in keeping alive local practices and crafts in the areas where they still survived. The Museum cooperated with centres of Adult Education to run weekend courses on the culture and life of key areas of Uganda. The first areas we chose were Teso in the north and Toro and Ankole in the southwest (Posnansky 1959). Rather than paying a fee to attend the courses, participants were encouraged to bring objects that held special meaning either to themselves or fellow members of the community. These objects, whose significance had changed over the years, and in some cases old photographs, reminded them of technologies or customs from their youth that they had forgotten in the rush to Independence and the exhortations to look toward the new nation state of Uganda. Many course attendees were schoolteachers, or worked in community development, so we knew that the impact of what they learnt would spread. In some cases the courses revealed to the participants knowledge about archaeological sites in the areas where they resided. In Teso many of the students who were unfamiliar with Stone Age rock art found it scattered in their area. This new knowledge was advantageous when the Uganda Ancient Monuments Board was established in 1964 and it was decided to schedule such sites as Nyero and provide them with limited protection from vandalism. It was realized that the archaeological sites and tools from the past provided a key into a previously ignored past.

The main problem with the folk museum initiative was that it depended on people helping people. There were no resources to provide for buildings, wages for staff to look after the museums, no money, and often no electricity for audio visual aids. Between 1970 and 1985 there was little regional development during this period of internal strife when a lack of basic security and roads and other services deteriorated. Help for the folk museum was low on any list of national priorities. When there was again stability in Uganda, after the troubles of the 1970s and 1980s, many new rock art sites were found since villagers knew what the National Museum or archaeologists were interested in finding. Folk museums and sites were attractions for tourists and provided fuel for the eventual initiation of courses on heritage studies and tourism in national universities. Archaeology for many schoolchildren and their teachers was no longer just 'stones and bones' but a method of exploring and rejoicing in their own past.

Museums, however, had many other jobs to do. The expansion of school services in the 1960s encouraged school visits to museums in both East and West Africa and played a major role in creating an awareness of the rich legacy of the countries they served. Very large numbers of school children gained information about their pasts, but the impact of the schools museum services was limited. Schools above the primary level were still sparse in some areas and rural schools often could not afford the buses to take them to the capital cities or large towns where museums were located. The involvement of University Institutes of Education, many of which had close relationships with the school programmes, resulted in useful teaching aids but there was a shortage of funds to make full use of aids such as circulated boxes of exhibits or audio visual equipment for otherwise effective programmes.

Both in East Africa and Ghana we found that it was critical to share our work and explain our methods of work and interests with the community we served when we had the opportunity, often many years after the event. Writing for a local public may not always advance one's career academically, but it is extremely important in helping people in different walks of life to be aware of what we are trying to do. We used local media, such as newspapers like the *People*, *The East African Standard*, *Farmer's Weekly* (Nakuru), and *The Rock* (Christian Council) in Kenya and the *Uganda Argus*, *Habari* (the Uganda Police bulletin), *New Vision* and *Monitor* in Uganda. When radio and television became fully established, students in Ghana like Emmanuel Agorsah gave talks and wrote short informative articles about our work at Begho. At the beginning of TV transmission in Uganda in 1961, a series was requested on the archaeology and monuments of Uganda while in Ghana we were able to talk about archaeology on discussion shows. By this means, a wider awareness was developed. People up country who had heard about our work often surprised me with their questions. These communications have continued and archaeologists like James Anquandah in Ghana have provided several comprehensive series of radio talks for the Ghana Broadcasting Corporation to very good effect.

The most success in integrating archaeology within communities occurred with the expansion of field archaeology after 1970. Previously, expatriates had undertaken most excavations. Few spoke the languages of the areas where they worked and most had a clear focus on the sites they were excavating rather than on the ethnographic context of their work. An obvious exception was Professor Thurstan Shaw whose work with the Igbo community, different families and individuals helped him to find, access and excavate the remarkable Igbo Ukwu sites that included a sacro-religious burial of a chief and what was possibly a shrine room (Shaw 1977; see Schmidt 2014). He based some of his interpretations on his shrewd use of ethno-archaeology. He helped members of the Anozie family, on whose compounds many of the sites were located, become acquainted with their ancestors. Eventually several of them became his colleagues in the research and discovery of new sites, several named after his informants or owners of the land. His love of the community and his work led to his election to a local chieftaincy *Onuna-ekwulu Ora of Igbo Ukwu* (the mouth that speaks on behalf of Igbo Ukwu). The respect in which he was regarded was evident in the large number of Nigerians who attended his funeral in Cambridge in 2014.

The major key to understanding the past is to integrate closely oneself into the community in which one is working. I personally was richly rewarded, in terms of cooperation, knowledge and long-term effects, in the research I conducted at the medieval and early modern market town/state of Begho in Ghana (Posnansky 2015), some 300 km northwest of Accra. From 1970 until 1975, we ran annual field schools at Begho. The University of Ghana funded a research centre, planned and built by our staff that housed 15 students and provided storage for both equipment and finds as well as providing some classroom space. A longitudinal survey of the social behaviour, crafts, and agriculture of the villagers was undertaken from 1970 until 1998 that involved students, staff and faculty of the University of Ghana and the Chief, elders and villagers of Hani (the contemporary town) (Posnansky 2004). Many of the informants provided labour on the sites, many voluntary joining every excavation we conducted from 1970 till 1979. Besides training students from the University of Ghana, the field schools also attracted students from other parts of Africa, Jamaica, Europe, and North America. From the beginning, students participated in three approaches to the past: archaeological excavation; ethno-archaeology in which we study present spatial relationships, technology and behaviour, social relationships, and religious practice; and finally, traditional history. In non-literate communities, much of the knowledge about the past, including the cycle of agricultural activities, is passed orally from generation to generation. Each clan or lineage may hold vital details about the past but every source of information cumulatively adds to a history often specific to the names of significant leaders. That knowledge is reinforced by praise songs at festivals, remembrances at funerals, and through the frequent meeting of the council elders, open to everyone. Every clan was at some time in the limelight, as all the clans had festivals attended by the whole village that highlighted something special in their traditions. Even the farm workers, Dagarti from northern Ghana, who helped with yam cultivation and harvest, had their day in the sun. The Ahohohene, chief of the strangers, a wing chieftaincy to which I was elected in 1975, represented them and other non-locals from the urban areas who came to Hani particularly as teachers. We had a festival at which I was installed. My deputy was the tro-tro (a modified lorry that took villagers to and from market up to a 40-mile radius) driver who was very much part of the Hani community, hailing from a village only 15 km away.

The longer a researcher lived and worked with the community, the more knowledge about the past they acquired. Villagers were happy to share their knowledge. Many had remarkable memories of different plants and parts of plants that they use for food, medicines, and in building. Some had a latent knowledge of literally 500–800 plants, animals and insects. These were not arcane memories of a semi-secret nature but valuable data that over the generations may be lost. By visiting or working in a community at different seasons, one can tap into useful information that during another season may not have crossed the mind of a resident. Much of the best information came from informal conversations, often in a relaxed evening location, rather than from previously prepared questionnaires that the informants sometimes found intimidating.

One key requisite that we found especially important was to request a respected chief who had been on his stool for a long period to endorse our need for help from both the community and the ancestors we were disturbing. The first request is made at a chief's council, libations are poured and the community learns about the archaeologists' goals. Later the chief asks the community to help the researchers. So, in preliminary fieldwork we often had up to 20 men helping us clear vegetation to expose a site – work they performed willingly as communal labour requested by the Chief. In our case, the chief, the Hanihene Kofi Ampofo II, was well respected in the area so villagers acknowledged him for his accumulated wisdom. Similarly, if the Chief wanted the ancestors to yield their secrets to the researchers, libations were poured at regular intervals such as when we wished to take a burial from the ground. When libations were poured, all those involved partook and all understood that this symbolized their willingness to be involved. Schoolchildren, particularly from the Middle School, helped on occasion by washing the potsherds. Many eventually joined our team as labourers. One benefit was that knowledge about our objectives, means of discovery, and some of our conclusions filtered through the village in an informal way.

The link between the Chief and Governmental representatives also ensured the cooperation of the people and indicated the Government's commitment to support our research. This was clearly in evidence when the Regional Commissioner opened the Research Centre in 1972. All the neighbouring chiefs came with their festive umbrellas, sword bearers, and in some instances their chiefly palanquins. Their presence acknowledged their support for the research and for the importance of the Chieftaincy at Hani as heir to the historic reality of the Begho State that had preceded it.

Attendance at the ceremony by the local population indicated support of their chief and reaffirmed the essential links that existed between the Chief, neighbouring chiefs, and the Central Government. Similarly, the attendance of the pro-Vice-Chancellor and other dignitaries from the national University at Legon signified the scholarly importance of the venture and the high regard in which the researchers were held in their own institution. All of those participating in the opening were stake holders, all had different motivations, but hoped to gain from that association, whether it was recognition of past glories, the hope for outside interest and perhaps future tourism, and importantly, a recognition of the value each party held for their conjoined pasts. An immediate result of the ceremony was the linking of the names of Begho – the site and the ancestral State – and Hani, its modern descendant. Both names now appear on official signboards and memoranda.

A small exhibition of the artefacts we found was arranged to accompany the opening gathering. This also provided a description of our interpretations while reconstruction of pots from shards demonstrated to villagers and chiefs from surrounding villages the importance of what we had been found and illustrated how history could be recreated. Students in the Department of Archaeology gained an appreciation of working with the local community. The locals were no longer just interpreters or casual informants but colleagues. They are proud of their ancestors. There has been much cross-cultural interaction between the villagers, gaining much from the students in their contacts (Posnansky 1993). Students trained at Begho have gone to other areas in Ghana and have similarly interacted with their hosts. Three years after the Research Centre opened, a small library was endowed by donations from the Lions community of our American staff member (Joanne Dombrowski). It became the meeting room for the middle school teachers. These multiple interactions provided extra stimulation for the village's cultural development and gave even more visibility to Hani, now a community with bore holes, a health clinic, electricity, and many other amenities that research participation helped stimulate.

One way in which closer interaction between the archaeological team and the community developed was through sport. In Hani we provided new goal posts, a good leather football and jerseys clearly recognizing Hani as their team. We played a series of games, often the Hani labourers working on the dig would join our team, at other times they strengthened the home team. Sports established great rapport. In Notse, Togo, the visitors fielded a basketball team. The locals were sceptical about women playing on our team but they proved enthusiastic opponents and learned to respect American gender equality. Certainly in West Africa sport is a great way for successful interaction to be switched from the purely archaeological/historical issues to social interaction particularly in the camaraderie of the get-together after the game.

An important caveat needs to be made. The experiences of community involvement discussed above apply largely to those areas where some continuity of population can be proved. Sites of the deeper past that include Stone Age and early agricultural sites rarely have descendants who have any knowledge of their predecessors. The work of discovery is thus a joint one. Many sites in Africa are dug with African students drawn from university departments of archaeology and history or students from overseas trained in departments of anthropology. They may be excavating far away from communities interested in enhancing their awareness of the past. Once trained, such students can contribute significantly to finding new sites like rock shelters, but often they need information that comes from general knowledge of archaeology, the environment, and recognizable artefacts. In West Africa this means an awareness that terra cotta 'cigars' are a clue to early agricultural occupations or that iron slag came from iron working – also knowledge held by members of rural communities that may help them to alert archaeologists to significant sites.

All the approaches I have discussed built up an awareness of the past. Archaeology at first seemed an arcane discipline taught to only a few students. But as numbers grew knowledge filtered down through the school system where many students eventually taught at still too few fully staffed secondary schools. Museums conserve and display finds and develop programmes to meet the requirements of schoolchildren. Pupils at school eventually gain a passing knowledge of the continuity of their culture. As the example from Ghana clearly indicates, the most effective way of communication is through the cooperation of researchers with communities around sites. But there are some provisos. In order for a community to be aware of what the archaeologists are doing, it is necessary for projects to last several years. It helps if the archaeologists can invest in the community, not necessarily by gift giving, but by sharing knowledge, providing opportunities and opening horizons. Whatever approach is taken, effectiveness is limited, a fact that is daunting for the archaeologist due to the relatively small areas in which field archaeology is conducted. In developed countries, most major centres of population have museums and there is a network of archaeologists able to respond to the need to protect threatened sites. In contrast, in the developing countries the impact of a research team is fairly local and the promise of follow-up work or regional museums is more restricted. There are a few exceptions, such as the National Museums of Kenya that has 18 museums and open-air museums as well as a staff of over a thousand. Though there are many logistical problems and a very large population to serve in Nigeria, nevertheless there are many regional hubs for antiquities research and museums providing public access. Interaction with the archaeologists can provide the community with role models to emulate, particularly if encouragement is provided.

One of the follow-up occasions that I always appreciate when I return to Ghana is to learn which villagers from Hani have visited their former colleagues on the staff of the Department of Archaeology when they come to the big city. It is also wonderful to hear of how many of the schoolchildren we knew advanced in their education beyond the middle schools of Hani. Our interaction certainly had an educational benefit. Continuity of interaction is extremely important. Far too often when the tents, equipment, and finds are packed, and the goodbyes said, the community know that they may never see the archaeologists again and loses interest. Far too often publications are produced outside of the country concerned and the community never knows the results of the work on sites they may have discovered and helped unearth. They have no access to libraries containing the results of the research. To counteract this aspect, I revisited the village of Hani 30 years after the last archaeological work and a dozen years after the last ethno-archaeological survey. I gave each person who had helped our work a privately produced volume (Posnansky 2010) that reproduced three of my major written pieces on Hani and Begho, including a special set of conclusions and nearly 100 photographs in colour that illustrated life in the village, ethno-archaeology, and excavations and arte-facts. Most of the recipients had never seen the photographs and multiple mementos of our work remains in the village. The volume documents the village in the 1970s, the Chief and Elders who were then so important, the roles of the church and schools, and the work of the farmers of the time. When we first arrived in 1970, all we had were a few notes on the oral history. The combined work of the community and the archaeological team has amplified that history and provided a heritage compendium for a community that is proud of its past and appreciative of its interaction with the crew from the local university they were not too sure about 45 years ago.

Disclosure statement

No potential conflict of interest was reported by the author(s).

Suggested citation

Posnansky, Merrick. 2017. "Archaeology and the local community in Africa: A Retrospective". In Special Series, African Perspectives on Community Engagements, guest-edited by Peter Schmidt. *Journal of Community Archaeology and Heritage* 4(2): page #s tbd.

References

Mire, Sada. 2007. "Preserving Knowledge, not Objects: A Somali Perspective for Heritage Management and Archaeological Research." *African Archaeological Review* 24: 49–71.

Posnansky, Merrick. 1959. "The Development of Regional Folk Museums and Adult Education." In *Proceedings of the Third Conference of Curators of East and Central African Museums, Kampala 1959*. Kampala: Uganda museum.

Posnansky, Merrick. 1982. "African Archaeology Comes of Age." *World Archaeology* 13: 344–356.

Posnansky, Merrick. 1993. "The Archaeologist and the African Community." *Akan Studies Council Newsletter* 6: 8–11.

Posnansky, Merrick. 2004. "Processes of Change – A Longitudinal Ethno-Archaeological Study of a Ghanaian Village: Hani 1970–98." *African Archaeological Review* 21: 31–47.

Posnansky, Merrick. 2010. *Reflecting on Begho and Hani, 1970–1998*. Los Angeles: Privately published.

Posnansky, Merrick. 2015. "Begho, Life and Times." *Journal of West African History* 1: 95–118.

Schmidt, Peter R. 2014. "Rediscovering Community Archaeology in Africa and Reframing its Practice." *Journal of Community Archaeology and Heritage* 1 (1): 38–56.

Shaw, Thurstan. 1977. *Unearthing Igbo-Ukwu*. Ibandan: Oxford University Press.

Seniority through ancestral landscapes: Community archaeology in the highlands of southern Ethiopia

Kathryn Weedman Arthur, Yohannes Ethiopia Tocha, Matthew C. Curtis, Bizuayehu Lakew and John W. Arthur

ABSTRACT
This article focuses on our collaboration with the Boreda of southern Ethiopia to document the ways in which their cultural heritage knowledge is entwined with Ochollo Mulato, one of their nine tangible senior ancestral landscapes or *Bayira Deriya*. Through the interface between oral traditions, life histories, and the archaeological record, we grew increasingly aware of the descendant community's wide range of alternative but equally valid memories and attachments to their ancestral lands. Articulated through the landscape at Ochollo Mulato, Boreda demonstrated to us the various historical paths for defending assertions of seniority between youths and elders and between farmers and craft-specialists.

Introduction

It was a cool clear day on the western escarpment of the Rift Valley in the Gamo highlands of southern Ethiopia. Kathryn and Yohannes spent the morning in Ochollo Mulato guided by three elders, Alemayehu Gunto, Chilga Chisha and Baredo Badeke, walking well-worn paths that spiral through ancestral geographies, crowning at Ochollo Mulato. We stood with our guides near a wall shielding the *Kalo Ogyiya*, the road that saves us from hunger, surrounded by the four peaks that form Ochollo Mulato.

The elders directed our eyes around the landscape we had just traversed. They referred to the different patches of forests where craft-specialists and farmers were buried; where they established temples to pray for success in war and hunting, and where the King lived, prayed in his sanctuary, and held assembly court. The peak to the east is the highest and now adorned with a bright blue tarp under which John, Matthew, Bizuayehu, and the landowners, who are sons of the elders, were excavating the ancient settlement site of Ochollo Mulato (Figure 1). We asked the elders, *what do you wish us to prepare and accomplish with all the histories we were collecting?* Alemayehu replied,

> We want the government to recognize the importance of our historical places, to help preserve these places and our culture for the next generation. The assembly places, temples, women's sacred forests, and men's sacred forests, we want to keep them. Our elders told us this history, this is not information we made up, and it is passed to us from long ago. We must protect our heritage for future generations so that they will know what we have achieved and remember how we lived and prospered. (25 May 2011)

Above, Alemayehu clearly articulates his desire to preserve his heritage, to have it nationally recognized, and to produce a written account for future generations. We are collaborating with him and

Figure 1. Excavations under blue tarps at the ancient settlement site of Ochollo Mulato. Provided by authors.

other elders to achieve these shared goals. The Gamo represent one of 56 nationalities in southern Ethiopia. Although there are no histories written in their Omotic language, Gamo heritage is revitalized through ritual practices and preserved in the memories of the elders. Alemayehu and other elders, who are among the first generation of Gamo to have a formal education, recognize the power and longevity of the written word and wish for their memories of historical practices and places to be preserved on paper. Archaeology also is well-entrenched as part of local and national discourse. Their knowledge of palaeoanthropological remains such as the early hominid fossil 'Lucy' instills an almost universal sense of national pride. For many Gamo, their local historic site of Ochollo Mulato imparts a sense of dignity, prestige, and seniority.

Our community-based archaeology project centres on one Gamo district, Boreda. For the last 10 years, the authors collaborated with many Boreda to facilitate our joint desire to produce a written historical text that would privilege their wisdom and combine it with archaeological knowledge. This article focuses on Boreda knowledge of their cultural heritage and the ways in which it is entwined with Ochollo Mulato (Figure 2), one of their nine tangible ancestral landscapes or *Bayira Deriya*. Bayira Deriya literally means the 'places of seniority.' The meaning of the term *bayira* is highly situational and may either refer to seniority as a title or be a predicate to describe a hierarchical relationship, such as elite, eldest or first (Sperber 1975a). As we spent more time at Ochollo Mulato, we came to appreciate how diversity in the potential meanings of *bayira* extended to the grounds titled Bayira Deriya. The descendant community's sense of seniority and prestige reflects a wide range of alternative memories and attachments in their relationship to their ancestral lands. Through the interface between oral traditions, life histories, and the archaeological record, we grew increasingly aware of the different but equally valid realms of knowledge significant to the development of various Boreda identities.

Our journey to community-based archaeology

Our journey to a collaborative heritage approach began similar to other Africanists with ethnoarchaeological research (e.g. Mapunda and Lane 2004; Schmidt 2010). Twenty years ago, John and

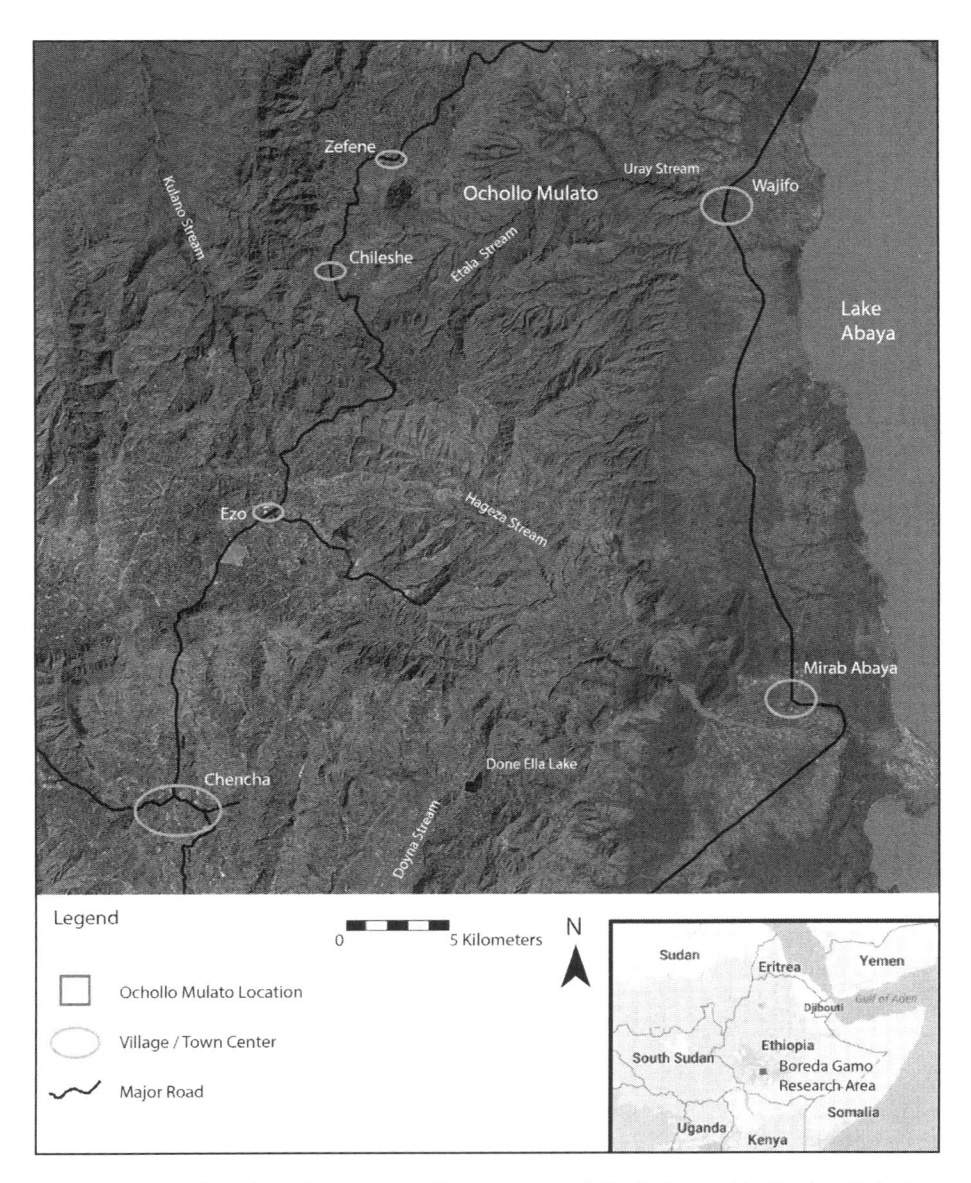

Figure 2. Map locating Ochollo Mulato adjacent tc Lake Abaya in southern Ethiopia. Designed by Matthew C. Curtis.

Kathryn's incorporation of life and generational histories into ethnoarchaeological studies of Gamo craft-specialists sensitized them to the connection between descendants and their heritage (Arthur 2006; Weedman 2006). In our preliminary conversations, many Gamo made it clear that their heritage was entangled with their memories of *Bene Woga* or old culture, ritual practices, and the landscape. In 2005, we returned to the Gamo highlands to begin a community-based archaeological project that would engage our anthropological skills to highlight the Boreda-Gamo perceptions of the development of their caste system. We were well aware that the dominant explanations for the segregation of farmers and craft-specialists among the Gamo and other southern Ethiopian peoples were national narratives touting conquests of the region by historic states centralized in northern and eastern Ethiopia and Eritrea (Levine 1974; Pankhurst 1999; Freeman 2001). In order to address potential archaeological indicators of inter-cultural interactions and possible conquests in the Boreda region, we invited Matthew Curtis (Curtis 2008, 2014), an archaeologist who studied the development of early complex societies in northern Ethiopia and Eritrea, to join our project. Matthew now co-directs Boreda archaeological excavation and mapping, exploring interests concerning regional expressions of sociopolitical complexity. Because our intention was to safeguard local histories, we collaborated at locations many Boreda identified as most significant historically and we proposed in archaeological research grants to examine the theories for caste development provided in Boreda oral traditions.

We were intimately concerned with respecting Boreda heritage rights in our project for personal and professional reasons. Personally, John and Kathryn felt the weight of pasts concealed, when the death of parents and grandparents disclosed our respective Choctaw and Jewish heritages. Histories that were intentionally hidden to protect us and our parents, spoke loudly to us about the power of the majority and the fragmentation of community. Concurrently, we witnessed in the late twentieth and early twenty-first centuries rising tensions between archaeologists and descendants, who were demanding legislative protection for their practices and histories (La Roche and Blakey 1997; Deloria and Wilkins 1999; Smith 1999; Weiner 1999; Watkins 2000; Funari 2001). During our project, Gamo in other districts became active in promoting their position as Indigenous peoples with 'Minority Rights Group International' (Mihlar 2008), and with the 'Sacred Land Film Project' (Tindall 2009), to protect their culture and sacred lands. One of our goals was to assess if the Boreda considered their ancestral landscapes to be threatened, and if so how we could assist them in protecting these places. In this regard, we had discussions with many Boreda elders, who cited that government road construction, agricultural expansion, and water development schemes had destroyed or impinged upon places important to their cultural heritage. We were fortunate that anthropologist Bizuayehu Lakew for the last 10 years was assigned to work with us as a representative of the regional government's Culture and Tourism Bureau. His extensive experience and knowledge of southern Ethiopian cultures was essential in the process of obtaining government protection for Ochollo Mulato. Driven by the Boreda community's commitment for conservation, we were interested in collaboration to ensure preservation of the archaeological sites, as well as their heritage practices and narratives.

We follow in the sentiments of Zimmerman (2005) that archaeologists need to refocus on the real people – the descendants – rather than on object-centred narratives and the *reconstructed people* in the archaeologist's mind. Certainly, we were influenced by the work of earlier Africanists who combined oral tradition and archaeology as a means of collaboration and decolonization (Shaw 1970; Posnansky 1979; Schmidt 1983). Heritage is often constituted in the intangibles: songs, narratives, dance, and experience that provide meaning for the tangible and reaffirms a sense of culture and personal history (Hollowell and Nicholas 2009; Jacobs and Porter 2012). These intangibles of heritage were initially invisible to us until we demonstrated our long-term commitment to the community (Heckenberger 2009; Gomes 2012). In part this was accomplished by our return in 2005, when John, Matthew, and Bizuayehu began our project by interviewing Gamo elders and met several Boreda community members interested in collaborating with us to document a history of places important to them. A year later Kathryn joined the project in Boreda, a community with whom she worked seven years earlier. After this absence her language skills were poor and she enlisted the assistance of Yohannes Ethiopia Tocha, who grew up in the region and possesses an intimate knowledge of Gamo language and culture. Yohannes helped Kathryn build her linguistic skills to articulate narrative meanings more effectively (e.g. Walz 2013, 83). His widespread social networks in the region and Kathryn's return to Boreda and renewal of many of her friendships, added richly to our Boreda partnerships. Boreda assign high value to external friendships based on the exchange of ritual, trade items, services, and information, referred to as *jala laga* (Tadesse 2004). The return of Kathryn and John demonstrated to many Boreda that we were invested in their communities and they began to share with us the locations and histories of their ancestral grounds, Bayira Deriya.

We are resolved to apprentice ourselves to the Boreda and their practices and ways of knowing the past to 'democratize knowledge production' (Smith and Wobst 2005; Atalay 2012, 3; Schmidt and Mrozowski 2013). This is admittedly a work in progress, however, because the various project specialists are still finishing their analyses concerning the Ochollo landscape and archaeology. We are now seeking funds to return to Ethiopia, when we will share our analyses with the Boreda community and learn what they think about them in light of *their* interpretation of the site.[1] While there are many particulars that make our experience distinctive, we hope that the Ochollo Mulato case study serves others working in Ethiopia and beyond as a reminder that a landscape may unfold the reasons behind people's varied perspectives concerning heritage (Dowdall and Parrish 2003; Chirikure and Pwiti 2008; Schmidt 2010). Articulated through the landscape at Ochollo Mulato, Boreda demonstrated to us the various historical paths for defending assertions of seniority (*bayira*) between youths and elders and between farmers and craft-specialists.

Elders and youth at Ochollo Mulato: ancestral or agricultural land

In 2005, the elder Alemayehu proudly directed John to Boreda's oldest settlement mound at Ochollo Mulato. Upon walking up to the mound, John was struck by its placement in the landscape perched with a perfect view of the Rift Valley below. Ochollo Mulato appeared as a mound with a thick, secondary growth of shrubs encircled by a series of old growth acacia and fig trees unencumbered by present day homes or agriculture. Alemayehu spoke enthusiastically, indicating that it was a large place that extended over 40 ha beyond the first settlement mound. Eroding from the settlement areas were stone hidescrapers, ceramics, and slag that John felt might hold significance for archaeological contributions for understanding the development of Boreda caste hierarchy.

In 2006, John and Matthew conferred with elders of the King's clan, who are recognized as the most senior or bayira within the elite farmer caste. We learned that their sons (Figure 3) were the actual landowners of Ochollo Mulato and it was imperative that we meet with them to discuss whether they wished us to excavate at the site. We spoke to the elders and their sons about archaeological methods and the potential for producing knowledge from the materials left in the ground by their ancestors. We requested their permission to excavate and asked if they would work with us to clear, map, and test excavate the site. They were fully supportive of a collaborative effort towards

Figure 3. Bizuayehu Lakew (centre), Matthew C. Curtis (far right) speaking with young farmers at Ochollo Mulato. Provided by the authors.

preserving their heritage and the elders gave us their blessings to excavate this site so that future generations would not forget their history. Work began with clearing the mound of secondary growth, but the elders insisted that we keep all primary trees intact, including their sacred fig trees.

When we returned to Ochollo Mulato in 2011 to conduct more extensive excavations, we were alarmed by the extent of farming that had occurred in the interim, some of which was beginning to encroach upon the central mound area. The absence of recent human disturbance of the site and our previous discussions with local Boreda led us to assume that the mound would be left intact for the future. We neglected to consider some major changes that occurred in the highlands that would explain differences in elders' and youths' attachments to the landscape. Many elders grew up in a period when they could freely practice their Indigenous religion based on ancestral and other spirits alongside attending the local Orthodox churches. Many of their sons, however, were born during or after the Derg Militant Socialist regime (1974–1991), which forbade Indigenous land-based practices and insisted that people join either Christianity or Islam. In addition, the Gamo highlands over the last two decades experienced an increase in land clearance for farming, a phenomenon closely related to wider regional and national economic and political changes in Ethiopia. We recognized an important tension in the situation. The young landholders who were appropriating the site with more intensive and extensive farming practices were the sons of the very elders who were considered their seniors and served as custodians of the traditions and stewards of Ochollo Mulato's landscape. It was apparent that further discussions were needed to discern if it was viable to excavate.

Kathryn and Yohannes arrived a few weeks later, and began by visiting the households of individual Ochollo Mulato elders to discuss their heritage associated with the site. It was at the request of the Ochollo Mulato elders, that Yohannes and Kathryn accompanied Bizuayehu to arrange a meeting between the elders, their sons the landowners, the Boreda Vice District Head, the Boreda Agricultural Officer, and the archaeologists. The meeting took place at the Ochollo Mulato settlement site and began with John speaking about the historical importance of the site as we understood it in the local and archaeological context and asking if the community shared in our vision to preserve it. Many of the young landowners expressed that they were interested in preserving the site, but it served as their only farmland and they were hoping the agricultural office would allocate them alternative farmland. The local government officials affirmed that they would witness the short-term payment agreement to compensate the landowners for their crops and salaries on the project. They qualified that they would need the national government to designate Ochollo Mulato as a historical place requiring protection, before they could allocate replacement farmland. At the meeting, one of the young landowners stood up and spoke loudly for everyone's attention declaring: *We agree completely, this is a historical place and you are experts, but it is our cultural heritage and if we do not protect it no one else will. We will protect it! Thank you.* Surrounding landowners and elders voiced their agreement and began gently to bump their shoulders against ours, a common Boreda gesture of friendship.

Boreda elders and youth both perceived the land as the medium for sustaining future fertility and well-being. For elders the future path was through preservation and rituals honouring ancestors and for youth the land was significant for crop production to feed and support their families. After long discussions, we reached an initial agreement with the young landholders that they would cease farming on the most sensitive areas of the Ochollo Mulato site area for two years in return for compensation for the loss of potential income. What might happen to Ochollo Mulato after the two-year agreement expired? Many Boreda elders continued to express concern about its future preservation. We were keenly aware that Ochollo Mulato's sustained preservation would require both community and formal state-sponsored preservation. Thus, we engaged regional (Bizuayehu) and national (Gezehegne Girma) representatives of Ethiopia's Authority for Research and Conservation of Cultural Heritage to broker an agreement with the landholders to stave off future farming in the central areas of Ochollo Mulato in return for comparable nearby farmland. Ethiopia and the Gamo highlands possess one of the fastest-growing human populations in the world, corresponding with an increased need to obtain fuelwoods for cooking and to clear forests for agricultural land, leading to deforestation and farmland erosion (Assefa and Bork 2014; Teshome 2014). Based on our experience at Ochollo,[2] in which increased demand for agriculturally productive land created a dispute over cultural heritage preservation, we believe that those invested in safeguarding their heritage landscapes in Ethiopia may meet similar challenges in the future. In this case, an agreement to preserve the site was reached in 2012 because the landholders, elders, project researchers, and the regional and national representatives of federal authority created an open and prolonged dialogue.

Elite men and Ochollo Mulato: legitimizing seniority and preserving independence

Elders Alemayehu, Chilga, and Baredo derive great pride and status as seniors in the community from their associated heritage at Ochollo Mulato. They suggested that Kathryn and Yohannes traverse the landscape with them (Figure 4). This approach allowed us better to experience the connection between their historic settlements, walls, and sentry posts and their narratives concerning their first king, King Borchay, and warfare. They encouraged us to take photographs, map, and record their memories concerning each place, as well as note what physically endured, such as trees, stones, and broken pots. Kathryn asked what they hoped we would do with all these artefacts of preservation. They replied that such preservation was needed to help the next generation and asked what we could offer. We suggested that we could make a film and write a book – perhaps for school-aged children. They, other Boreda, and local schoolteachers we worked with liked these ideas and they continue to assist us in the creation of a book that will be in the national language, Amharic, Gamocalay, and English.[3]

Kathryn's and Yohannes' immersion in the landscape with elders Alemayehu, Chilga, and Baredo began at the summit of Ochollo Mulato, the first ancient settlement. The elders conveyed that here was where *Borchay the first King made a fire to signal eight other men and their families to proceed up from the lowlands* (25 May 2011). As members of the King's clan, they declared descent from the first settlers on this landscape and as such they were bayira or seniors. This pattern would repeat in our discussions with elite lineages at the other eight highland Bayira Deriya. King Borchay, the elders said,

Figure 4. (left to right) Kathryn Weedman Arthur, Yohannes Ethiopia Tocha, Alemayehu Gunto, Chilga Chisha, Baredo Badeke, and John W. Arthur discussing the history of Ochollo Mulato at the ancient settlement. Provided by the authors.

lived in a lush open field near a spring at the northwestern base of Ochollo Mulato. When we arrived, the conversation's demeanour and volume changed. Chilga stood with his hands clasped behind his back and spoke in hushed tones. *This is the Ka'o Keta, the former residence of the first King, sacred ground, no settlement, no farming, and no animal grazing is permitted.* The other two men nodded and we proceeded to walk slowly across the grasses, the men held their heads slightly bowed in reverence until we arrived on the northern edge of the King's property. We stopped at a small mound no larger than 10 by 20 m deforested of its prior stand of large fig trees. We had arrived at the *Ka'o's Bura*, the King's sanctuary. Later, the King's former spirit-medium would divulge to us that the King's sanctuary was where she communicated with the King's ancestral spirits to warn him of future misfortunes and the means to allay them. Chilga offered that the King conveyed current problems and issues foretold by the spirit-medium to elder men of the farmer caste by gathering them at his assemblage court, *Bareto Yaha Debusha*. We then walked up the steep mountainside to the King's assemblage court and here our tour of Ochollo Mulato ended for the day. We learned more about the activities here from another highly respected Boreda elder:

> I know all the elders. In the past we went to the King's assemblage court in Mulato and we all met there during the Bonfire festival and this is how I know the story of Borchay and Ochollo Mulato. (Deha Dola 28 June 2011)

The Borchay tradition was common knowledge among elder farmers, members of the elite caste group who participated in the project. They stated it was a true story of their fathers' fathers, who annually heard the King recite his lineage's history commemorating the arrival of their founder. As Giya Fanikasha (26 May 2006) emphasized: *Borchay was king of all of Boreda, the first in Boreda.* Most Boreda farmer elders agreed that Borchay was bayira, the first, the one to whom they accord prestige. *Bayira* is a key concept associated not only with Borchay, but with the term they chose to represent themselves within Ethiopia – 'Gamo'. After the Ethiopian Emperor Menelik II's conquest of the Gamo highland area in 1897, the peoples of the region were given the national name 'Gamu', which, like many names ascribed by conquerors, is derogatory and literally means in the Amharic language, 'they stink' (Woldemarium 2013). The Derg Militant Socialist government (1974–1991) encouraged a new pronunciation of the name aligning the pronunciation with the Gamo's own word for lion (*gamo*). Gamo directly refer to the lion as bayira or the most senior. In doing so, they ascribe the qualities of a lion, such as its prestige, strength, and dominance with their culture, thus reconstituting their identity with a prideful sense of seniority (*sensu* Sperber 1975a, 1975b). When discussing lions, Boreda men also stated that only the King and men of his lineage had the right to wear lion skin regalia. Farmer men legitimatize their senior status in society through displaying their lion hides, claiming descent from Borchay and his followers, and for owning and defending the ancestral lands, Bayira Deriya.

The place where the first Boreda King settled, Ochollo Mulato, is a toponym meaning *the place where people were saved in war*. Like the other eight Boreda ancestral landscapes, Ochollo Mulato bears the scars and ruins of conflicts with the animal and human worlds in defence of Boreda sovereignty. In discussions and tours of Bayira Deriya with men of the farmer caste, Kathryn and Yohannes noted that their narratives often matured into tales of their triumphs in hunting and warfare. Boreda histories are reminiscent of other Gamo oral traditions that tend to emphasize warfare to protect their autonomy (Olmstead 1975, 226–227; Bureau 1979; Abélès 1981, 40–42). Historical records indicate that between the fifteenth and nineteenth centuries, the Gamo were invaded by the Oromo, subsumed under the Kucha and Kafa polities, and eventually integrated into the northern Amhara Ethiopian Empire (Bureau 1976; Marcus 1994, 19–29). The Borchay tradition often ascribes monikers to Borchay's followers that emphasize their origin from these external polities.

> Borchay came from Mande Gergeda [Sidama and Oromiyaa] and he was the first settler at Ochollo Mulato. He came with 8 other clans, including the Amhara, Gondo [Oromiyaa], and Woreta [Amhara]. (Kuta Kunta 8 July 2011)

The various versions of the Borchay tradition suggest that the Boreda originated from the north and east from the territories of the Amhara, Oromo, Sidama, Kucha, and Kafa. It became evident as we walked the landscape of Ochollo Mulato and the other ancestral landscapes that while King Borchay left his homeland to the east and settled peacefully at the top of Ochollo Mulato, these landscapes harbour protective architecture.

Many Boreda recalled that the sentry posts, fortified walls, trenches, berms, and cemeteries at Bayira Deriya are manifestations of intra-regional conflict between Gamo polities. Gamo oral traditions offer that historically, the 40 Gamo political districts engaged in conflict not over land, but over future military and agricultural service (Olmstead 1975; Abélès 1981).

When we descended from Ochollo Mulato, with Alemayehu, Chilga, and Baredo on a footpath named the road that saves us from hunger, we encountered a small open plain overlooking Lake Abaya and the Rift Valley below – the *mitta*. A mitta is a former wooden enclosure described throughout the Gamo highlands as a lookout to defend against attack (Olmstead 1975; Abélès 1977). These sentry posts conjured memories of honour and prestige for battles won, and were also the locations where the ancestors empowered men's spears for hunting, prior to its outlaw in 1980. As Deha Dola, an elder in Zonga Boreda, stated:

> In past times, people hunted animals for their hides and most of the time to get the title that would make us very famous. (12 June 2007)

Elder men were eager at every visit from us to recount their ancestors' past hunting and warfare adventures, bringing out their spears, elephant-hide shields, and lion and leopard capes of prestige – implements employed for hunting and defending their autonomy at the sentinel posts, berms, trenches, and walled ancestral landscapes. As we walked with elders throughout Boreda, they pointed out these large, walled earthworks and commented on the implied intensive labour and their protective locations surrounding the mountaintop settlements. They led us under canopies of remnant forests that concealed deep narrow trenches easily twice our height and over the high berms, where, they stated, their ancestors buried their victims of war where they fell. The oldest of the Boreda cemeteries is at Ochollo Mulato, the 'giving burial ground' or *Ema Dufo* which the elders said embraces the remains of men and women who lost their lives during Borchay's time. When warriors and hunters survived battles and hunts, there were elaborate rites honouring the men with feasts and praise songs (Olmstead 1975; Abélès 1977). At Boreda ceremonies held long after a warrior/hunter's death, his descendants performed commemorative songs in which he was compared to men of other prestigious polities such as the Amhara, Kucha, or Oromo; polities that national narratives insist conquered the Gamo.

Bayira Deriya memorialize the feats of Boreda founders and the heroes who defended their communities against other Gamo polities. Elite farmers enlist the past through oral traditions and rituals of warfare and hunting at ancestral landscapes to reinforce their claims of direct descent from first settlers and prestigious warriors, thus reinforcing their present-day seniority and prestige.

The first fire at Ochollo Mulato: farmers and craft-specialists contesting seniority

Elite farmers' claim to be the first settlers is disputed by craft-specialists, particularly surrounding the history of who ignited the first fire at Ochollo Mulato. The first firing place occupies a small terrace on the southern edge of Ochollo Mulato mound. Standing there, one of the elders of the King's clan desired a more reverent tone and announced loudly to the giggling children around us and a few curious and talkative adults, *elders and small children these are your historical places, it was larger and flat with more sacred trees but now suffers from erosion, be respectful*. Silence ensued and the elder elaborated, offering that when Borchay arrived he established the first fire here. The fire wafted smoke into the air that signalled that it was safe for the others to come. Since this time, Boreda farmers have honoured Borchay and the first settlers with an annual Bonfire festival, *Tompe*.[4]

> At the Bonfire festival, a father gave each of his sons a firestick and we all went to Ochollo Mulato to celebrate in June to the first firing place. This holiday reminded us of the first fire. (Kuta Kunta 8 July 2011)

Fire is an essential aspect of ritual life, and the order in which the nine Boreda communities light the fire during the Bonfire festival signals their settlement order. We attempted to corroborate the chronologies of their ancient settlements using radiocarbon dating. Their chronology begins with the first highland occupation during the time of King Borchay at Ochollo Mulato, a site with deposits spanning seven centuries between Cal AD 1270–1950, reaffirming their heritage that this site is the earliest Bayira Derre (singular of Deriya) in Boreda (Arthur et al. 2010). Unfortunately, with poor preservation due to extensive erosion at the other mountain settlement sites, chronometric dates could not confirm a detailed timeline for the subsequent settlement orders outlined in oral traditions. Boreda elders, confident in their accounts, are not troubled by the inability of archaeology to provide detailed settlement dates.

Fire signals settlement and social order and Boreda farmers and craft-specialists both claim their heritage through the first fire at Ochollo Mulato. Most farmer accounts of the Borchay tradition concur that he established the social order. As one elder told us, *the story of Borchay is more about the arrival of our culture —rather than a story of human migration* (26 May 2012).

> Borchay gave names to the farmer, leatherworker, and the potter-smith castes, for all people, but the man who started the first fire was of the potter-smith caste. (Chilga Chisha 24 May 2011)

Interestingly, even some farmer narratives accord the first fire to the potter-smith caste rather than to farmers, though it is implied that their king gave the potter-smith the order to build the fire. Farmers argue that only men and women of prestige had the privilege to enter the sacred groves, as Borchay did, and ignite the first fire. At least one lineage of the potter-smith caste contested the farmer caste's Borchay tradition, offering their story of settlement and prestige.

> Farmers know that it is the potter-smith caste who have the knowledge of fire. In the past, the potter-smith caste and the farmer lived together at Mulato, but then the farmer forced us to leave there. We have a saying from the first man's house smoke arises. (2011)

Today, smoke often arises from the fires utilized for the production of pottery, heating and shaping metals, and hafting stone tools for processing leather goods. Fire is essential to a craft-specialist's livelihood. Craft-specialists generally focused on their individual lineage histories and rarely confirmed a shared oral tradition regarding craft-specialists' first settlement at Bayira Deriya. The absence of a shared oral tradition among craft-specialists speaks to the depth of their repression. Most craft-specialists live far from the ancestral landscapes and we actively had to seek them out to participate in the project. Their narratives converged with each other and with farmers on their past oppression by farmers and prohibition from ancestral land.

> The farmers forced us to live in the swamp areas and on the edge of the mountain [Ochollo Mulato] and took the fertile lands. Always we were on the edge and they gave us very little food for our effort. (2011)

> They could not enter the sacred forest. They sat on the edges for wedding, mourning, and ritual induction ceremonies. We did not marry. We still do not marry. The farmers are senior and keep rules, keep their dignity. (2007)

Farmer narratives also forward a history in which they both justify the segregation of craft-specialists and at the same time elevate them to the historic status of kings in the Iron Box tradition. None of the craft-specialists that we spoke to knew this oral tradition and when we told them about it, they would nod and often smile offering something to the effect of, *so we were right we came first*! Giya Fanikasha, an elder man, who was renowned in the region for his knowledge of Boreda heritage, provided the most detailed accounting of this tradition, few other farmer elders could corroborate but they were clear in their respect for Giya's knowledge.

> Yes, I told them last time about leatherworkers and potters-smiths. In ancient times they were of the King's family. So in earlier times when the spirits lived in the world, the leatherworker and potter-smith took his son … they put him in a small iron box and they threw him in the water. [When the spirits learned this, they] said to them, in this world you have no authority and year after year you will live under the others. So in this case, craft-specialists and

farmers do not eat together, they do not live together, and they do not marry together. (Giya Fanikasha 26 and 29 May 2006)

This oral account outlining the heritage of segregation between farmers and craft-specialists is deeply entangled with the history of their contact with Amhara Christians. Some elders elaborated on the narrative offering that in the past the elite buried their deceased in boxes with iron nails, which the Amhara Christians introduced to the region during the time of Emperor Haile Selassie's reign (1916–1935). Historically, many Boreda buried their deceased in only a white cloth. They believed that an iron box would prevent an individual from transforming physically into the earth and spiritually into an ancestor. Iron is essential to Boreda agriculture for its use as hoes, axes, and plows that penetrate the earth in symbolic reproduction, maintaining fertile fields and hence human fertility. However, in this oral tradition, craft-specialists overstepped their boundaries by using iron to disrupt rather than instigate fertility. The spirits' punishment for their misuse of iron as a violation of the natural order was to demote craft-specialists to a low status and restrict their interactions with farmers to prevent further disruption of fertility. The exchange and conflict of power over key resources, such as iron, used to maintain the fertility of the soil, food sources, and human fertility, is present in other Eastern African oral traditions (Schmidt 1997). The tensions between farmers and craft-specialists are deeply entwined with their heritage connected to their ancestral landscapes.

Conclusion

Collaboration with descendant communities may reveal a wide variety of (even conflicting) perspectives concerning preservation and interpretation (Waterton 2005; Chirikure and Pwiti 2008; Straight, Lane, and Hilton 2015). Certainly, our community collaborations in the Boreda highlands of Ethiopia highlight how individuals can differentially derive a sense of seniority and prestige through the landscape. For many Boreda, Bayira Deriya activate emergent tensions between elites of differing generations over land use and preservation and amid craft-specialists and farmers concerning identity and prestige. We learned that most non-elite craft-specialists express their historical unity under narratives that emphasized their oppression, and quietly contest elite narratives that attempt to erase their presence at founding settlements.

Nonetheless, farmers own the land at Bayira Deriya, and as the social elite they historically control the dominate narratives surrounding these ancestral landscapes. Their sons also draw privilege and status through these ancient settlements and battlegrounds and initially challenged their fathers' desire to preserve the ancestral landscapes, preferring its use for agriculture production. Future archaeological researchers in Ethiopia should consider changes in land-use when mitigating cultural heritage resources with communities.

In this particular instance, we could bring together the diverse perspectives of Boreda farmers and craft-specialists and local, regional and national officials to preserve and excavate one of their Bayira Derre (singular of Deriya), Ochollo Mulato. We look forward to completing (and sharing with the Boreda) the archaeological story that is emerging through our analysis, and working together to build historic knowledge of the region.

It is a privilege to be entrusted with Boreda knowledge of their history and ancestral landscapes. Scholarship on the continent has long demonstrated that including descendent community perspectives is necessary to disrupt tropes that previously misidentified their roles in African history, and to restore prestige and dignity to African identities (Shaw 1970; Posnansky 1979; Wilmsen and Denbow 1990; Schmidt 1997). Bayira Deriya provide further evidence of the social-political complexity built by African peoples prior to colonial contact, and animate a variety of narratives through which the Boreda reconstitute their prestige and seniority. For many Boreda, acquiring prestige and seniority requires transformation for people, things, and landscapes such as Bayira Deriya. Bayira Deriya were once historic settlements that became battlegrounds and then sacred landscapes and agricultural fields. Change is essential to the Boreda way of knowing the world (Arthur 2013) and as we move forward in our collaboration with Boreda men and women, we expect that future interpretations and associations with Bayira Deriya will continue to be dynamic and inclusive of the divergent perspectives and desires within their communities.

Notes

1. When writing these grant proposals, we used Boreda histories to underpin our proposed theories for interpreting these sites, rather than Western-derived archaeological models.
2. At this writing, there are no other works published in Ethiopia that discuss that population pressure and increasing need for farm land, deforestation, and erosion, and how they impinge on heritage preservation. We believe that this issue will be increasingly important in the future.
3. We are planning to print the book ourselves and provide copies to the community at that point. This book will not be online because very few people in the community have access to the internet, and most are still without electricity. In addition, two of the co-authors (Kathryn Arthur and Yohannes Tocha) plan to translate all of our articles for the local community, and to seek funding to build a small cultural centre.
4. *Tompe* was a June festival associated with their Indigenous religion and practices that was later conflated with the national New Year celebration with a bonfire in September.

Acknowledgements

Heartfelt thanks go towards the Boreda who with compassion and enthusiasm collaborated and shared their present and past lives with us and to them most of all we hope this work brings pride, honour, and dignity. We also would like to thank the program officers and reviewers at the National Science Foundation (award numbers 0514055 and 1027607), National Endowment for the Humanities (award number RZ-50575-06), and the University of South Florida for providing funding for this project. We extend our deep gratitude for the assistance of the personnel of the offices at Ethiopia's Authority for Research and Conservation of Cultural Heritage particularly our national representative Gezehegne Girma; the National Museum of Ethiopia; and the Southern Nations, Nationalities, and Peoples Region's Bureau of Culture and Information in Awassa, Arba Minch, and Zefine.

Disclosure statement

No potential conflict of interest was reported by the authors.

Citation information

Arthur, Kathryn Weedman, Matthew C. Curtis, Bizuayehu Lakew, and John W. Arthur. 2017. 'Seniority through ancestral landscapes: community archaeology in the highlands of southern Ethiopia'. Special Series, African Perspectives on Community Engagements, guest-edited by Peter R. Schmidt. Journal of Community Archaeology and Heritage 4(2): page #s tbd.

References

Abélès, Marc. 1977. "La guerre vue d' Ochollo." *Revue Canadienne des Études Africaines* 11 (3): 455–471.

Abélès, Marc. 1981. "In Search of the Monarch: Introduction of the State among the Gamo of Ethiopia." In *Modes of Production in Africa: The Precolonial Era*, edited by Donald Crummey and C. Steward, 35–67. Beverly Hills, CA: Sage Publication.

Arthur, John W. 2006. *Living with Pottery: Ethnoarchaeology among the Gamo of Southwest Ethiopia.* Salt Lake City: Foundations of Archaeological Inquiry, University of Utah Press.

Arthur, Kathryn Weedman. 2013. "Material Entanglements: Gender, Ritual, and Politics among the Boreda of Southern Ethiopia." *African Study Monographs (CAAS Supplemental)* 47: 53–80.

Arthur, Kathryn Weedman, John W. Arthur, Matthew C. Curtis, Bizuayehu Lakew, Joséphine Lesur-Gebremariam, and Yohannes Ethiopia. 2010. "Fire on the Mountain: Dignity and Prestige in the History and Archaeology of the Boreda Highlands in Southern Ethiopia." *SAA Archaeological Record* 10 (1): 17–21.

Assefa, Engdawork and Hans-Rudolf Bork. 2014. "Deforestation and Forest management in Southern Ethiopia: Investigations in the Chencha and Arbaminch Areas." *Environmental Management* 53 (2): 284–299.

Atalay, Sonya. 2012. *Community-Based Archaeology: Research with, by, and for Indigenous and Local Communities.* Berkeley: University of California Press.

Bureau, Jacques. 1976. "Note sur les Eglises du Gamo." *Annales d'Ethiopie* 10: 295–303.

Bureau, Jacques. 1979. "Notes Sur L' Histoire Contemporaine des Gamo d'Ethiopie Meridionale." *Abbay* 10: 201–204.

Chirikure, Shadreck, and Gilbert Pwiti. 2008. "Community Involvement in Archaeology and Cultural Heritage Management." *Current Anthropology* 49 (3): 467–485.

Curtis, Matthew C. 2008. "New Perspectives for Examining Change and Complexity in the Northern Horn of Africa during the First Millennium BCE." In *The Archaeology of Ancient Eritrea*, edited by Peter R. Schmidt, Matthew C. Curtis, and Zelalem Teka, 329–348. Trenton, NJ: Red Sea Press.

Curtis, Matthew C. 2014. "Aksum: Ethiopian Royal Trading City." In *Cities that Shaped the Ancient World*, edited by John Julius Norwich, 110–113. London: Thames & Hudson.

Deloria Jr., Vine, and David E. Wilkins. 1999. *Tribes, Treaties, and Constitutional Tribulations.* Austin: University of Texas Press.

Dowdall, Katherine M., and Otis O. Parrish. 2003. "A Meaningful Disturbance of the Earth." *Journal of Social Archaeology* 3 (1): 99–133.

Freeman, Dena. 2001. *Initiating Change in highland Ethiopia: Causes and Consequences of Cultural Transformation.* Cambridge: Cambridge University Press.

Funari, Pedro P., 2001. "Public archaeology from a Latin American Perspective." *Public Archaeology* 1 (4): 239–243.

Gomes, Denise M. C. 2012. "Amazonian Archaeology and Local Identities." In *Ethnographies of Archaeological Practice: Cultural Encounters, Material Transformations*, edited by Matt Edgeworth, 148–160. Lantham, MD: AltaMira Press.

Heckenberger, Michael J. 2009. "Mapping Indigenous Histories: Collaboration, Cultural Heritage, and Conservation in the Amazon." *Collaborative Anthropologies* 2 (1): 9–32.

Hollowell, Julie, and Nicholas, George. 2009. "Using Ethnographic Methods to Articulate Community-based Conceptions of Cultural Heritage Management." *Public Archaeology: Archaeological Ethnographies* 8 (2–3): 141–160.

Jacobs, Jennifer, and Benjamin Porter. 2012. "Excavating Turath: Documenting Local and National Heritage Discourses in Jordan." In *Ethnographies & Archaeologies, Iterations of the Past*, edited by Lena Mortensen and Julie Hollowell, 71–88. Gainesville: University of Florida Press.

La Roche, Cheryl J., and Michael L. Blakey. 1997. "Seizing Intellectual Power: The Dialogue at the New York African Burial Ground." *Historical Archaeology* 31 (3): 84–106.

Levine, Donald N. 1974. *Greater Ethiopia: The Evolution of a Multiethnic Society.* Chicago: The University of Chicago Press.

Mapunda, Bertram and Paul J. Lane. 2004. "Archaeology for Whose Interest-archaeologist or the Locals?" In *Public Archaeology*, edited by Nick Merriman, 221–223. London: Routledge.

Marcus, Harold G. 1994. *A History of Ethiopia.* Berkeley: University of California Press.

Mihlar, Farah. 2008. *Voices that must be Heard: Minorities and Indigenous People Combating Climate Change.* London: Minority Rights Group International Brief Reports. http://minorityrights.org/wp-content/uploads/2015/07/MRG_Brief_ClimateC.pdf

Olmstead, Judith. 1975. "Agricultural Land and Social Stratification in the Gamo Highlands of Southern Ethiopia." In *Proceedings of the First U.S. Conference on Ethiopian Studies*, edited by H. G. Marcus. 223–234. East Lansing: African Studies Center, Michigan State University.

Pankhurst, Alula. 1999. "Caste in Africa: The Evidence from Southwestern Ethiopia Reconsidered." *Africa* 69: 485–509.

Posnansky, Merrick. 1979. "Excavations at Begho, 1979." *Nyame Akuma* 15: 23–27.

Schmidt, Peter R. 1983. "An Alternative to a Strictly Materialist Perspective: A Review of Historical Archaeology, Ethnoarchaeology, and Symbolic Approaches in African Archaeology." *American Antiquity* 48 (1): 62–79.

Schmidt, Peter R. 1997. *Iron Technology in East Africa: Symbolism, Science, and Archaeology.* Bloomington: Indiana University Press.

Schmidt, Peter R. 2010. "Social Memory and Trauma in Northwestern Tanzania." *Journal of Social Archaeology* 10 (2): 255–279.

Schmidt, Peter R., and Stephen A. Mrozowski, eds. 2013. *The Death of Prehistory*. Oxford: Oxford University Press.

Shaw, Thurston. 1970. *Igbo-Ukwu: An Account of Archaeological Discoveries in Eastern Nigeria*. London: Faber Institute for African Studies.

Sperber, Dan. 1975a. "Paradoxes of Seniority among the Dorze." In *Proceedings of the First U.S. Conference on Ethiopian Studies, 1973*, edited by Harold G. Marcus, 209–222. East Lansing: Center for African Studies, Michigan State University.

Sperber, Dan. 1975b. *Rethinking Symbolism*. Cambridge: Cambridge University Press.

Smith, Linda T. 1999. *Decolonizing Methodologies: Research and Indigenous Peoples*. London: Zed Books.

Smith, Claire, and Hans M. Wobst. 2005. *Indigenous Archaeologies: Decolonizing Theory and Practice*. London: Routledge.

Straight, Bilinda, Paul J. Lane, Charles E. Hilton. 2015. "'It was Maendeleo that Removed them' Disturbing Burials and Reciprocal Knowledge Production in a Context of Collaborative Archaeology." *Journal of the Royal Anthropological Institute* 21 (4):391–418.

Tadesse, Wolde Gossa. 2004. "Having Friends Everywhere. The Case of the Gamo and Hor." In *The Perils of Face: Essays on Cultural Contact, Respect, and Self-esteem in southern Ethiopia*, edited by Ivo Strecker and Jean Lydall, 289–310. New Brunswick, NJ: Transaction Publishers.

Teshome, Menberu. 2014. "Population Growth and Cultivated Land in Rural Ethiopia: Land Use Dynamics, Access, Farm Size, and Fragmentation." *Resources and Environment* 4 (3):148–161.

Tindall, Ashley. 2009. "Gamo Highlands: Sacred Land Film Project". Accessed 3 November 2014. http://www.sacredland.org/gamo-highlands/.

Walz, Jonathan R. 2013. "Routes to history: Archaeology and Being Articulate in Eastern Africa." In *Death of Prehistory*, edited by Peter R. Schmidt and Stephen A. Mrozowski, 69–92. Oxford: Oxford University Press.

Waterton, Emma. 2005. "Whose Sense of Place? Reconciling Archaeological Perspectives with Community Values: Cultural Landscapes in England." *International Journal of Heritage Studies* 11 (4): 309–325.

Watkins, Joe. 2000. *Indigenous Archaeology: American Indian Values and Scientific Practice*. Walnut Creek, CA: AltaMira.

Weedman, Kathryn J. 2006. "An Ethnoarchaeological Study of Hafting and Stone Tool Diversity among the Gamo of Ethiopia." *Journal of Archaeological Method and Theory* 13 (3): 188–237.

Weiner, James F. 1999. "Culture in a Sealed Envelope: The Concealment of Australian Aboriginal Heritage and Tradition in the Hindmarsh Island Bridge Affair." *Journal of the Royal Anthropological Institute* 5 (2): 193–210.

Wilmsen, Edwin and James Denbow. 1990. "Paradigmatic History of San-speaking Peoples and Current Attempts at Revision." *Current Anthropology* 31 (1):489–524.

Woldemarium, Hirut. 2013. "Revisiting Gamo: Linguists' Classification Versus Self Identification of the Community." *International Journal of Sociology and Anthropology* 5 (9): 373–380.

Zimmerman, Larry J. 2005. "Real People or Reconstructed People? Ethnocritical Archaeology, Ethnography, and Community Building." In *Ethnographic Archaeology, Reflections on Stakeholders and Archaeological Practices*, edited by Christopher Matthews and Quetzil Castenada, 183–204. Lanham, MD: AltaMira Press.

Community archaeology and heritage in coastal and Western Kenya

Chapurukha M. Kusimba

ABSTRACT

We have conducted research on the histories of slaving in Kenya, the growth and demise of urban centres along the Kenya coast, and the origins of inter-ethnic conflict and warfare in the Mount Elgon region since 1986. Our engagement with Swahili and Bukusu peoples of Kenya has blossomed into strong bonds of friendship and trust. We are fully aware that what we write has been and continues to be a collaborative effort between our host communities and ourselves. This paper reports aspects of my experiences and discusses how they have influenced how I approach and interpret the past and balance the often-conflicting perspectives and expectations of stakeholders.

Introduction

Major advances in method and theory have refined ways of knowing and interpreting the past, bringing us ever closer to the Binfords' wish that 'the past is knowable' (Binford and Binford 1968, 28). Yet outstanding issues in the practice of archaeology remain. Indigenous communities still view archaeologists suspiciously in many parts of the world (Nicholas 2010). Many view their western counterparts as primarily engaged in artefact-driven research that often fragments the materials excavated, leading to the invention of unrecognizable histories of indigenous experiences. Three decades ago, Peter Schmidt called for an overhaul in the research practice of anthropological archaeology:

> One of the most critical issues facing archaeology in Africa (and North America) today is the need to perform research on problems that are significant to the historical self-identity of living peoples, particularly those descended from the prehistoric and historic populations we study. As anthropologists, we cannot continue to perpetuate Western paradigms that militate against local historical sensibilities. This is particularly true of the practice of archaeology in the colonized world; it is even more poignantly relevant in Africa because of the colonial history of the West on that continent. (Schmidt 1983, 63, 2014, 37)

The slow pace of incorporating community archaeology into mainstream archaeology threatens the future of one of the few disciplines whose overall mission is to understand and resurrect voices from the past. As a discipline, archaeology's future will be sustained through a seamless collaboration and cooperation of stakeholders (Atalay 2012; Schmidt 2017; Schmidt and Pikirayi 2016). Is full stakeholder commitment to (re)writing the histories, protecting both tangible and intangible heritages, marketing heritage, and balancing the needs of contemporary communities – local, national, and global – achievable? What individual and institutional roadblocks prevent the attainment of a decolonized archaeology in Africa? How can an archaeology that integrates all voices and stakeholders thrive in Africa? We illustrate the complexities of contested history and heritage with a case study from Kenya coastal community first reported about 22 years ago (Kusimba 1996) and the potential for community engagement with an example from Western Kenya.

Broadly defined, community archaeology is an 'engagement in formal collaboration with tribal organizations that help determine research design, project methodology, and interpretation of results' (Murray et al. 2009, 65). Community archaeology transcends inclusion of stakeholders in field and heritage research as consultants, and entails building co-equal partnerships and collaborations in designing research agendas and funding; in data collection and analysis; and in interpretation and publication (Atalay 2012; Heckenberger 2008, 2009; Murray et al. 2009, 65; Nicholas, Welch, and Yellowhorn 2008, 293). In Alaska and the American Southwest, community archaeology is nearly mainstream (Colwell-Chanthaphonh and Ferguson 2008; Kerber 2003; Silliman 2008) and archaeologists ignore indigenous voices and perspectives at their own peril (Nicholas 2010).

Despite advances, vestiges of colonialism continue to privilege Western interpretations over indigenous ones. Across Africa, the exclusion of native intellectual voices in the writing of the African past is an ongoing phenomenon and standard practice that has raised the problem of the future of a discipline that continues to silence the voices of the people it purports to write about (Ndlovu 2009; Schmidt 2009; Schmidt and Walz 2007; Schmidt and Karega-Munene 2010). Most papers read at conferences, for example, including those held in Africa, still do not include African collaborators. Perhaps even more troubling is that the western scholars continue to be much more concerned with 'science' leaving the task of community archaeology and heritage management to their African colleagues (Ichumbaki 2016). Scholarship that goes out of its way to exclude local intellectual voices only guarantees its own illegitimacy and hastens the demise of long-term bridge-building that is so crucial for realizing community archaeology and heritage.

In another example, for the past three decades, Professor Felix Chami and his colleagues at University of Dar es Salaam, Tanzania, have dedicated efforts to the systematic research and the training of students from East and Southern Africa. Pioneer studies in the archaeology of urbanism in Eastern and Southern Africa had undervalued African agency. Professor Chami and his students have reversed perspectives that delegitimized African agency in the making of their own histories. However, like other academic programmers in Africa and to a lesser extent, everywhere these days, the Department of Archaeology and Heritage at University of Dar es Salaam has struggled to maintain a robust research and training agenda. To their credit, both faculty and students regularly publish their research in regional and international outlets (Chami 2000, 2004; Juma 1996, 2004; Sinclair, Juma, and Chami 2006).

Thus, when archaeologists from the University of Oxford received a generous European Research Council (ERC) grant through the Sealinks Project, there was jubilation that many of the questions raised by previous researchers, including those at University of Dar es Salaam, would finally be addressed. Many East African scholars assumed that any collection or field-based research carried out at previously explored sites would be collaborative and inclusive. Permit-granting agencies in East African countries require all research to be affiliated to local educational or research institutions. They encourage but have not made it mandatory for foreign scholars to collaborate with local scholars. The protocol for conducting research at previously investigated sites is to work in consultation and/or collaboration with previous researchers unless they are deceased.

Much to the disappointment of the archaeological community in East Africa, the Sealinks project did not make serious efforts to include local archaeologists who have previously worked or have ongoing active research in Tanzania and Kenya. Publications emerging from these projects, in particular those that have revisited sites investigated by Professor Chami and his colleagues, appear to be more concerned with delegitimizing the University of Dar es Salaam's contributions in East African archaeology. While this is not altogether novel, Sealinks' exclusion of still active researchers is an unusual demonstration of neo-colonial arrogance. To illustrate

The Sealinks project recently returned to the site of Ukunju Cave on Juani island, Mafia—originally excavated by Chami in 2000 (Chami 2000, 2004) –to collect new data relating to early settlement, subsistence, and trade in the archipelago. Our small-scale excavations emphasized the recovery of high-resolution cultural, archaeobotanical and zooarchaeological evidence, allowing us to begin addressing their research themes. Here we report our preliminary findings from the site where we reopened the original main trench (Trench 1) (Chami 2000, 2004) and dug to the lowest, unexcavated deposits to bedrock. The results outlined here, while in focus, inform wider debates about the earliest phases of East Africa's maritime settlement and the Indian Ocean engagement. (Crowther et al. 2014, 23)

As noted above, restudying contested sites or materials should involve collaboration with previous excavators unless the original excavator is deceased. However, in the cases in Tanzania, Sealinks has targeted sites Unguja Ukuu (Juma 2004), Juani primary School Site (Chami 1998, 2001), and Ukunju Cave (Chami 2000, 2004) for re-excavation without involving their still-active colleagues (Crowther et al. 2014).

Would this practice be tolerated in England or sanctioned in the USA or Canada? This careerist practice not only violates long-established protocols of cooperation and collaboration but also inhibits the dismantling of frontiers, a goal begun during the Panafrican Congress of African Prehistory and Related Studies in the 1940s (Kusimba 2016). But in East Africa, a well-funded team of Western researchers has alienated a leading academic and teacher. The absence of collective objection to these re-excavations is particularly disquieting and a commentary on the colonial legacy of archaeological practice. We listen to the silence – as the sense of community erodes when ethically questionable practices persist. There are more than 400 sites on the Swahili Coast, yet these sites are re-excavated as if early research lacked the imprimatur of legitimacy.

Community archaeology's overall goal of collaboration between indigenous and foreign archaeologists is good for the discipline's future. On the East African coast, for example, extensive archaeological surveys have revealed an extremely rich cultural and ecological heritage consisting of built spaces and domesticated landscapes (Freeman-Grenville 1958; Garlake 1966; Wilson [1978] 2016, [1980] 2017). The east African coast's urban landscape of 400 towns arose from demographic pressures, regional trade and exchange, and innovations in technology. Western scholarship had denied agency of local indigenous peoples in these developments, but credited colonists from the Middle East (Chittick 1974, 1984; Kirkman 1964; Pradines 2004). The identity of the founders of the Swahili maritime state is still contested.

Contemporary research must be sensitive to perspectives that appear to delegitimize or throttle local perspectives. From a community archaeology perspective, one could argue that our community of archaeologists is split asunder, with some still pursuing a neo-colonial paradigm and another one, the anticolonial paradigm. The former is well funded and controls publication channels and the 'peer review' process. The latter struggles, often with limited resources and publishing opportunities. The outcome is, as Ndukuyakhe Ndlovu (2016) argues, an old archaeological praxis that cloaks itself in a fashionable garment called inclusivity.

In a recent volume on community archaeology, contributors articulate the problems they encounter in their attempts to develop community archaeology and heritage (Schmidt and Pikirayi 2016). In extreme cases, there is a systematic effort to marginalize and undermine local scholarship. Secrecy surrounds the formation of research teams and selections of editorial board membership. In some cases, the very implementation of community archaeology is still reliant upon external funding (Chirikure and Pwiti 2008). Structures and instrumentation for generating local fundraising efforts and donor cultivations remain weakly developed and in some cases, non-existent. Worse, structures to encourage corporate giving are few or non-existent. I now turn to two cases studies to explain why community archaeology fails and succeeds.

Why community archaeology fails: land grants on the Kenya coast

When communities, local leadership, and archaeologists, have competing agendas in heritage management, the likely outcome is failure and community suffering. I illustrate this with two examples with which I have been intimately involved.

Between 1986 and 1993, I worked as a research scientist at the National Museums of Kenya. During that time, I was engaged in several archaeological and heritage management projects both as an employee of the National Museums of Kenya and later as a graduate student (Kusimba 2009; Grande 2017, 177–179). These experiences thrust me into the midst of socio-economic dynamics that nearly destroyed the communities where I worked along the Swahili coast. In 1993, I presented a paper entitled *Kenya's Destruction of the Swahili Cultural Heritage*, at a conference organized by the Center for African Studies at the University of Florida. I decried the wanton destruction (through corrupt land grabbing) of Kenya's coastal heritage sites, many of which had significant archaeological values. I highlighted government complicities, a weak and corrupt judicial system, weak antiquities laws, and nepotism in hiring and promotion at the National Museums of Kenya, a government institution invested with safeguarding both the tangible and intangible heritage of the nation on behalf of the people of Kenya (Kusimba 1996).

I was the first archaeologist to note openly Kenyan society's complicity in depriving the Swahili of their heritage and rights as citizens of Kenya. Colonial era perspectives about the Swahili erroneously and cynically cast them as Arabs, and had served the selfish interests of those in power, who wanted to profit from the return of Swahili land to the colonizer at the expense of indigenous Swahili. President Moi was in power. Corruption in government circles was tolerated and government impunity was at an all-time high in the 1990s. In fact, Kenyan society had fully embraced what social justice activist Koigi wa Wamwere has called 'the curse of negative ethnicity' (Wamwere 2003).

The conference paper later published (Kusimba 1996) in the volume Plundering Africa's Past (Schmidt and McIntosh 1996), discussed illegal possession and repossession of land, destruction of immovable heritage sites, and the National Museum's ineffectiveness in managing that heritage. I argued that the perpetrators of the destruction used historical and archaeological knowledge that had silenced the voices of the indigenous peoples of the coast, creating a caricatured historical landscape that denied agency to local peoples. A show of solidarity with the Swahili communities, my paper elicited anger amongst some when I revealed local collaboration with government and foreign investors to steal Swahili land. I was also warned that the then notorious secret service had come to Fort Jesus Museum looking for me. Some colleagues at the National Museums of Kenya were annoyed because they felt that institution was presented as complicitous, leading to isolation costly to my personal and professional identity.

During the colonial period, it was common practice for local elites to invent traditions to justify their legitimacy (Mafeje 1973). On the Swahili coast, local elites invented traditions to align with a patrilineal Arab descent, which at the time carried privilege. Political independence reversed fortunes for those who had shunned their African identities in favour of Arab identities (Alpers 1984, 680; Menon 1978, 44–46). They found themselves second-class citizens, their wealth – in massive land holdings – at the mercy of those who sought to settle old scores. What has transpired since 1996?

The Alawy family struggles to regain ancestral land on Wasini Island (1968 – present)

One community, the Alawy (or BaAlawy) family of Wasini Island had lost all their land in 1968 and spent 27 years appealing for its return. The Wasini case epitomized the savage inequalities that existed in Kenya at the time and the polarization within coastal communities that presented tense and dangerous contexts for community collaborations.

The island of Wasini is located on the Kenyan coast in Kwale County. It has historically been home to two communities, the Wavumba and the Wachifundi (Hollis 1900; McKay 1975; Stanish and Kusimba 1996). The island's earliest settlements date to the thirteenth century (Wilson [1980] 2017, 6). The island's oral history constructs a complex narrative of the evolution of polities on the Southern Kenyan coast. Often these narratives credit the founding to a handful of Shirazi (Persian) immigrants who settled here in the late first millennium (Hollis 1900; McKay 1975). These oral traditions silenced the local Segeju and Mijikenda narratives of state formation (Allen 1993). It was the rendering of the peoples' history that was to have adverse consequences.

During the nineteenth century, a Diaspora community from India and Oman settled on the coast and cheaply acquired large tracts of land where they established large coconut plantations using enslaved African labour. Local elites became increasingly marginalized, relative to these Omani and Indian immigrants (Hollingsworth 1960; Ramchandani 1980). More radical transformations on the coast began during the Oman colonial period, especially in Zanzibar, Lamu, and Mombasa at the height of plantation slavery (Cooper 1977; Glassman 1995; Croucher 2014; Stockreiter 2015). During this period, the socioeconomic and political power of the local elite, *Waungwana*, declined (Alpers 1984; Gray 1975, 156–169; Middleton and Campbell 1965, 26–28). Edward Alpers' (1984) proposal that Omani overlords exploited slave labour and created a cash economy that devastated local indigenous elites (and especially adversely affected women) is persuasive. In Zanzibar, the now famous stone town 'grew from a small Hadimu town to a large, multi-ethnic town of perhaps 25,000 people at mid-century and continued to expand thereafter' (Alpers 1984, 679). The distinction between stone town and the rural residences often built on privately owned plantations increasingly came to symbolize subservience, service, and even servitude: a place to draw cheap labour to the indigenous population and a retreat for the 'fast paced' life of the emerging metropolis of Zanzibar under the Omani sultanate (Allen 1981; Alpers 1984, 680; citing Menon 1978, 44–46). Similarly, Randall Pouwels concluded, in his study of Islam and Islamic leadership in the coastal communities of Eastern Africa, that before the middle of the nineteenth century, 'civilization' was linked intimately to the local concepts of Islam and was embodied linguistically by the word *uungwana*. This concept, he argued, like James Allen and Wilson (1982) and Allen (1993), was quite distinct from any notion of 'Arabness':

> "Civilization" and Arabness, in fact, seem to have become associated after the mid-nineteenth century when the Busaidi dynasty in Zanzibar began to have a cultural, as well as a political, impact on coastal communities. It was sometime after the 1860s and 70s then, that civilization was characterized less and less by *uungwana* and its implications concerning parochial concepts of Islam, and was gradually replaced by the word *ustaarabu*—in other words—to be like an Arab. (Pouwels 1979, 187–188; cited by Alpers 1984, 680–681)

These colonial-era tensions re-emerged in the 1960s following Kenya's political independence. A presidential directive to revise land adjudication provided an opportunity for pay back and land grab (Leo 1984). The issuance of title deeds enabled access to credit finance and the right to sell or buy land and settle anywhere in the country. The new system contradicted traditional practices of communal ownership, which accorded use rights to all, and prohibited individual sale of land (Prins 1967). Privatization overturned traditional farming practices.

The case of Wasini is particularly poignant here, because it illustrates the negative power of ethnicity and nationalism. In a reversal of fortunes, families who benefitted from being 'Arab' in colonial times were targeted by the postcolonial land adjudication programme of 1968. Among these families was the BaAlawy clan. Family members understood that their relocation was temporary and that they would soon return home, because they had valid titles for the land issued by Her Majesty the Queen's Colonial Office. So, many moved to nearby villages and towns such as Vanga, Shimoni, Gazi, and Mombasa with relatives. By 1993, their case against the Kenya Government illegal adjudication and repossession of their land had not yet been brought to the courts for a hearing. Judge after judge postponed this case as the state was still gathering evidence.

In March 1995, I received news that the Alawy family had won the case and the judge had authorized the government to rescind the titles previously issued by the Lands Commission as illegal and order fresh adjudication. The defendants, who included old and new residents who had occupied the land since the 1968 adjudication, vowed not to comply with the judge's ruling. In the same year, land adjudication officials from the Ministry of Lands, accompanied by the police, set off to Wasini to resurvey the island, a necessary process before issuance of new title deeds. As the government lands survey and the Alawy family members prepared to board the boat to the island, they received news that Wasini residents were armed and ready to confront government officials and fight to the last person. Government officials aborted the exercise.

The court order of 1995 has yet to be complied with, some 22 years later. The government claims insecurity as the primary reason for inaction. In the meantime, large portions of the island are now developed, presenting a further conundrum to compensating current owners. Many of the original perpetrators and victims have died, leaving their descendants landless and displaced or illegal occupiers.

The Wasini case illustrates how powerful stakeholders can exploit archaeology and history. I have shown how early studies created the coastal heritage as a landscape of foreign settlers who exploited local communities. This 'othering' continues to have a debilitating effect on descendants like the Alawy family, whose presumed foreign ancestry in postcolonial Kenya now compels them to defend their legitimacy as an African people and their culture as authentically African.

Sustaining tradition through production and consumption of pottery in Bungoma County today

My second case study illustrates the potential of a community-engaged anthropology in fostering empowerment. The study takes place in Bungoma County in Western Kenya where we have worked since 2003 (Kusimba, Yang, and Chawla, 2015; Makila 1978; Osogo 1966; Wagner 1949; Wandibba 1985). Although the county is one of the major water catchment systems of Lake Victoria, rapid population growth has resulted in large-scale deforestation, declining soil fertility, and low agricultural yields. A decrease in size of land holdings has created tensions, conflicts, and violent land conflicts. Like many regions in East Africa, Bungoma County was devastated by the HIV/AIDS pandemic, which left many orphans, and restructured family lives (e.g. Schmidt 2010).

Despite the winds of modernity that have swept the countryside over the past two generations, the making and use of traditional pottery continues to thrive in Western Kenya among the Luo, Luyia, Iteso, Pokot, Nandi, and other Kenyan communities. In Bungoma County, nearly 50 potters are actively engaged in pottery making. Demand for pottery is high and potters distribute their wares across the county and in neighbouring regions in the North Rift Valley. However, the high fuel requirements to produce pottery are now threatening the future of pottery production.

Consumption of traditional pottery in Bungoma County lifeways

Surveys of 600 households revealed that 17 per cent of the households are women-headed (Table 1).

Our study revealed that pottery making was the only surviving craft monopolized by women, but that its future was under assault. Potters were young mothers in their early 20s to grandmothers in their 70s. Many elderly potters were widowed, household heads, and primary providers of their household income. Income generated from pottery enabled them to pay school fees, clothing, and other household basics for their families. Although they owned land, the yields from it could only keep them food secure for at least 7 months of the year. Pottery sales sustained them during periods of food scarcity and shortage.

In contrast to general perceptions, traditional pottery is still profoundly important in western Kenya and is imbued with cultural meanings around gender (Nangendo 1994). People use traditional

Table 1. Women-headed households (in bold) in Bungoma County.

Marital status	Number	Percentage
Married	487	81
Widowed (W)	49	**8**
Separated (W)	46	**8**
Cohabitation	13	2
Divorced (W)	5	**1**

pots for keeping water, storing grains, cooking certain food delicacies, and for ritual purposes. Nearly one-third of the local household utensils are ceramic. Furthermore, the demand for pottery for flower-pots and other decorative/aesthetic needs has increased. Whereas we saw a craft that was likely to continue, potters saw an unsustainable craft, whose future was grim without intervention and innovation.

Threats against sustainability of the pottery production

Pottery in Bungoma County is open-fired using firewood and wet swamp grass. Wet grass is a redu-cing agent in the open kiln. Each firing requires one whole tree and at least five bags of grass. Potters must purchase and transport both of these resources to their homes. Competition for the trees and wet grass is high, as over 95 per cent of households in the county use firewood for cooking. During the dry season, cows compete with potters for grass.

Potters were concerned that the rising cost of fuel coupled with the decline in swampland threa-tened their industry. If the current 50 potters worked on a full-time basis for 50 years, they would exploit 150,000 mature trees, which have taken more than 75–100 years to grow (Table 2). The fact that nearly every household uses firewood for cooking creates extremely dire conditions for the sustenance of traditional pottery.

Fuel shortages threaten pottery making. In the words of Mama Robai, a 72-year-old semi-retired potter:

> We must build a new kiln with every new firing so we must gather all the necessary materials that are needed. These materials include firewood and wet grass which we must buy, hire labour to cut, and transport home. Dis-tances are ever increasing because trees are no longer available in our area. Most people now grow vegetables and sugarcane in the swamps leaving very few areas fallow. Even where grass is available, we compete with cows. Since our kilns are constructed in the open, they are susceptible to inclement of weather. We must fire our pottery during the sunny days. If it rains during the firing operation all the pots will explode due the sudden changes of temperature resulting in heavy losses. Those large shards you see over and the ones I now use as funnels in the kiln are recycled from previously failed firing operation when torrential rains came before the firing cycle was completed. (Robai Mayeku, June 2015)

Mama Robai appealed to us for assistance in finding fuel-efficient firing practices.

Community archaeology in Bungoma County

Bungoma County potters were aware that the high cost of fuel, including firewood and wet grass, rendered the craft unsustainable and sought our assistance in exploring more fuel-efficient firing techniques. We carried out research on the various kiln designs from around the world, and with potters' input we picked the different elements that were useful in each kiln design and incorporated it into the experimental kiln that we would built on one potter's compound. If successful, all potters in the area would adopt the kiln.

In the summer of 2015, we collaborated with the potters and local masons to build a small exper-imental kiln in the home of Mama Robai. The kiln cost US $ 2000 including all the materials (Figure 1).

Table 2. Postulated number of mature trees used by a single potter to fire pottery over 100 years.

Days	Years	Trees	No. of pots
1		1	100
7		2	200
14		3	300
21		4	400
30		5	500
365	1	60	30,000
3650	10	600	300,000
18,250	50	3000	1,500,000
36,500	100	30,000	3,000,000

Figure 1. Experimental kiln built in the home of Mama Robai. Provided by author.

At the launch of the experimental kiln on 14 July 2015, we invited local government officials including area chiefs, legislators, and the County Governor. We used the occasion to sensitize the community to the impact of climate change and rapid population growth.

The County Governor invited us to submit a proposal to build modern fuel-efficient kilns for potters. Besides eliminating the need for wet swamp grass, this kiln could reduce consumption of firewood by 70 per cent and enable potters to work full-time year-round.

Discussion: imagining community archaeology and heritage in Africa

The potential for community archaeology and heritage – the coming together of academics and communities with governments, to build strong collaborative and coequal programmes to study the past and sustain livelihoods – requires patience and time to build trust. Community archaeology challenges us to transcend traditional boundaries that separate professional archaeologies, heritage managers, and local communities (Fontein 2006). It demands embracing inclusivity and sensitivity to short- and long-term effects of archaeology's engagement with the community, and it calls upon professional archaeologists to listen to and engage with other voices, including government, for change. Doing this will lead us to avoid engaging in what Carol McDavid (2002) has referred to as archaeologies that hurt (see also McDavid 2007).

Self-awareness of the legitimacy of our research and the potential for abuse should compel us to engage local communities in the creation of knowledge at all levels. My research on the coast involved issues that highlighted the ancestors of most the coastal peoples, their language, cultures, and everyday traditions (Kusimba 2016, 113–114). Colonial and postcolonial narratives that show professional indecisiveness about the identity politics have had and may continue to have the undesirable consequence of supporting and abetting the ongoing human rights abuses of Muslim Kenyans. We must recognize the potential undercurrents that inevitably influence interpretation of the archaeological record. Our ongoing work in Bungoma County is unveiling the power of listening to local collaborators for a change.

In sum, the future of community archaeology as practised in Africa is tremendous (Schmidt 2017; Schmidt and Pikirayi 2016). Our colleagues and our students continue to be feted and fed on many occasions by our local collaborators. Their generosity and cooperation is unfolding into a reciprocal process and might explain why local communities have permitted us and, in some cases, encouraged us, to conduct sensitive research. Community archaeology's potential for addressing old as well as emerging questions, such as climate change, technological innovation, migration, domestication, trade, conflict and warfare, and identity formation, is tremendous. We must give back to the communities that enabled us to create new knowledge and sustain our careers.

Funding

This work was supported by National Endowment for the Humanities [2012–14], National Science Foundation [BCS 9615291, BCS 0106664, BCS 0352681, BCS-1030081, SBR 9024683, BCS 0648762] and IIE J. W. Fulbright Sr. Scholars Program [2002–3, 2012].

Suggested citation

Kusimba, Chapurukha M. 2017. 'Community Archaeology and Heritage in Coastal and Western Kenya'. Special Series, African Perspectives on Community Engagement, guest-edited by Peter R. Schmidt. *Journal of Community Archaeology and Heritage* 4 (3): page 218–228.

References

Allen, James de Vere. 1981. "Swahili Culture and the Nature of East Coast Settlement." *International Journal of African Historical Studies* 14 (2): 306–334.

Allen, James de Vere. 1993. *Swahili Origins: Swahili Culture and the Shungwaya Phenomenon*. Oxford: James Currey.

Allen, James de Vere, and Thomas H. Wilson. 1982. "From Zinj to Zanzibar: Studies in History, Trade and Society on the Eastern Coast of Africa." *Paideuma* 28. Franz Steiner Verlag, Wiesbaden.

Alpers, Edward A. 1984. "'Ordinary Household Chores': Ritual and Power in a 19th-Century Swahili Women's Spirit Possession Cult." *The International Journal of African Historical Studies* 17 (4): 677–702.

Atalay, Sonya. 2012. *Community-based Archaeology: Research With, by, and for Indigenous and Local Communities*. Berkeley: University of California Press.

Binford, Sally R., and Lewis R. Binford, eds. 1968. *New Perspectives in Archaeology*. Chicago, IL: Aldine Publishing Company.

Chami, Felix A. 1998. "A Review of Swahili Archaeology." *African Archaeological Review* 15 (3): 199–218.

Chami, Felix A. 2000. "Further Archaeological Research on Mafia Island." *Azania: Archaeological Research in Africa* 35 (1): 208–214.

Chami, Felix A. 2001. "Chicken Bones From a Neolithic Limestone Cave Site, Zanzibar: Contact Between East Africa and Asia." In *People, Contact and the Environment in the African Past*, edited by Felix A. Chami, Gilbert Pwiti, and Chantal Radimilahy, 84–97. Dar es Salaam: Dar es Salaam University Press.

Chami, Felix A. 2004. "The Archaeology of the Mafia Archipelago, Tanzania." In *African Archaeology Network: Reports and Views*, edited by F. A. Chami, G. Pwiti, and C. Radimilahy, 73–101. Dar es Salaam: Dar es Salaam University Press.

Chirikure, Shadreck, and Gilbert Pwiti. 2008. "Community Involvement in Archaeology and Cultural Heritage Management: An Assessment from Case Studies in Southern Africa and Elsewhere." *Current Anthropology* 49 (3): 467–485.

Chittick, Neville H. 1974. *Kilwa: An Islamic Trading City of the EAST AFRICAN COAST*. Nairobi: British Institute in Eastern Africa.

Chittick, Neville H. 1984. *Manda: Excavations at an Island Port on the Kenya Coast*. Nairobi: British Institute in Eastern Africa.

Colwell-Chanthaphonh, Chip, and T. J. Ferguson, eds. 2008. *Collaboration in Archaeological Practice: Engaging Descendant Communities*. Lanham: Altamira Press.

Cooper, Frederick. 1977. *Plantation Slavery on the East Coast of Africa*. New Haven, CT: Yale University Press.

Croucher, Sarah K. 2014. *Capitalism and Cloves: An Archaeology of Plantation Life on Nineteenth-century Zanzibar.* New York: Springer.

Crowther, Alison, Mark Horton, Anna Kotarba-Morley, Mary Prendergast, Eréndira Quintana Morales, Marilee Wood, and Ceri Shipton. 2014. "Iron Age Agriculture, Fishing and Trade in the Mafia Archipelago, Tanzania: New Evidence From Ukunju Cave." *Azania: Archaeological Research in Africa* 49 (1): 21–44.

Fontein, Joost. 2006. *The Silence of Great Zimbabwe: Contested Landscapes and the Power of Heritage.* London: University College London Press.

Freeman-Grenville, G. S. P. 1958. "155. Some Recent Archaeological Work on the Tanganyika Coast." *Man* 58: 106–112.

Garlake, Peter S. 1966. *The Early Islamic Architecture of the East African Coast.* Memoir of the British Institute of History and Archaeology in East Africa. Nairobi: Published for the Institute by Oxford: Oxford University Press.

Glassman, Jonathan. 1995. *Feasts and Riot: Revelry, Rebellion, and Popular Consciousness on the Swahili Coast, 1856–1888.* Portsmouth: Heinemann.

Grande, Lance. 2017. *Curators: Behind the Scenes of Natural History Museums.* Chicago, IL: University of Chicago Press.

Gray, John M. 1975. *History of Zanzibar, from the Middle Ages to 1856.* Westport, CT: Greenwood Press.

Heckenberger, Michael J. 2008. "Entering the Agora: Archaeology, Conservation, and Indigenous Peoples in the Amazon." In *Collaboration in Archaeological Practice: Engaging Descendant Communities,* edited by Chip Colwell-Chanthaphonh and T. J. Ferguson, 243–272. Lantham, MD: AltaMira Press.

Heckenberger, Michael J. 2009. "Mapping Indigenous Histories: Collaboration, Cultural Heritage and Conservation in the Amazon." *Collaborative Anthropologies* 2: 9–32.

Hollingsworth, Lawrence W. 1960. *The Asians of East Africa.* Nairobi: Macmillan.

Hollis, A. Claud. 1900. "Notes on the History of Vumba, East Africa." *Journal of the Anthropological Institute of Great Britain and Ireland* 30: 275–297.

Ichumbaki, B. Elgidius. 2016. "A History of Conservation of Built Heritage Sites of the Swahili Coast of Tanzania." *African Historical Review* 48: 43–67.

Juma, Abdulrahman M. 1996. "The Swahili and the Mediterranean Worlds: Pottery of the Late Roman Period from Zanzibar." *Antiquity* 70 (267): 148–154.

Juma, Abdulrahman M. 2004. *Unguja Ukuu on Zanzibar: An Archaeological Study of Early Urbanism.* Uppsala: Department of Archaeology and Ancient History, University of Uppsala.

Kerber, Jordan E. 2003. "Community-Based Archaeology in Central New York: Workshops Involving Native American Youth." *The Public Historian* 25 (1): 83–90.

Kirkman, James. 1964. *Men and Monuments on the East African Coast.* London: Lutterworth Press.

Kusimba, Chapurukha M. 1996. "Kenya's Destruction of Swahili Cultural Heritage." In *Plundering Africa's Past: The Erasure of Cultural Patrimony,* edited by Peter R. Schmidt and Roderick J. McIntosh, 201–224. Bloomington: Indiana University Press.

Kusimba, Chapurukha M. 2009. "Practicing Postcolonial Archaeology in Eastern Africa from the United States." In *Postcolonial Archaeologies of Africa,* edited by Peter Schmidt, 79–92. Santa Fe: School of Advanced Research Press.

Kusimba, Chapurukha M. 2016. "The Swahili and Globalization in the Indian Ocean." In *The Routledge Handbook of Archaeology and Globalization,* edited by Tamar Hodos, 104–122. London: Routledge.

Kusimba, Sibel B., Y. Yang, and Nitesh Chawla. 2015. "Family Networks of Mobile Money in Kenya." *Information Technology in International Development* 11 (3): 1–21.

Leo, Christopher. 1984. *Land and Class in Kenya.* Toronto: University of Toronto Press.

Mafeje, Akin. 1973. *Agrarian Revolution and the Land Question in Buganda.* The Hague: Institute of Social Studies.

Makila, Fred E. 1978. *An Outline History of Babukusu of Western Kenya.* Nairobi: Kenya Literature Bureau.

McDavid, Carol. 2002. "Archaeologies that Hurt; Descendents that Matter: A Pragmatic Approach to Collaboration in the Public Interpretation of African-American Archaeology. Special Issue on Community Archaeology, edited by Yvonne Marshall." *World Archaeology* 34 (2): 303–314.

McDavid, Carol. 2007. "Beyond Strategy and Good Intentions: Archaeology, Race, and White Privilege'." In *Archaeology as a Tool of Civic Engagement,* edited by Barbara J. Little and Paul A. Shackel, 67–88. Walnut Creek: AltaMira Press.

McKay, William F. 1975. "A Precolonial History of the Southern Kenya Coast." Unpublished PhD thesis, Boston University.

Menon, Ramachandran. 1978. "Zanzibar in the Nineteenth Century: Aspects of Urban Development in an East African Coastal Town." Unpublished Master's thesis, University of California at Los Angeles.

Middleton, John, and Jane Campbell. 1965. *Zanzibar: Its Society and its Politics.* Oxford: Oxford University Press.

Murray, Wendi F., Nicholas C. Laluk, Barbara J. Mills, and T. J. Ferguson. 2009. "Archaeological Collaboration with American Indians: Case Studies from the Western United States." *Collaborative Anthropologies* 2: 65–86.

Nangendo, Stevie Moses. 1994. "Daughters of the Clay, Women of the Farm: Women, Agricultural Economic Development and Ceramic Production in Bungoma District, Western Province, Kenya." PhD thesis, Department of Anthropology, Bryn Mawr College, Philadelphia, University Microfilms, Ann Arbor, MI.

Ndlovu, Ndukuyakhe. 2009. "Transformation Challenges in South African Archaeology." *The South African Archaeological Bulletin* 64 (189): 91–93.

Ndlovu, Ndukuyakhe. 2016. "Old Archaeology Camouflaged as New and Inclusive?" In *Community Archaeology and Heritage in Africa: Decolonizing Practice,* edited by Peter R. Schmidt and Innocent Pikirayi, 136–152. London: Routledge.

Nicholas, George P. 2010. "Seeking the End of Indigenous Archaeology." In *Bridging the Divide: Indigenous Communities and Archaeology into the 21st Century*, edited by Caroline Phillips and Harry Allen, 233–252. Walnut Creek: Left Coast Press.

Nicholas, George P., John R. Welch, and Eldon C. Yellowhorn. 2008. "Collaborative Encounters." In *Collaboration in Archaeological Practice: Engaging Descendant Communities*, edited by Chip Colwell-Chanthaphonh and T. J. Ferguson, 273–298. Walnut Creek: Altamira Press.

Osogo, John N. 1966. *A History of the Baluyia*. Nairobi: Oxford University Press.

Pouwels, Randall. 1979. "Islam and Islamic Leadership in the Coastal Communities of Eastern Africa." PhD diss. University of California, Los Angeles.

Pradines, Stéphane. 2004. *Fortifications et urbanisation en Afrique orientale* (British Archaeological Reports International Series 1216). Oxford: Archaeopress.

Prins, Adriaan Hendrik J. 1967. *The Swahili-speaking Peoples of Zanzibar and the East African Coast: (Arabs, Shirazi and Swahili)* (Vol. 2). London: International African Institute.

Ramchandani, R. R. 1980. *India and Africa*. London: Humanities Press.

Schmidt, Peter R. 1983. "An alternative to a Strictly Materialist Perspective: A Review of Historical Archaeology, Ethnoarchaeology, and Symbolic Approaches in African archaeology." *American Antiquity* 48: 62–79.

Schmidt, Peter R., ed. 2009. *Postcolonial Archaeologies in Africa*. Santa Fe: School for Advanced Research Press.

Schmidt, Peter R. 2010. "Social Memory and Trauma in Northwestern Tanzania: Organic, Spontaneous Community Collaboration." *Journal of Social Archaeology* 10 (2): 255–279.

Schmidt, Peter R. 2014. "Rediscovering Community Archaeology in Africa and Reframing its Practice." *Journal of Community Archaeology and Heritage* 1 (1): 37–55.

Schmidt, Peter R. 2017. *Community-based Heritage in Africa: Unveiling Local Research and Development Initiatives*. New York: Taylor & Francis.

Schmidt, Peter R., and Karega-Munene. 2010. "An Africa-informed View of Postcolonial Archaeologies." In *Handbook of Postcolonial Archaeology*, edited by Jane Lydon and Uzma Z. Rizvi, 215–225. Walnut Creek: Left Coast Press.

Schmidt, Peter R., and Innocent Pikirayi. 2016. *Community Archaeology and Heritage in Africa: Decolonizing Practice*. London: Routledge.

Schmidt, Peter R., and Jonathan R. Walz. 2007. "Re-representing African Pasts Through Historical Archaeology." *American Antiquity* 72 (1): 53–70.

Schmidt, Peter R., and Roderick J. McIntosh, eds. 1996. *Plundering Africa's Past: The Erasure of Cultural Patrimony*. Bloomington: Indiana University Press.

Silliman, Stephen W., ed. 2008. *Collaborating at the Trowel's Edge: Teaching and Learning in Indigenous Archaeology*. Amerind Studies in Archaeology (Book 2). Tucson: University of Arizona Press.

Sinclair, Paul, Abdurahman Juma, and Felix Chami. 2006. "Excavations at Kuumbi Cave on Zanzibar 2005." In *The African Archaeology Network: Research in Progress*, edited by John Kinahan and Jill Kinahan, 95–106. Dar es Salaam: Dar es Salaam University Press.

Stanish, Charles, and Chapurukha M. Kusimba. 1996. "Archaeological Research and Community Participation." Society for American Archaeology Bulletin 14 (3): 6–8.

Stockreiter, Elke. 2015. *Islamic Law, Gender, and Social Change in Post-Abolition Zanzibar*. New York: Cambridge University Press.

Wagner, Gunther. 1949. *The Bantu of North Kavirondo, Vol.1*. Oxford: Oxford University Press.

Wamwere, Koigi. 2003. *Towards Genocide in Kenya: The Curse of Negative Ethnicity*. Nairobi: Mvule Africa Publishers.

Wandibba, Simiyu. 1985. *History and Culture in Western Kenya: The People of Bungoma District through Time*. Nairobi: Gideon S. Were Press.

Wilson, Thomas H. [1978] 2016. *Swahili Monumental Architecture and Archaeology North of the Tana River*. Nairobi: National Museums of Kenya.

Wilson, Thomas H. [1980] 2017. *The Monumental Architecture and Archaeology of the Central and Southern Kenya Coast*. Nairobi: National Museums of Kenya.

Contests between heritage and history in Tanganyika/Tanzania: Insights arising from community-based heritage research

Peter R. Schmidt

ABSTRACT
Ongoing collaborative heritage research in northwestern Tanzania engages partners from diverse backgrounds, from craftsmen and common folk to a sitting king and his royal clan. Such diversity has revealed intangible heritage in two adjacent kingdoms. In Kihanja Kingdom, the physical structures of Kanazi Palace appear to dominate the heritage landscape, yet, ethnographic and archaeological collaborations revealed that Kihanja kings engaged in heritage performances that preserved ritual knowledge the Christian church erased. Written records further misrepresented these subaltern practices, and were at odds with heritage values enshrined in practice and the archaeological record. In Bukara Kingdom, the ravages of HIV/AIDS led to the loss of oral traditions, thus obscuring a significant massacre by German troops over a century ago. By revisiting oral accounts recorded 48 years ago, we (with local participants) were able to correct the written record and justify their efforts to preserve and interpret human remains at Mazinga cave.

Introduction and background

Over the last 48 years I have explored, through ethnography and archaeology, heritage meanings among the Haya people who live along the western shore of Lake Victoria. This essay builds on my previous treatment of participatory community-based research and its affinities to and differences from other community projects in Africa and around the globe. One theme that emerges is that community is not homogeneous, not a neat collection of nucleated residents of like-mindedness. African villages are just as diverse as those in rural settings elsewhere. Class, gender, social, and age differences deeply complicate our efforts to respond to community needs while ensuring participatory approaches that cross these boundaries.

How the Haya people represent their heritage must start with the writing of a local historian, F. X. Lwamgira, known for his *History of the Kings of Kiziba* (1949a). Lwamgira poignantly captured how the Haya conceptualize their heritage, outside of any authorized heritage discourse recognized in the West:

> I want to state that our former grand parents *did know how to write*. Many people wonder how I have managed to gather the historical information contained in this book. Ask the keepers of the kings' burial places, they will tell you how these places were established; enquire about sacred trees and you will be told how they came about, inquire about palace buildings ... You will quickly understand that even if our ancestors did not write on paper, still they wrote down historical facts by signs and symbols which they left behind in the hands of guardians. These guardians make sure that their historical significance should never disappear. It would be a shameful act to destroy all the burial and sacred places. (Lwamgira 1949a, 3–4; emphasis added)

Lwamgira clearly articulates that Haya heritage lies in chains of memory, wherein oral traditions are passed across generations, along with knowledge about royal burial places, shrines trees, and other sacred places. It is not the places alone that make up heritage. Rather, it is the oral traditions and rituals attached to these places that evoke profound emotions and memories of the past, contributing to Haya identity. The oral traditions and ritual practices (that is, intangible heritage) linked to such places define the Haya world of heritage, a condition that Lwamgira saw as threatened by the destruction of sacred places. For Haya culture, then, oral traditions are a mainstay of heritage identity.

Oral traditions are one way of constructing interpretations of the past. They changed over time for social and political reasons, sometimes at an accelerated pace when political motives led to their manipulation to satisfy special interests (see Schmidt 1978, 2006, 2013). In this sense, they resemble Western historiography, also shaped by intellectual fads and the socio-political values of the era in which history is written. In the West, many have come to consider the spoken word more subject to such transformation than the written word (Nora 1989). While metaphorical infusions are an important part of oral genres, we should not mistake their inclusion as an erasure of their historical integrity, given histories such as Mesopotamia, where the rigours of oral tradition preservation over hundreds, even thousands of years were made vital through continuous performance (Schmidt 2006, 2013).

Nora (1989) writes that memory is life borne by living society, and history is reconstruction, always problematic and incomplete. This dichotomy ignores parallel processes of reconstruction in oral transmission, but also warns us about relying only on written records to characterize heritage practices in the past. Here, I illustrate such dangers and suggest that alternative sources, oral traditions as well as ethnographic and archaeological inquiries, may provide more credible ways to understand heritage values in Africa.

I draw on two examples from the Kingdoms of Kihanja and Bukara (formerly Maruku under the British) in Buhaya (Figure 1). The first is a story about the intangible heritage insights that emerged from a collaborative heritage project (a weaving of oral tradition, archaeological, and restoration elements) at Kanazi Palace, Kihanja Kingdom. The second is a story about the loss of oral traditions in the nearby Bukara Kingdom – loss driven by extreme conditions of social stress, disease, and poverty linked to the ravages of HIV/AIDS. Local indigenous knowledge about a significant massacre by German troops during the colonial period was unrecorded in official accounts, and reclaimed by collaborative community heritage research.

The period I discuss runs from the turn of the 20th century throughout the next 115 years, a period when colonial standards and missionary values dominated the representations appearing in the written record. I argue that colonial period records and their later historical interpretations have seriously distorted Haya heritage values, and that it is only through a careful examination of *how heritage values were practiced*, both in religion and in the telling of oral traditions, that we can come to a more plausible understanding of how heritage values changed and were preserved.

I demonstrate how, even under transformed circumstances, there is much to learn from community-based participatory research (Atalay 2012; Schmidt 2017). Oral tradition archives – no different from documentary archives in their importance – have the potential to illuminate past heritage practices erased or distorted in written accounts.

Kihanja Kingdom: heritage research into Kanazi Palace

Participants

Our first focus is Kanazi Palace of Kihanja Kingdom, a kingdom the German colonial administration (1890–1916) highly favoured. King (Mukama) Petro Nyarubamba, ensconced there between 1958 and 2010, held important heritage knowledge about the palace. At his prompting and request, in 2008 I and other collaborators embarked on research into the heritage of his royal palace, an engagement that arose from the king's desire to restore it. Since the German colonial government's

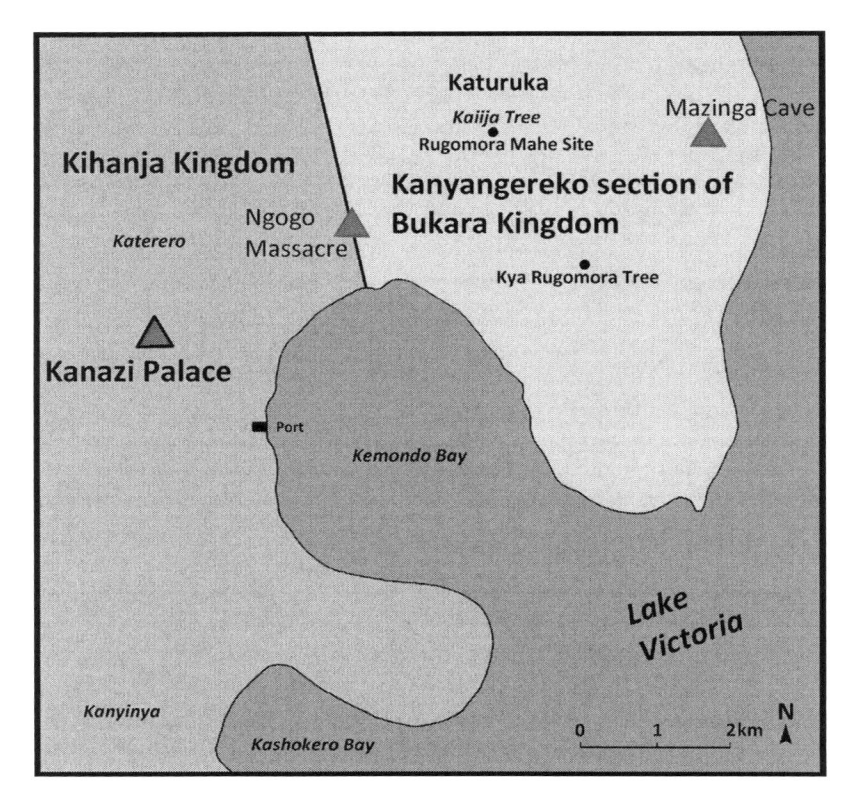

Figure 1. A map of the Kemondo Bay area, with Kanazi Palace to the west of the bay. Kihanja Kingdom was divided from Bukara Kingdom, to the east and including the Kanyangereko peninsula, by a river that ran north to south into Kemondo Bay. Provided by author.

construction of Kanazi Palace in 1905, it had declined into a state of severe degradation. Restoration alone, however, was meaningless without understanding its heritage values.

King Nyarubamba of the Hinda clan (the former royal clan) shared his personal history in several long interviews that threw important light on traditional religious practices. His and other oral testimonies provided insights into how traditional heritage values continued during a time when there was overwhelming change in Haya culture. Many residents of nearby Kanazi village and scattered around the former Kingdom of Kihanja did not view Kanazi Palace positively. I was keen to incorporate assessments of change and dynamism, not simply valorize what was once an unpopular royal lineage. Memories were strong about the reign of King Kahigi II (1890–1916), who enforced German government-issued decrees and collected taxes, imprisoning those who failed to pay. Memories about a 1950s political movement against the elitism of the Hinda clan also left bitterness (Curtis 1989).

Therefore, working with the royal clan and its history of popular opposition during late colonial times presented several ethical dilemmas, among them the possible reification of royal oppression. Uzma Rizvi captures what were then my ethical concerns: 'Most decisions to maintain and reify power structures are not maliciously intended, but they are the byproducts of prioritizing research over inequality and disenfranchisement, and, in a callous sense, of prioritizing our research over the present, past, or future of others' (Rizvi 2015, 159).

This concern compelled me to include, additionally, people from outside the royal family and clan as participants. I drew on oral interviews with non-royals and on observations of and interactions with those engaged in daily embodied practice during the palace's restoration – the craftsmen who gathered materials, fabricated them into forms consonant with early colonial modes of construction, and engaged in a constant discourse about the context in which these activities occurred. As they performed daily activities, craftsmen provided a significant counter-balance to elite views.

Because I was able to gather insights from different social and economic groups, *together* my participants constituted a 'community of interest', a diversity spread over a large geographical area. I first describe the physical Kanazi palace and the written records associated with it, and then discuss the intangible heritage values that emerged from community engagements.

The physical Kanazi Palace

Once a grand edifice (Figure 2(a)), Kanazi Palace may be one of Tanzania's most unusual and important indigenous colonial structures of the German colonial era. It is an example of colonial bricolage, a mixture of the structure and function of indigenous palaces with German colonial administrative architecture. The rectangular court building at Kanazi departs from the round shape of a traditional *nyaruju* palace (Figure 2(b)), with brick/plaster pillars that mimic the large tree-like post inside a traditional palace against which key leaders sat during judicial events. The throne platform at Kanazi was elevated to the left of the entrance, like the elevated thick bundle of mat-enclosed grass left of the traditional entrance.

Kanazi Palace, local heritage, and the written record

First occupied in 1905 by King Kahigi II of Kihanja Kingdom (Figure 3(a) and (b)), Kanazi Palace was built on land that Kyamutwara Kingdom (immediately to the north) previously administered. The German colonial administrations handed over the land to King Kahigi when he outwitted the Kyamutwara King by planting guns in his palace (Lwamgira 1949b; Austen 1968), about 10 years before the current palace's construction.

The territorial growth of Kihanja Kingdom meant a concomitant growth in tax revenues, and the need for closer German surveillance that was not possible at Kahigi's distant capital on the Kamachumu plateau (60 km from German headquarters). A four-room building was the first residence, later added onto to make the royal court. After he moved to the main residence, the larger rooms of the suite became Kahigi's regalia store (Nyarubamba 17 September 2010, Kanazi), later used by his successors for similar purposes, until the building began collapsing in the early 1980s.

Heritage embedded: examples

Our research showed that strong *intangible* values associated with indigenous religion make Kanazi Palace distinctive, more than its physical buildings or written history. With little knowledge circulating within the immediate villages about the palace, it was important to elicit Haya heritage discourses that went beyond stories about a ruthless administration followed later by colonial representations about irresolute political administrations.

Kahigi II and his burial estate

As a backdrop to life at Kanazi Palace, I first want to highlight a story about King Kahigi's death. It does not take place at Kanazi Palace, but involves a second palace that King Kahigi used. The story is stunning in the strength of its moral principles and loyalty, and also illustrates how a vivid narrative can persist in *heritage* memory and how King Kahigi resisted identity with Kanzai Palace. I then return to Kanazi Palace itself.

There is no burial estate (*gashani*) at Kanazi for any of the five Kings of Kihanja over the last century. King Kahigi II's burial estate was located to the west of Kanazi in a village (Ibwera-Rubungo) where he had a second, traditional palace. More information about this palace came to light when Petro Nyarubamba and others repeatedly shared the story of Kahigi's death (e.g. Solomon Mukende, Kamachumu-Bulembo, 13 April 2011).

Figure 2. (a) Kanazi Palace residence before restoration in 2008; (b) The royal court of Kanazi Palace before restoration in 2010. Photograph by author.

Made an Obersultane in 1905 (Austen 1968) and given the rank of 'major' in the German army,[1] Kahigi was the most successful opportunist amongst his contemporaries. He was foremost a cagy and clever negotiator who played German administrators to gain as much land and wealth as possible. Loyal to his end, he was not ready to bend to British administrators when they summoned him to their headquarters in Bukoba in 1916. On the Bukoba parade ground he met D. A. Baines, the first British Political Officer. Baines accused him of murdering the King of Karagwe and his nine sons. Kahigi's administration of Karagwe Kingdom was controversial, but the accusation was false and deeply offensive. He strongly denied the charge. Many versions of oral traditions are unanimous in relating that Baines then slapped him, a public humiliation. He immediately departed for his home

Figure 3. (a) King Kahigi II as a freshly minted officer in the German army; (b) King Kahigi in his later years, also in military dress. Photograph by author.

village in Kamachumu, not Kanazi: 'Returning to his birthplace in Kamachumu, he announced that he would never work for bastards like the British, and then committed suicide by poison' (male elder, 4 April 2011, Kamachumu). This widespread story is at odds with the truncated British version of what transpired:

> Kahigi had not lost his touch. At his first meeting with a British officer he secured a promise to continue the large tax rebate which the Germans paid to Haya chiefs. But later in the year Kahigi died and his sub-imperialism, so brilliantly sustained, collapsed overnight. (Iliffe 1979, 253)

Iliffe's analysis captures Kahigi's political astuteness, but completely misses the reason for his death. The *consistent and widespread* heritage knowledge about how Kahigi died, which emerged in our research but not in historical records,[2] provides a powerful alternative to the British gloss about his treatment and his death.

This contradiction between local intangible heritage and history provoked us to examine more closely other historical representations of the Kings of Kihanja. Kahigi II used his traditional palace as a retreat, free from the direct gaze of German administrators and free from the chills of cold, breezy palace rooms at Kanazi. It grew to significant size and prosperity in part because of labour from those who failed to pay their poll tax. Following his suicide and 'burial' in 1916, his traditional palace first functioned as the ritual *Buchwankwanzi* house, the venue in which the king once consulted his diviners and counsellors and, after his death, where his regalia and memorabilia were carefully curated, venerated, and used in rituals of renewal featuring Kings' spirits as snakes during New Moon ceremonies overseen by female ritual authorities (Schmidt 2017).

Intangible heritage evidence for religious practices at Kanazi

I now return to Kanazi Palace itself and its role in the expression of traditional religion, heritage performances that occurred during widespread conversion to Christianity, or Islam, among most Haya. In our interviews, King Nyarubamba spoke openly about his ancestors' attitudes toward religion, including his grandfather Kahigi's severity toward those who left traditional religion and his 'caning of Muslims' (Nyarubamba, 17 September 2010, Kanazi). His memories captured Kahigi's well-known antipathy toward foreign religions, particularly Christianity. For example, Kahigi initially refused to give attractive land to missionaries. Instead he gave them a marshy piece of land unsuitable for their mission (Cory 1959), only to relent later with a small, more suitable grant. He steadfastly opposed religious conversion throughout his reign.

We learned more about Kahigi in relation to the palace from our interactions with the craftsmen. In early 2010, Ernest Kobwota, an elder, took us on a tour of Kanazi palace, stopping to share his knowledge about a very large *Buchwankwanzi* house once situated behind the main house and contiguous to the current kitchen (Kobwota, 15 March 2010, Kanazi, deceased). A *Buchwankwanzi* in this setting, on palace grounds, is used by a living king as a divining house as well as a meeting house for close advisors. King Perto Nyarubamba maintained another, smaller *Buchwankwanzi* at Kanazi used for rituals performed for *Cwezi* (ancient, ancestral) gods.

We clearly understood that this structure was contemporary with another traditional palace (*nyaruju*) once standing at the northeastern corner of the main residence, thus dating back to Kahigi II. Kobwota's information about indigenous religious performances inside the palace compound led to significant insights about where heritage values, once in universal practice, lie hidden at Kanazi Palace. The fact that Kahigi's successor, Alfred Kalemera (1916–1943), continued to maintain and use this large *Buchwankwanzi*, as did his successors up to Henrico Bwogi (1944–1958), is a powerful commentary on the vitality of indigenous religious beliefs through the twentieth century *within the palace precincts*. This is a significant sign of heritage values preserved, literally fenced off against the transformed and Christian-dominated world in which most local religious practices disappeared under aggressive attack as satanic (Sundkler 1980).

Religious heritage affirmed by material evidence

Our first restoration efforts, working in close collaboration with local craftsmen, focused on the removal of overburden from collapsed mud walls of Kahigi's first residence attached to the royal court. The craftsmen proved to be among the most involved stakeholders, and participated in this construction. During this process, they carefully observed and documented any objects that appeared at the original floor level, below the recent debris. Their insights about objects in relation to Kanazi heritage were informed by an intimate connection to its physical presence in their neighbourhood and knowledge of indigenous material culture. The evidence that emerged from the two large rooms of this suite showed the palace to be a place of religious refuge, where heritage meant (as other Haya also understood and used heritage) rituals and oral narratives performed at sacred places, rituals and oral performances that, at Kanazi, continued as vital but secret forces.

One morning in March 2011, the craftsmen greeted me with a request to inspect several corners of the former regalia rooms where they located objects of interest. There was an intriguing array of ritual items in the corners of the two large southern rooms (Schmidt 2011). The excavators carefully defined a ritual *kishwa*, receptacle (Figure 4(a)) for cowry shells (Figure 4(b)). The meanings of these objects and their association are well known in Haya culture, and here the craftsmen observed that the cowries were offerings to a *Cwezi* (ancestral) spirit. King Nyarubamba earlier described a similar vessel – a ritual brazier – when discussing his kingly duties vis-a-vis *Cwezi* spirits:

> … It will be like this: you should treat it this way. Then the king fulfilled these directives. He offered the required materials to the priest. The priest put them in the *mushozi* [a vessel] in which were placed the offerings that [in turn] were placed within the *Cwezi* residences in the *kiikaro*. (Nyarubamba, 18 September 2010, Kanazi)

As part of our collaboration, Nyarubamba recalled other ritual cowry uses when he travelled the kingdom making offerings at sacred sites: 'For example, in Kihanja [Kingdom], Kamachumu in Kanoni village. There, too, I placed a cowry shell' (Nyarubamba, 18 September 2010, Kanazi). In another corner were several patent medicine bottles, carefully placed to avoid harm, suggesting that these modern materials marked a ritual bricolage – new objects assigned meanings from a traditional ritual healing repertoire (see Schmidt 1996, 1997 on ritual bricolage).

The craftsmen found iron objects in three of the remaining six corners of the two rooms. Iron in Haya heritage holds significant reproductive potency (Schmidt 1997), with ritual importance in royal life and legitimacy at Kanazi. During a new King's installation, the candidate would enter the forge, take the bellows, and produce iron. As he departed the forge, people hailed him as the Iron King of Kihanja, whereupon he announced, 'I am Iron' (Nyarubamba in *The Tree of Iron*, McNeil, Muhley, and Schmidt 1988). It is customary that iron would be part of a royal ritual assemblage and its associated heritage values. A documented spear butt is part of the royal ritual regalia, symbolic of power and inter-generational continuity. Equally potent is a hoe, the power of which lies in its tie to reproduction of society – a tool central to the production of food. The last iron object was a section of automobile manifold, its substance announcing its power yet its original function obscuring its heritage message. According to local partners, it relates to narratives about King Kelemera as an aficionado of auto-mobiles. He and his successors are widely known to have favoured fancy automobiles, with Kalemera

Figure 4. (a) A *kishwa*, or vessel intended for ritual offerings, from King Kahigi's regalia rooms at Kanazi Palace; (b) Cowry shells left as ritual offerings at the *kishwa*. Photograph by author.

often pictured with his black Buick and other luxury cars. Among the relics of his reign curated at the Kanazi museum is a crank handle for starting cars.

Most importantly, this extraordinary assemblage signals royal engagement in ritual practices with *Cwezi* ancestors – a strong continuity of indigenous religious practices, despite memberships in Christian churches and the *widespread disappearance* of similar practices. Kanazi palace was therefore a sanctuary for the maintenance of indigenous religious practices, a heritage now viewed as threatened by villagers who, alarmed at the loss, have initiated projects to protect and preserve shrines and their oral traditions (Schmidt 2010, 2014a, 2017).

Such observations and ethnographic collaborations in multi-site settings allow us all to see how the Kings at Kanazi were preservationists of traditional religious practices and beliefs over the entire twentieth century. Our interactions with King Petro Nyarubamba reinforced this point. His willingness to share and discuss the activities and duties of the king to propitiate *Cwezi* ancestors and maintain their shrines through the performance of appropriate rites was key to understanding a once vital Haya heritage, now virtually erased. No matter what pressure Kings faced from the church, it was their duty to ensure the kingdom's well-being and prosperity.

Other perspectives, other partnerships: understanding the role of modernity in erasing heritage beliefs

As the first phase of the Kanazi Palace restoration ran its course, we found memories of the palace itself to be fragmentary and historical accounts sparse. Both deficiencies compelled us to make further archaeological inquiries. With the agreement of clan elders, we engaged three additional categories of partners: students from the University of Florida, members of the royal family at Kanazi, and an archaeologist previously trained in Katuruka village (see Schmidt 2017).

The excavation results helped us to understand the role that modernity had in obscuring heritage beliefs and their performance at Kanazi Palace. Excavations at the locale of the *Buchwankwanzi* (as noted before, a king's divining/meeting) house produced large earthenware vessels suitable for serving many people, possibly feasting events. There, as well as the locale of Kahigi's traditional palace before 1905, we documented fancy painted ceramics and English gin consumption (Schmidt 2016). Kingly office under colonial rule ensured great prosperity and luxury goods. Redistribution of tribute faded, replaced by wealth accumulation. By 1920, King Alfred Kalemera (1916–1943) received tribute from each subject, plus one month's labour (later dropped by the British), and in 1927 Kelemera had an income of 2,773 pounds a year (Iliffe 1979, 283). Of all the Haya Kings, the Kihanja king received the most generous British gratuity, equal to the salary of a senior British civil servant (Lumley 1976), which elicited critical observations: 'Their extravagance is deplorable and futile … large automobiles, expensive lounge suits and Paris dresses for their wives' (Dundas to Cameroon [1927?] TNA 215/50; cited in Iliffe 1979, 283).

Beneath the window dressing of modernity, however, strong threads of heritage practice kept traditional religion alive while it withered outside the palace walls. Artefacts recovered in one of the two tribute storage rooms inside the court provide a vivid commentary on elite consumption – a large variety of discarded auto parts. These were taken to an elderly Haya mechanic, who identified parts from a Land Rover, Peugeot 403, and even a Willis jeep. These finds dated to the period when the court was used as a garage, according to Nyarubamba (13 November 2008) (Schmidt 2016, 2017).

These archaeological results indicate that elite rural consumption during colonial times was more expansive than previously documented. As chiefs, nobles, and common folk ate their meals on banana leaves, the royal family used fine china, enhancing their prestige in a world that otherwise highlighted their diminished political influence. Conspicuous consumption of expensive goods marked a new era of wealth display by the royal elite, not possible before colonialism. These opportunistic adoptions of the material trappings of modernity starkly contrast with the Kings as stewards of heritage, tenaciously performing religious rites on a regular basis for 125 years during the colonial and postcolonial periods.

Other insights into the illusion of modernity

Had we not been conscientious about listening to and learning from our collaborators, then the trappings of modernity would have obscured past and still-active heritage values practiced at Kanazi, assuring them a subaltern profile. We were able to document religious heritage at Kanazi because of daily interactions with King Nyarubamba and his performance of rites at multiple shrines.

I discussed earlier the location of what one elder called the very large *Buchwankanzi* divining house behind the main residence, which King Kalemera and his successor(s) continued to use, as did King Henrico Bwogi (1944–1958) when our partner Ernest Kobwota saw it in the 1940s. King Kalemera's maintenance of this important religious structure is at odds with an assertion by a colonial official that Kalemera destroyed an important *Cwezi* shrine in Butakya (to the SW) in celebration of his conversion to Christianity in 1919. A 1922 British report, for example, says that Kalemera had the most important *Cwezi* shrine to Wamara at Butakya burned after his 1919 conversion to Christianity (Iliffe 1979, 261 and ft. nt. 4), a representation that has apparently distorted local religious heritage practices. As part of his official duties, Kalemera made regular tribute offerings to this and other *Cwezi* shrines. Research partners in Butakya (another 'community of interest') remember it differently: 'missionaries came, pitched tents near the shrine, and destroyed it with the help of several collaborators'; a significant counter-testimony to the British report (Field notes, 15 March 2011, Butakya). Kalemera's patronage of these powerful *Cwezi* diviners and allies was both political (countering political rivals) and an integral part of fulfilling expectations for performance of heritage practices.

These testimonies by local descendants and heritage experts demonstrate how privileging a report written three years after the fact by a British officer (who was apparently drawing on rumours) betrays a profound misunderstanding of the Butakya shrine. Characterizing it as a haven for renegade spirit mediums, those ritual officials in fact served the Mukama at the 'killing rock', an execution centre for those committing serious violations of traditional law out of sight of colonial law.

Kalemera's official conversion in 1919 occurred at the same time that several other Kings converted (Sundkler 1980), a political move to gain the favour of British authorities. Historical accounts, particularly those painted with a religious brush, also obscured his continuing indigenous heritage practices. Bishop Sundkler, the first Lutheran Bishop in northwestern Tanzania, relates several stories that amplify Kalemera's devotion to Christianity while denying his indigenous beliefs. Sundkler relates a tale of youth that went on a rampage after Kalemera converted:

> But youngsters wish to be radical; they attacked what was old and traditional. Feeling strong in their group fellowship, they entered the shambas [farms] on the mountain and kicked aside the little discreetly-placed Wamara huts. … rebellious, swinging, drumming youngsters with a smell of hashish about them, on their way to the future – together with the king – towards a Jesus religion … . (Sundkler 1980, 65)

This highly romanticized rendering of youth on a hashish-inspired Christian rampage is an imaginary elaboration 40 years later about alleged events, filtered through the interpretative lenses of two stalwart church members. We must read between the lines of such reports to see the cleverness of Kelemera's public activities, apparently used to obscure the continuous practice of indigenous religious beliefs inside the palace and at key shrines. Whatever his characterizations by Christian pastors, Kalemera taught *Cwezi* rites to his son and successor Petro Nyarubamba, who years later continued to perform them in his role as a legitimate king.

Kalemera's real attitude toward Christianity emerges with his extreme discomfort with missionary activity near his palace, particularly by two African pastors – one known for his extreme antipathy to the 'satanic practices' of indigenous religion. Kalemera (like his father, Kahigi II) did not want mission activities in the precinct of his palace, surely a risky business for a King who was following indigenous beliefs. Sundkler admits (1980, 66) that 'Kalemera, though baptized, did not appear to take Christianity very seriously' [and] 'feared that an evangelist from abroad … might be plotting against him'. Eventually Kalemera gave this pastor a 'splendid farm', thus removing him from Kanazi palace and freeing himself from Christian surveillance.

Multiple partnerships

Our multiple partnerships, incorporating accomplished craftsmen working on the physical structures as well as both royal and non-royal participants, added diverse heritage values that were difficult to see when we embarked on the Kanazi Palace project. Heritage values played out daily with obeisance paid to the *Cwezi* ancestors. At every turn, one is confronted by traditional religious practices – at the shrines in the contemporary *nyaruju* palace, the shrine in the *Buchwankwanzi* house behind the court (Figure 5), multiple shrines maintained behind the main house, a shrine in Kalemera's house, and a special shrine (*ekiikaro*) in the back room of the main house where the recent King's regalia are kept.

The deep and enduring respect that Kanazi kings paid to *Cwezi* spirits is a defining characteristic of heritage preservation in the face of rapid cultural change. These performances were acts of resistance and affirmation, fulfilling ages-old heritage responsibilities. The Hinda Kings continued to be *Cwezi* devotees, right into the twenty-first century, following beliefs and ethical principles under attack from the Christian church. King Nyarubamba, taught by his father Kalemera, fulfilled his New Moon responsibilities by travelling around the entire kingdom to all the major *Cwezi* shrines, ' … at that time I had my car. I went all over the kingdom. Moreover the people had faith in me. They gave me sheep and other materials for the offerings'. In his view, and evidently his predecessors as well, there was no difficulty being a Christian and engaging in *Cwezi* rites: 'Christ's religion is new. Ours is traditional,' and their compatibility rests in 'what is forbidden by Christ's followers is also forbidden by the Cwezi' (Nyarubamba, 18 September 2010, Kanazi).

Archaeological evidence, oral testimonies, and ethnographic observations at Kanazi palace all affirm that the Kihanja Kings continued to practice indigenous rites *long after* they became Christian churchgoers and extraordinary consumers of prestige goods. The presence of multiple active shrines within the palace grounds today underwrites what we view in the archaeological record – a serious undermining of historical representations about the Kihanja Kings and their engagement with traditional religious practices. Kanazi Palace continues as a refuge for heritage preservation, hidden from common view, secreted from the sanctions of the church, yet an integral part of the physical fabric and heritage of Kihanja Kingdom.

Figure 5. A ritual Buchwankwanzi house maintained by King Petro Nyarubamba behind the royal court at Kanazi Palace. Photograph by author, with permission of Petro Nyarubamba.

Heritage erased, history whitewashed – the Ngogo massacre and Mazinga cave

The HIV/AIDS pandemic has taken a disproportionate toll on the villages along the western coast of Lake Victoria (e.g. Lwihula et al. 1993; Lugalla et al. 1999; Ndamugoba et al. 2000; Mutembei 2001). Almost an entire generation of elderly male keepers of oral tradition fell to AIDS, leading to a severe rupture in chains of transmission for heritage knowledge (Schmidt 2010, 2014a, 2014b, 2017). My second example emerges from the losses this rupture caused, and also reflects the tension between heritage practices and history as constructed by Western observers. It too features King Kahigi, this time through his involvement in the affairs of neighbouring Bukara Kingdom.

Not long after the Katuruka initiative's launch (Schmidt 2010, 2014a, 2017), we learned that students at nearby Nyarubale Primary School had found human bones. A teacher who asked pupils to bring bones to class for a biology lesson was surprised to see human skulls and long bones when he expected chicken, goat, and cattle bones. Students had removed the bones from a rock shelter at Mazinga waterfall about 2 km away towards Lake Victoria (see Figure 1). In a school storeroom, we observed a significant number of mostly complete and partial skulls as well as many long bones and several fragments of pelvises. We returned to visit the Mazinga rock shelter site in February of 2010 with student guides, finding a beautiful tropical pool and waterfall fringed by red moss (Figure 6(a)). Crossing a shallow pool and clambering over the talus to rock ledges (Figure 6(b)), we observed additional materials on a narrow ledge about 2 m deep. The presence of a *kishwa* (brazier), similar to that found in King Kahigi's regalia rooms, marked ritual practices associated with Bacwezi spirits. A visiting forensic dentist found that most individuals were males ranging between 20 and 50 years old. Several of the skulls had punctures and fractures that seemed to be inflicted by high calibre bullets – 45 calibre or larger.

Benjamin Shegesha, the project director of the Katuruka village heritage initiative, shared with me his desire to find ways that this site – now attached to the academic identity of the school – might figure into the revitalization and renewal of diminished intangible heritage in the region, a primary focus of the Katuruka project (Schmidt 2010, 2014a). Yet the site presented an ethical issue: notwithstanding the eagerness of the school community as well as the neighbouring community to develop the site as a heritage destination, how could we justify such participation in Mazinga Cave without adequate interpretive context? The Mazinga site and the school's involvement had the advantage to recuperate knowledge of a 'dark heritage' of the community (McDavid 2002; Logan and Reeves 2009), but we agreed that without context the site might become a place of a negative 'dark' heritage, ignoring local heritage and appealing to visitors' obsessions with the macabre.

Figure 6. (a) The rock ledges called Mazinga Cave, where human remains were placed after losses in battle; (b) The waterfall contiguous to Mazinga Cave. Photograph by author.

Occasional visits with the headmaster over several years developed the idea that the Mazinga site should be protected, for possible use as an educational heritage site with potential to earn income for the school. What continued to elude us was why human bodies were placed in this exposed setting. Interviews during the Katuruka project revealed nothing about the origins of the Mazinga remains. These interview questions, however, prompted my memory of stories told me in 1969 by local elders who had discussed a major massacre of local residents by Germans at the turn of the 20th century– oral traditions once a vital part of heritage in this part of Buhaya. I wondered, was there possibly a link between the bones left at Mazinga and the stories I heard years ago?

Written history and heritage once remembered

In my search for knowledge about a major massacre near the border of Kihanja and Bukara Kingdoms, I first turned to written accounts of Haya history (e.g. Cory 1959; Austen 1968; Curtis 1989) pertaining to German military activities possibly tied to the Mazinga cave remains. I found only elisions and glosses about serious incidents of German repression. Among the silences was the virtual erasure of historical knowledge about a conflict between Kishebuka – the King of Bukara Kingdom – and the German administration, with assistance from King Kahigi II of Kihanja who lived at Kanazi palace. No published histories mentioned when German troops crushed Kishebuka's forces in a massacre below Kanazi Palace, with help from the African police of King Kahigi II.

Both written and oral chronicles mention King Kahigi's scheming against his neighbour and kinsman, King Kishebuka, when conspirators hid guns at Kahigi's direction in the house of Kishebuka's prime minister and then reported it to the Germans (Austen 1968, 48). This resulted in the German transfer of the Kanyangereko section of Bukara to Kahigi II. The period in question, between 1898 and 1902, was during the administration of Franz Richter,[3] locally known as Bwana Korongo (crane or stork).

Some minor insights into what happened to Kishebuka come from F. X. Lwamgira, whose writings included a Kanyangereko history (Lwamgira 1949b). This history whitewashes colonial atrocities (Lwamgira was a colonial client extraordinaire), but does mention how King Kahigi II betrayed Kishebuka, causing Kishebuka to lose the Kanyangereko section to Kahigi (Lwamgira 1949b, 19–21). The account mentions nothing about another incident in which Kishebuka came into violent conflict with Richter and King Kahigi II of Kihanja Kingdom.

Local evidence of a massacre

After returning from the field in 2010, these silent historical writings compelled me to re-examine the archived oral traditions I recorded in 1969.[4] A grandson of one of the principal participants once provided a riveting story:

> They met the Germans at their camp in Ngogo. When the German officer Hauptmann Lionel [Richter ?] [see note 1] saw the Bakara and their leaders, he asked for their Mukama. *When he asked who was Mukama, [the Katikiro – Prime Minister] said that he was, and within moments he had been shot dead with a pistol by the German officer. Then the German African askaris [soldiers] present started firing into the seated crowd; the askaris had tried to warn the people, but their signs had not been understood. Of the hundreds there, there were only a few survivors. It took the relatives of the dead nine days to retrieve and finish burying their dead at the same place. Some were not buried, and their skulls could be seen for years thereafter.* (Bandio, 5 November 1969, Maruku; emphasis mine)

There is no ambiguity about the events of this fateful day in Haya history. Even more specific accounts explained the event:

> When [Kishebuka's troops] arrived, a German asked them where Kishebuka was. Gradually, they were looked over by Korongo as he searched for Kishebuka. As he asked for Kishebuka, the Katikiro spoke up and announced that he was [the Mukama]. ... *When Korongo learned that Kishebuka was not present, he was very angry and ordered his askaris to open fire. The Abendere were the first to die, then the Bakara. Those who escaped the deadly fire were those*

who happened to be standing in the proximity of Korongo. Those not killed by rifle fire were killed by the Bahamba [citizens of Kihanja Kingdom ruled by Kahigi II) *and their spears.* Those who escaped to Kiizi (near the Whites) were not killed but those who went to Kitembe forest were pursued and killed by the Bahamba (there and two other forests—Rugege and Kyamakonge). After this slaughter, the Germans went to Kahigi's kikale in Kanazi, Kihanja. (Rusinga, 29 November 1969, Maruku; emphasis mine)

Hundreds died in this massacre,[5] occurring during the latter part of Richter's command and about the time of the gun incident involving Kahigi's intrigue during 1901.[6] Most of the dead came from Kanyangereko and Maruku, two large communities stretching over 6 km on a peninsula protruding into Kemondo Bay, and contiguous to Mazinga cave. The presence of unburied bodies relates to a taboo that forbade *village* burial of those defeated and thus contaminated in battle; their bodies were placed in caves or holes (Lwamgira 1949a). This explains why some families placed bodies in Mazinga cave. Large calibre bullet wounds to the heads of several victims in Mazinga cave affirm a strong relationship between this massacre and Mazinga cave. Osteological examinations illuminate that the gunshot entry wounds to crania showed characteristic spalling, affirming initial analysis of death by shooting for several of a minimum of 14 individuals placed on the ledge (Daniels 2013).

Thus, oral traditions, one of the most highly valued forms of intangible heritage among the Haya, provided powerful testimony about traumas suffered under the German colonial regime (Schmidt 2010, 2014b, 2017). Two generations ago, these vivid and highly detailed narratives about this atrocity had been an integral part of heritage performance, providing a commentary on change that the Haya no longer express as part of their heritage identities. Published accounts of events leading up to the massacre are opaque and *completely omit any mention* of the Ngogo genocide (Figure 1).

Once an active part of daily story telling in some families, and central to heritage identities in Bukara, this form of heritage is no longer passed on reliably from generation to generation. How was it possible, after only five generations, that the memory of such a major event disappeared? While a variety of possible explanations arose for this forgetting, the most viable explanation parallels the experience we had come to understand in nearby Katuruka village: these oral narratives are no longer performed because of broken chains of transmission arising from the ravages of HIV/AIDS and the deaths of elderly keepers of oral traditions (Schmidt 2010, 2014a, 2014b, 2017).

Thus, the Mazinga cave heritage project became a corrective measure to reclaim once vital heritage expressed through multiple oral traditions. Emotive and detailed story-telling from five decades ago affirm the significance of these events in the intangible heritage of Buhaya – a remarkable antidote to the silences of written history.

Community and development of interpretation

In 2013, additional collaborative planning with the headmaster, assistant headmaster, elders who participated in interviews and project assessments, and the school board chairman, led to a blueprint for a heritage exhibition about this colonial-era heritage. The project brought students, teachers, and the school to the centre of activities, taking over management and using the exhibition for educational purposes. After contributing their ideas about the possible meaning of Mazinga cave, prominent elders in surrounding villages keenly supported the idea of featuring an exhibition of the Mazinga skeletal materials, arguing that it would be beneficial to the village as well as the school. These perspectives on exhibiting human remains initially surprised me, causing me to re-examine my discomfort (based on professional sensitivity to indigenous peoples whose ancestral remains were used as Western fetishes). Haya culture, however, valorizes the exhibition of ancestors, long a part of the respect and celebration of Kings, most notably the exhibit of the skull of King Rugomora III of Kihanja (d. 1890).

The advice and commentaries of local research collaborators led to a plan to exhibit evidence from Mazinga cave with interpretation sensitive to community needs. Local stakeholders concurred that the Mazinga site needed to be multi-functional, to present death in keeping with Mazinga being a place for remembrance, and to enhance educational experiences that may evoke contemplations on colonialism (McDavid 2002; Logan and Reeves 2009). Of particular importance to many local participants – school staff, villagers, business people, and other educators – was that the experience should reveal the impact of colonial policies at a local level while also remembering community ancestors. Through the persistent encouragement and needs of a small primary school, a profoundly important part of once vital Haya heritage finally emerged from the silencing forces of history and disease during the last century.

Conclusion

Both examples discussed – stories of a palace and a cave – demonstrate that heritage studies among African cultures must account for powerful intangible characteristics. Lacking the materiality of the built environment, such heritage is more vulnerable to change and manipulation. We have discussed and illustrated how written accounts of African heritage often misrepresented heritage values by privileging religious and political values of the West. Our collaborative research shows that by working with diverse 'communities of interest' we are able to bring alternative perspectives to bear on how heritage was performed and lived in days past. Under conditions of intense culture change, including conversion to Christianity and the social ravages of HIV/AIDS, heritage practices have been lost and hidden. Yet, with the inclusion of recorded oral traditions and extant knowledge about the past, we are able to recover heritage values that once played vital roles in the daily lives of the Haya people.

Notes

1. Obersultane was a paramount chief. Some when telling stories about Kahigi II refer to his rank as 'major'.
2. There is a reference, cited in Austen (1968, 121), regarding a rumour about suicide.
3. The rank of Hauptmann or Captain was used by the Haya themselves. Accustomed to addressing the German commandant as Hauptmann, they also treated 'Bwana Korongo'. According to Austen (1968, 273), he was in fact Lieutenant Franz Richter.
4. Research into this issue is continuing; German archives for this period of German administration must be consulted. The focus in this chapter is that all later historical representations of this period omit any mention of the loss of so many lives during the Kishebuka-Kahigi/German conflict.
5. There may appear to be an alternative view – that Herrmann's campaign against Mkotoni of Smaller Kyamtwara in 1895 (and in which King Kahigi was complicit) led to killings in caves (Austen 1968), but the narrative content, timing, and geography are wrong.
6. 'Captain' or Lieutenant Franz Richter was implicated in another massacre in 1907 of 200 people in the southern highlands of Tanganyika, an event that precipitated the Maji Maji rebellion (Iliffe 1979).

Disclosure statement

No potential conflict of interest was reported by the author.

Suggested citation

Schmidt, Peter R. 2017. "Contests between Heritage and History in Tanganyika/Tanzania: Insights Arising from Community-Based Heritage Research." In Special Series: African perspectives on community engagements, guest-edited by Peter R. Schmidt. *Journal of Community Archaeology and Heritage* 4(2): page #s tbd.

References

Atalay, Sonya. 2012. *Community-Based Archaeology: Research with, by, and for Indigenous and Local Communities*. Berkeley: University of California Press.

Austen, Ralph A. 1968. *Northwest Tanzania Under German and British Rule: Colonial Policy and Tribal Politics, 1889–1939*. New Haven, CT: Yale University Press.

Cory, Hans. 1959. *History of the Bukoba District*. Mwanza, Tanganyika: Lake Printers.

Curtis, Kenneth. 1989. "Capitalism, Fettered: State, Merchant, and Peasant in Northwestern Tanzania, 1917–1968." PhD diss., University of Wisconsin.

Daniels, Rosemary. 2013. "Report on the Oestology of Human Remains at Mazinga Cave." Unpublished ms.

Iliffe, John. 1979. *A Modern History of Tanganyika*. Cambridge: Cambridge University Press.

Logan, William, and Keir Reeves. 2009. "Introduction: Remembering Places of Pain and Shame." In *Places of Pain and Shame: Dealing with 'Difficult Heritage*, edited by William Logan and Keir Reeves, 1–14. London: Routledge.

Lugalla, J. L., M. A. C. Emmelin, A. K. Mutembei, C. J. Comoro, J. Z. J. Killewo, G. Kwesigabo, A. I. M. Sandstrom, and L. G. Dahlgren. 1999. "The Social and Cultural Contexts of HIV/AIDS Transmission in the Kagera Region, Tanzania." *Journal of Asian and African Studies* 34 (4): 377–402.

Lumley, E. K. 1976. *Forgotten Mandate: A British District Officer in Tanganyika*. London: C. Hurst and Co.

Lwamgira, Francis Xavier. 1949a. *Amakuru G'Abakama ba Kiziba [History of the Kings of Kiziba]*. G. Kamanzi, trans. Kashozi. Tanganyika: Rumuli Press.

Lwamgira, Francis Xavier. 1949b. *Amakuru G'Abakama ba Kanyangereko [History of the Kings of Kanyangereko]*. G. Kamanzi, trans. Kashozi. Tanganyika: Rumuli Press.

Lwihula, G. K., L. Dahlgren, J. Killewo, and A. Sandstrom. 1993. "AIDS Epidemic in Kagera Region, Tanzania – the Experiences of Local People." *AIDS Care* 5 (3): 347–357.

McDavid, Carol. 2002. "Archaeologies that Hurt; Descendants that Matter: A Pragmatic Approach to Collaboration in the Public Interpretation of African-American Archaeology." *World Archaeology* 34: 303–314.

McNeil, Peter, Frank Muhley, and Peter Schmidt. 1988. *The Tree of Iron*. Providence, RI: Foundation for African Prehistory and Archaeology.

Mutembei, Aldred. K. 2001. *Poetry and AIDS in Tanzania: Changing Metaphors and Metonymies in Haya Oral Traditions*. Leiden: Research School of Asian, African, and Amerindian Studies, Leiden University.

Ndamugoba, D., M. Mboya, K. Amani, and K. J. Katabaro. 2000. *The Impact of HIV/AIDS on Primary Education in Bukoba Rural and Kinondoni Districts of Tanzania*. Dar es Salaam: UNICEF.

Nora, Pierre. 1989. "Between Memory and History: Les Lieux de Mémoire." *Representations* 26: 7–24.

Rizvi, Uzma Z. 2015. "Decolonizing Archaeology: On the Global Heritage of Epistemic Laziness." In *Two Days After Forever: A Reader on the Choreography of Time*, Reader for the 56th Venice Biennale, Cyprus Pavilion, edited by Omar Kholeif, 154–163. Berlin: Sternberg Press.

Schmidt, Peter R. 1978. *Historical Archaeology: A Structural Approach in an African Culture*. Westport, CT: Greenwood Press.

Schmidt, Peter R. 1996. "Reconfiguring the Barongo: Reproductive Symbolism and Reproduction among a Work Association of Iron Smelters." In *The Culture and Technology of African Iron Production*, edited by Peter R. Schmidt, 74–127. Gainesville: University Press of Florida.

Schmidt, Peter R. 1997. *Iron Technology in East Africa: Symbolism, Science, and Archaeology*. Bloomington: Indiana University Press.

Schmidt, Peter R. 2006. *Historical Archaeology in Africa: Representation, Social Memory, and Oral Traditions*. Walnut Creek, CA: AltaMira.

Schmidt, Peter R. 2010. "Trauma and Social Memory in Northwestern Tanzania: Organic, Spontaneous Community Collaboration." *Journal of Social Archaeology* 10 (2): 255–279.

Schmidt, Peter R. 2011. *Kanazi Palace Restoration: A Foundation for Sustainable Heritage Tourism in Kagera Region*. Dar es Salaam: Foundation for African Prehistory and Archaeology.

Schmidt, Peter R. 2013. "Oral History, Oral Traditions and Archaeology: Application of Structural Analysis." In *Oxford Handbook of African Archaeology*, edited by Peter Mitchell and Paul Lane, 37–47. Oxford: Oxford University Press.

Schmidt, Peter R. 2014a. "Rediscovering Community Archaeology in Africa and Reframing Its Practice." *Journal of Community Archaeology and Heritage* 1 (1): 38–56.

Schmidt, Peter R. 2014b. "Hardcore Ethnography: Interrogating the Intersection of Disease, Human Rights, and Heritage." *Heritage and Society* 7 (2): 170–188.

Schmidt, Peter R. 2016. "Historical Archaeology in East Africa: Past Practice and Future Directions." *Journal of African History* 57 (2): 183–194.

Schmidt, Peter R. 2017. *Community-Based Heritage in Africa: Unveiling Local Research and Development Initiatives*. London: Routledge.

Sundkler, Bengt. 1980. *Bara Bukoba: Church and Community in Tanzania*. London: C. Hurst & Co.

Community involvement and heritage management in rural South Africa

Nthabiseng Mokoena

ABSTRACT

Located in the former Transkei homeland of the apartheid era, now the Eastern Cape Province, Matatiele is one of many disadvantaged though culturally rich communities in South Africa. Both the government and academics have neglected the region for decades. The Matatiele Community and its Mehloding Community Trust needed to understand community views about a proposed heritage centre. Therefore, I conducted research (including interviews) to understand the various communities' perceptions of what they regard as heritage, including their views on heritage management and the significance of rock art. In this paper, I outline the complexities of rock art management within an area whose inhabitants do not relate to the 'western' meaning of heritage, as well as the significance of involving community perspectives to achieve a better understanding of the dynamics surrounding heritage and its management. Communities' perspectives this study have informed heritage management strategies that are relevant for Matatiele.

Introduction

Along the foothills of the Maloti-Drakensberg Mountains, in the Eastern Cape of South Africa, is a community that has a population of 203,843 out of 54 million South Africans (Statistics South Africa 2014). Matatiele is particularly culturally rich and is still rooted in its traditions. Like many South African communities, the Matatiele communities are defined by diverse cultural groups. Lying along the eastern border with Lesotho, cultural influences of the Basotho among the Matatiele communities are significant along with influences imparted by Xhosa, Sesotho, Phuthi, Hlubi, Griqua, Bhaca, Afrikaner-, and English-speaking descendant communities. The main cultural groups forming the core focus of the research I discuss here are the Xhosa, Sotho, Phuthi, and Hlubi. As with many ethnic groups in southern Africa, these Bantu-speaking peoples moved into southern Africa to find San-speaking groups (for a detailed review of South African history see Mitchell 2002). Culture contact has been prevalent among these different groups (Derricourt 1977, 195; Jolly 1996; Challis 2012, 12) and, thus, one finds similarities in certain aspects of their culture. The cultural differences I highlight here are mainly traditional norms which heritage managers and researchers need to understand when investigating heritage and management strategies for these communities.

The living communities of Matatiele had, prior to the project described here, established the Mehloding Community Trust (http//www.mehloding.co.za) (henceforth Mehloding), a community tourism venture that runs an adventure trail and three chalets across Matatiele. Mehloding approached the Matatiele Archaeology and Rock Art (http//www.marasurvey.com) (MARA) project at the University of Witwatersrand about the possibility of establishing a rock art centre comprising displays of San rock art found in Matatiele. Later, Mehloding accepted MARA's advice to establish a heritage centre instead of the rock art centre, and Mehloding's major concern was the role that communities could play in the establishment and development of the project. Therefore, I joined MARA in 2013 to conduct a community-inclusive *heritage* management project as part of my Master's Degree research at the University of the Witwatersrand (Mokoena 2015). Because the heritage centre was a community project, my aim was to understand the communities' views on the proposed heritage centre; that is, to identify and assess stages of how a community-inclusive heritage management project could be achieved. I wanted to see whether the communities accepted the proposition of a heritage centre and, if so, to determine how they would want to be involved and how their heritage would be represented in the project. The rationale for this direct community research was to incorporate community views into the decision making and planning stages of the project. As such, it is situated within broader heritage discourses which explore and support community involvement in heritage management processes (see Chirikure and Pwiti 2008; Schmidt and Pikirayi 2016).

As a rock art specialist, I was especially concerned about the management of rock art sites in the Alfred Nzo area. As a member of the Bantu-speaking communities in southern Africa, specifically the Basotho, I knew the ignorance that some of our people have towards San rock art (Mokoena 2012; see also Mallen 2011). My earlier honours research had looked into the interpretation of San rock paintings of a site in the Foothills of Lesotho (Mokoena 2012). While tracing the site in Lesotho I interacted with local communities who expressed their unawareness of the meaning of the paintings. The communities knew that the paintings were made by 'Baroa' the San, but did not know why they were painted. Indeed, this ignorance had led to what (in some cases) is regarded (by heritage 'authorities') as vandalism (Mokoena 2015).

Rock art and heritage in Southern Africa

Like in many areas in southern Africa, San rock art is a dominant part of the Matatiele landscape. The San community is an indigenous hunter-gatherer community that utilized various regions across southern Africa. What makes San rock art distinctive is the accessibility of its religious symbolism, interpreted by scholars who used ethnographic records (Vinnicombe 1976; Lewis-Williams 1981b, 1986). In contrast to early colonial views that San rock paintings were just 'a direct and simple response to the artistic desire or an innate artistic predisposition to recreate objects or things people saw in nature' (Mguni 2015, 3), research has revealed that the art is religiously symbolic. The religious symbolic meaning behind San rock art has been debated since the 1960s (Vinnicombe 1967; Lewis-Williams 1981a; Biesele 1993; Solomon 1997; Lewis-Williams et al. 2000). Starting in the 1970s, research by such as Lewis-Williams (1981b); and Vinnicombe (1976) revealed a deeper significance in the meaning of rock paintings. The paintings depict images or events that happen in the spiritual world as experienced by the painters, who are believed to possess the ability to travel through the spirit realm (Vinnicombe 1976; Pearce, Namono, and Mallen 2009). The San interacted extensively with the Bantu-speaking communities, interactions that are depicted in the art (see Figure 1) and in the cultural practices and language of living communities (King 2014). When European groups moved into the region, they also interacted with the San, as revealed by depictions of European clothing, weapons, and even horses (Vinnicombe 1976; Challis 2009).

Theoretical approaches to community involvement

Archaeology in the colonial African context was an expression of 'white' privilege, and in South African remained as such until the end of apartheid (Shepherd 2003, 2005). The introduction of archaeology in South Africa was highly political and deeply embedded in achieving colonial agendas (Schmidt 1995, 125; Shepherd 2002, 198). Tensions created by apartheid led to mistrust of archaeology among informed South Africans, particularly because many academic disciplines

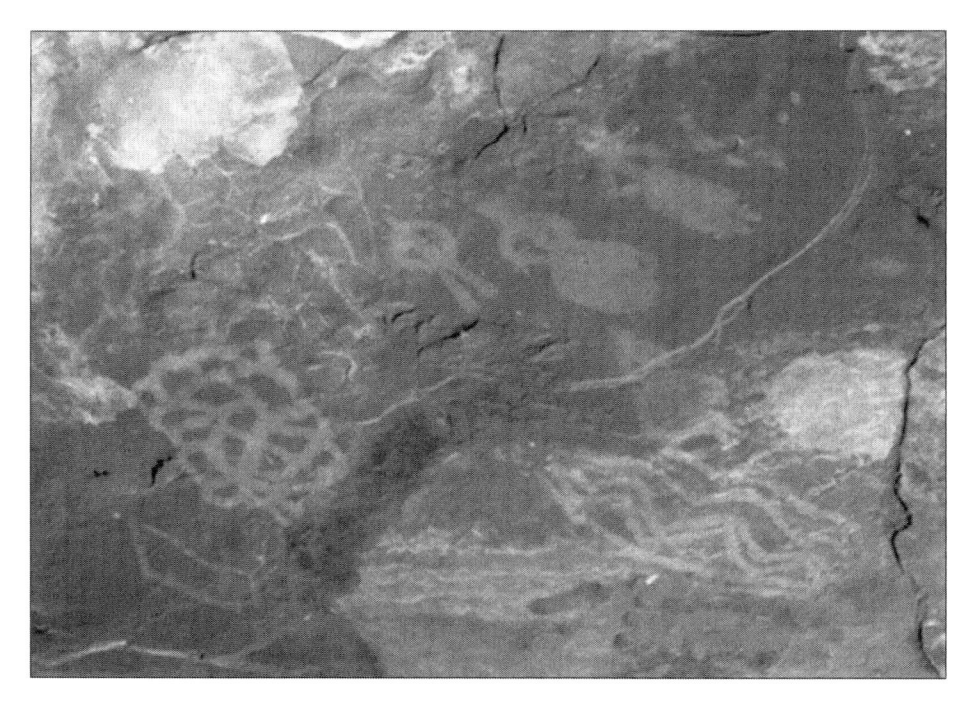

Figure 1. Finger paintings depicting images of human figures dressed in what appears to be European dress code. Provided by MARA.

were spear-headed by white researchers. Archaeology as a result was viewed, by South African scholars and others, as a colonial enterprise that did not take into account the different histories of African communities, and in particular did not promote multivocality (Hall 2005; Shepherd 2005; Ndlovu 2009; Lane 2011), much less seek the consent of those communities. Post-colonial archaeologies, on the other hand, emphasize subaltern communities that have been silenced by colonial archaeologies (Jopela 2011; Schmidt 2014b).

Echoing similar colonial dynamics globally, African communities were not recognized as having the agency to construct their own histories, which led to the marginalization of living communities. To correct these past injustices, post-colonial researchers highlight problems where research did not accommodate views of stakeholders, focusing particularly on communities residing next to research areas and those displaced by land alienation under colonial conditions (Pwiti and Ndoro 1999; Shepherd 2005; Chirikure and Pwiti 2008; Ndlovu 2009; Schmidt 2009, 2014b). Inclusion of communities means acknowledgement of their past and present cultures, and incorporating these into research (Andah 1995; Chirikure and Pwiti 2008; Jopela 2011; Jopela and Fredriksen 2015, 2).

Commitment to ethical responsibilities within the discipline is central in addressing past injustices. One of the primary roles that archaeologists and heritage managers play is to steward heritage and archaeological material (see Lynott 1997; Bendremer and Richman 2006; Beaudry 2009), and to do it in such a manner that the interpretative frameworks reflect multiple perspectives open to constant evaluation and change. Research promotes public outreach and education as part of interpretation and responsible, ethical protection of archaeological and heritage resources (Mazel 1982; Jopela and Fredriksen 2015).

Even with such shifting values, power imbalances within African archaeological research and management still prevail (Shepherd 2002; Schmidt 2009), and there is still concern over the authoritative nature of interactions between professionals and communities (Taruvinga and Ndoro 2003).

How then are communities' views incorporated in archaeological research and heritage management? Rural Matatiele provides an opportunity for a deeper discussion that incorporates all aspects of heritage in collaboration with local communities. Inclusion by archaeologists and heritage managers of the different community members in projects that affect them directly or indirectly is best practice towards addressing ethical responsibility for archaeology and heritage management. Such ethical practice in the implementation of projects that protect heritage will mean a reduced risk of compromising the most affected parties (Colwell-Chanthaphonh and Ferguson 2008; Atalay 2012; Schmidt and Pikirayi 2016).

In order to attempt community involvement in Matatiele, I conducted interviews and called community meetings in order to address communities' perceptions on heritage, rock art sites, and the establishment of a heritage centre within their community. Fieldwork took place in three different villages in Matatiele (Figure 2), as described below.

The dynamics of community-involved heritage management: methodologies

Heritage management is complex. It is helpful in the South African context to break down the meanings. Archaeologists and heritage practitioners have been criticised for 'protecting only those aspects of sites that heritage managers consider important, in most cases, excluding other aspects of heritage' (B. Smith 2006; Jopela and Fredriksen 2015, 3). In the case of Zimbabwe, for instance, colonial and early post-colonial approaches to heritage management did not account for the contribution of traditional local heritage management strategies (Fontein 2006; Chirikure and Pwiti 2008). Management strategies for archaeological sites such as Mapungubwe and Domboshava, for instance, did not involve communities that are linked to the sites (Taruvinga and Ndoro 2003; B. Smith 2006; Chirikure et al. 2010, 34).

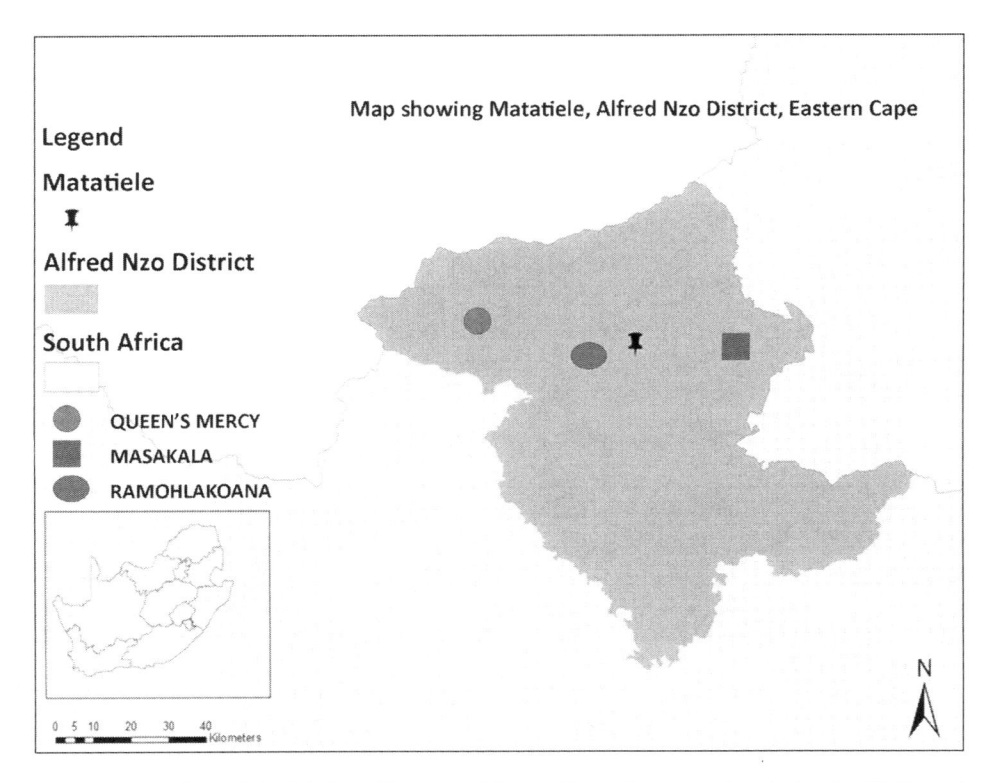

Figure 2. Map showing villages of Masakala, Ramohlakoana, and Queens Mercy, where research took place. Provided by author and Mncedisi Siteleki.

The case of Domboshava is an unfortunate reminder of what may go wrong if, during a heritage project, communities are ignored. Management staff at Domboshava covered a hole in the shelter that houses bees, but locals regard the hole as part of rain-making (B. Smith 2006, 327). Covering the hole sparked anger in the community, prompting a local to cover the rock art at Domboshava with brown enamel paint (B. Smith 2006, 327).

Recognizing the limitations of southern African archaeology and heritage management, researchers now understand the significance of exploring management systems used by living and past communities as alternative heritage management strategies (Chirikure and Pwiti 2008; Ndlovu 2009; Jopela 2011). Part of exploring such management systems is involving local communities' views.

Traditional management systems are, for instance, based on daily use and systems of meaning that reach into pre-colonial times by African communities; they were put in place to ensure respect and protection of places of spiritual cultural importance (Pwiti and Mvenge 1996; Manyanga 1999; Ndoro 2001; Pwiti et al. 2007; Sheridan and Nyamweru 2008). Places such as the Matopo Hills in Zimbabwe, the Vumba Mountains in Mozambique, and the Chongoni Rock Art World Heritage Site in Malawi (Ndoro 2001; Ndlovu 2009; Jopela 2011) are examples of how traditional practices ensure the viability of heritage locales in southern Africa and elsewhere in Africa.

Many southern African communities continue to make use of rock art sites as places of worship or for rain-making (Ndlovu 2009; Jopela 2011). Management of such heritage sites should acknowledge both past and present values of people who infuse them with cultural values. Under such valuations of sacred territory, community involvement in the management of heritage sites is compelling and ensures that formal systems of heritage values held by researchers or heritage practitioners do not overpower those of living communities (Jopela and Fredriksen 2015).

'Communities' are best defined as fluid, non-homogenous, and locally defined (Tully 2007). They also must include stakeholders who are affected either directly or indirectly by research (cf. Watson 2007; Fouseki 2010; Chirikure et al. 2010; Jopela and Fredriksen 2015). Therefore, the first step in an ideal methodological approach for successful community involvement in heritage management is to identify the values espoused *by* affected communities. One way to do this is to listen to community members to understand how they regard heritage (L. Smith 2006; Schmidt 2014b). Oral traditions can be crucial in doing this (Echo-Hawk 2000).

The study conducted by Posnansky in the 1960s in Ghana required direct participation of local communities and local researchers, hence they were regarded as critical participants in his research (Schmidt 2014a). Community-involved heritage management may also involve the public in the protection, valuing, and caretaking of heritage resources (Chirikure and Pwiti 2008). Identifying stakeholders is a critical first step.

Community involvement and heritage management in Matatiele

The study I conducted in Matatiele was, as noted above, mandated to identify pragmatic methods of community involvement in the context of heritage management. My main goal was to study how a community-inclusive heritage management plan may be implemented. The main objectives for my research included: (1) identifying how Matatiele communities represent their 'heritage' and also their knowledge of San rock art and rock art sites; (2) identifying appropriate methods of rock art conservation and protection of selected rock art sites informed by the communities of Matatiele; and (3) implementing educational outreach sessions by holding community educational gatherings. In order to compile both qualitative and quantitative data, my questions were both open-ended and structured.

The questions I designed were meant to construct individual perceptions of heritage and archaeological materials. For the first phase of research, I organised meetings with chiefs and different headmen so as to obtain permission to visit individual households during fieldwork. Following meetings with the chiefs, I held community gatherings hosted by headmen and chiefs in different villages where residents were informed about the project. Members of each residential community were informed by their chiefs and headmen that if they had knowledge about rock art sites in their area, they should be forthcoming and communicate this knowledge. During the first meetings with local chiefs and headmen, I made enquiries about which rock art sites around their villages (c.f. Mokoena 2015). Some individuals mentioned that they knew about the rock art sites because they encountered them while herding.

In the second phase of fieldwork I focused on interviews with a wide variety of informants, including chiefs, traditional healers, teachers, and youths. I selected informants according to the likelihood that they might have knowledge of San rock art as well as the diverse meanings of heritage. Traditional healers in southern Africa, for example, are known to use elements of the landscape. Matatiele is also one of the areas in South Africa where communities continue to practice male initiation – a key heritage activity of great interest to these communities. With assistance from the MARA team that consisted of local heritage technicians, researchers, and students, I held public discussions regarding the values of heritage and how best to manage it. The final phase also incorporated outreach and educational sessions informed by results from interviews. For the educational sessions, I designed posters that highlighted the significance of heritage.

I conducted interviews in different households and during meetings where informants were comfortable. A total of 140 interviews were conducted in three villages. Table 1 shows a breakdown of the number of participants interviewed in each village.

Public perceptions on heritage and rock art in Matatiele

Defining heritage in ways that incorporate different perspectives was crucial in my research. I asked collaborators in Matatiele to list and define what they regarded as heritage. In most southern African languages, there is no single word for 'heritage.' As a native southern Sotho speaker, I already knew the complexities of using 'heritage' as a fixed concept, so I used Sotho proxies: culture, traditions, and religion. Xhosa interpretations, including the alternative use of the word 'heritage,' were conducted by two of the field heritage technicians trained by MARA. Both of my field companions mentioned that the word 'heritage' is tricky to translate, but we agreed that culture, religion, and traditions should be communicated.

Among the responses given by participants about what they regarded as heritage, initiation was featured. Seventy-seven per cent of the interviewed members of the community mentioned initiation as part of their heritage compared to the 23 per cent that mentioned traditional food, attire, games, and music. In an interview with one of the employees at Mehloding, I realized the importance of initiation: 'The first thing you should know is that initiation is very big in our community. I am also initiated. Even the deep Christians are initiated' (Ntate Puseletso Lecheko, Matatiele, December 2013).

I will now concentrate on initiation because it is a strong example of how tangible and intangible aspects of heritage coalesce. Initiation is significant heritage for the Matatiele communities, an observation further emphasised during community gatherings. Initiation occurs in rock shelters, some of which have rock art and other archaeological evidence. Emphasis on values such as initiation illustrates that heritage management principles requires taking into account any spiritual or cultural values attached to rock art shelters by living and ancient communities of Matatiele.

I also asked Traditional healers what they regarded as their heritage. All of the interviewed healers mentioned that healing was integral to their heritage. Spiritual healers use rock art sites as places where they connect with their ancestors (also see Jopela 2011; Siteleki 2014). A traditional herbalist from Matatiele revealed that rock shelters are home to some of the herbs he uses to heal his clients.

Table 1. Number of villages where interviews were conducted.

Village	Number of selected sub-villages	Number per sub-village
Queens Mercy	13	5–10
Masakala	4	5–10
Ramohlakoana	3	5–10

Some traditional spiritual healers also chip off paint to mix with other herbs to make medicine (also see Siteleki 2014).

> There is a relationship between rock art and the plants I use. I use the paint to mix with plants when making certain medicine. The San people are my ancestors, and I draw power from them. They sometimes come to me when I am in trance (Mzwandile Radebe, Matatiele, December 2013).

These healers believe the paintings are powerful and thus can heal. A similar revelation appears in ethnographies, describing how people touched paintings to heal (Jolly 1986; Lewis-Williams 1986). In conventional academic orthodoxy, chipping off paint damages resources and, thus, creates a conservation problem. Communities such as Matatiele represent their heritage through the use of rock art. This tension between official policy and indigenous use poses a dilemma. Our joint study shows the need to consider how conflicts with government management policies may be resolved by employing management plans that are sensitive to local values and systems of heritage management, perhaps reserving areas with less visibility and significance where such practices may continue unrestricted – a position that inevitably will rouse an 'authorized heritage discourse' (L. Smith 2006) that privileges preservation above all other values.

In order to initiate appropriate rock art management strategies, it is necessary to investigate possible impacts of management principles – indigenous or otherwise – on the rock art. Having identified anthropogenic rock art conservation issues in Matatiele, it was imperative to have conversations with other related communities to learn of their perception of rock art and rock art sites in the region. Rock art sites in many southern African areas are considered sacred places for both religious and traditional purposes (Pwiti and Mvenge 1996; Maradze 2003; Ndoro 2003).

When I asked informants if they knew of the presence of rock art sites in Matatiele, 72 per cent of those that said 'yes', while 28 per cent said 'no', out of a sample of 140 individuals. Out of the 72 per cent that knew of rock art sites, only 15 per cent had seen rock paintings, despite the fact that most respondents were born and raised in Matatiele. A follow up question explored whether people knew the makers of the art. Seventy-four per cent of the respondents who knew about rock art knew who made the art, 13 per cent did not, and 14 per cent did not give a definite answer. These responses provided insights into local knowledge of the landscape. We learned that females are not intimate with their wider environment; many have not explored their landscapes even from their childhood, with only a few young women who explored farther afield when performing chores. Importantly, young males who looked after their families' animals, and thus had opportunities to explore their environment, had observed rock art sites.

During the interviews, I asked respondents whether they regarded rock art sites as sacred, since research has shown that San rock art is spiritual and is considered as valuable heritage. Sacredness in the local languages (Sesotho and isiXhosa) means places of religious and cultural significance, values captured by a research assistant who said, 'We regard places such as praying pools and rock art sites as sacred because in our cultures (Sotho, Hlubi, and Xhosa), and religion they are holy' (Puseletso Lecheko, Matatiele, June 2014). An 84-year-old elder from the Hlubi group claimed ancestral connection with the San: 'I use rock art sites to connect with my ancestors and give thanks. I reconnect with my culture, my heritage every time I go there. Therefore, for me and my family rock art sites are sacred' (Teboho Maboloka, Matatiele, 7th December 2013).

Fifty two per cent of interviewees responded that they regarded rock art sites as sacred, 24 per cent said they were not sacred, and the other 24 per cent did not know. The sacredness of rock art sites according to the Matatiele communities is determined by the type of activities that take place in these locales. Rock art sites and rock shelters in general are used for initiation, as healing sanctuaries, as historical places (Mokoena 2015), and as places where everyday activities occur.

Rock art shelters in rural pastoral communities such as Matatiele are incorporated into social and economic activities. Rock shelters (with or without paintings) are used for sheltering animals and herders, as pastures for rural Matatiele are located deep in the mountains where rock art sites are also located. The mountains are part of their social survival for they use them as initiation places, pastures, shelter for their animals, and as the places where they harvest wild vegetables.

Community outreach in Matatiele – community involvement strategy

In this heritage management project, I attempted to give local values primacy and control in determining heritage meaning. As such I followed the lead established by other projects, including the Waanyi Women's project in Australia (Smith, Morgan, and van der Meer 2010), and Sonya Atalay's work at Çatalhöyük in Turkey (Atalay 2007, 2010). My Matatiele interviews yielded similar positive results, and will inform any future heritage project about local values and how people would contribute to the management and research into their heritage. To ensure participatory research, interviews were not sufficient. Therefore, I introduced the idea that interviews be examined in an open forum, where all could actively participate by contributing their particular understanding. There was also a need to discuss the results and collectively highlight important observations that came out of the interviews.

Outreach sessions in Matatiele were held in three main villages: Ramohlakoana, Queens Mercy, and Masakala. The sessions reported on the interview results and discussed how best to manage heritage (Figures 3 and 4). The second purpose of the meetings was to present pamphlets and posters that promoted the significance of protecting and maintaining heritage values.

During communal meetings in the main villages, individuals emphasised the importance of initiation as a crucial part of the identity of their communities. The conversations that we held during these gatherings confirmed community perceptions about the use of rock shelters for use during initiation. Chief Lepheane, a principal chief of Ha-Ramohlakoana, said

Figure 3. Community gathering (*pitso*) at the Masakala village. Provided by MARA.

Figure 4. Pamphlets and posters distributed to school representatives during community meetings. Provided by MARA.

> Male initiation is a very important and a big part of our community. It is our heritage and as you can see part of my job is to check and approve that any young male who goes to the initiation school is of accepted age. (Chief Lepheane, Matatiele, 26 March 2014).

He said this while filling a form for one of the young males who was scheduled to undergo initiation that summer.

In another public meeting at Nkau village, one of the attendees, a teacher from a local school emphasized that:

> I am glad that you asked this community about their heritage and the use of rock shelters because in our culture initiation is very important, it is part of our lives and we use rock art shelters for this activity. Men and boys not initiated and females are not allowed to go to the mountains during initiation period. It is important that you in your profession also understand that you need to consult the chief before you set off into the mountains to search for heritage so that you will not infringe on our culture and also so that you are under the protection of this community through the chief (Thabo Lepolesa, Matatiele, 25 March 2014).

Initiation is very private in these communities, so I had to research through talking to chiefs and elders to become familiar with the initiation season in the Matatiele region. It is crucial that any heritage management plan instigated in these communities include every aspect of protecting initiation and embracing it as the identity of the communities of Matatiele.[1]

Discussion

Effective heritage management is achievable through involvement of affected communities (Marshall 2002; Chirikure and Pwiti 2008; Chirikure et al. 2010). Community-involved heritage management becomes effective once the project is defined from perspectives of those affected by the heritage project. Traditional healers and some members of the communities regard rock art sites as part of their heritage and the ways they act out and talk about that heritage allows understandings of how they manage their heritage. In the case of the proposed heritage centre, communities shared their perceptions on the manner in which their heritage should be represented and also what roles they are willing to play in the maintenance and protection of their heritage, as well as more general attitudes about the proposed centre. Management strategies that follow the perceptions of those involved and living nearby are destined to be much more effective than any arising outside these communities. Conversations with communities provided a clear idea of what they regard as heritage and how best to manage it, namely, that rock art sites must include a strong respect for these places as sacred sites, with all of the respect for traditional practices and rituals that such recognition demands. Local ritual practices, such as the removal of paint, are an integral part of what makes these sites vital, living heritage. Management policies must be reconstructed to account for the fact that if the performance of this heritage is prevented, then such sites will lose their heritage values among the very populations for which they are so important for spiritual well-being.

All approaches to heritage management are an endeavour to uphold ethical responsibility. Important factors include the importance of listening to all parties that are likely to be affected by potential heritage management or archaeological projects. The Matatiele case shows that projects should be implemented only after eliciting the ideas of all affected parties and incorporating their practices and concerns into any management strategy or interpretive treatment.

Understanding heritage from the perspectives of communities helps in the identification of what they consider heritage outside the 'authorized heritage discourse' (L. Smith 2006), which privileges 'expert' values over those of local communities, and tends to limit appreciations of heritage to what is primarily material. Initiation is the primary point of heritage identity for the Matatiele communities. The use of rock art sites for various purposes, including spirituality (healing), initiation, and animal sheltering, are also part of their heritage. Management of rock art sites, therefore, should be implemented in a way that considers current heritage meanings. A management plan that incorporates all dimensions of the heritage of these living communities is necessary. Rock art shelters as I have defined them make up an important part of the social and political fabric of the heritage of the people of Matatiele. Rock shelters are home to initiation, spiritual retreats, animal sheltering, and harvesting of vegetable matter. Heritage values and materials will not survive if impacted parties are not involved in the plans to address management of places they still use.

Regardless of the sacred qualities of rock art shelters, not everyone, given the diversity of these communities, sees them as such. Only traditional healers and those involved in initiation regard these places as sacred, a value attached by virtue of the cultural practices and beliefs associated with these sites. Any management plan needs to account for the spiritual and cultural values of these sites, and not only the physical manifestations of cultural practices. One of the key observations that emerges from this and other studies is that current cultural and religious activities carried out in these sites help maintain the values of rock art and any associated archaeological sites (Ndlovu 2009; Jopela 2011).

Addressing different stakeholders (such as educators in Matatiele) puts heritage managers or archaeologists in positions to understand what kind of impact their research will have on different members of the communities. Having identified the significance of providing schools with materials that promote the different aspects of heritage, any future heritage management endeavour needs to account for such benefits. Interacting with educators has given us an additional picture of the level of knowledge they have with regard to rock art and its makers, expanding our comprehension of what type of educational resources are useful in identifying the protection of heritage resources.

Dialogues with specific members of the community who play pivotal cultural roles proved to be important in understanding local principles of effective heritage management. Chiefs and traditional healers for instance opened understandings of how to negotiate the use of heritage spaces, particularly the use of rock art sites. Chief Lepheane of Ha-Ramohlakoana was very supportive of the idea of protecting rock art sites. He suggested. 'I can organize a pitso where you can talk about the protection of the rock paintings. We can also move a bit further from the boulder where we hold the community male meetings' (Chief Lepheane, Matatiele, December 2014). Although the statement comes from one of the elite, the fact that the chief was willing to consult with community members and advise on the significance of protecting rock art sites (and rock paintings), shows that rock art management can be achieved with the assistance of those who have organizational powers and skills. There is a danger of not involving those individuals who directly make use of the rock art as part of their heritage, but if a wide range of collaborators/stakeholders are consulted (for example, traditional healers, who use rock art sites and the rock art for spiritual purposes), then there is a greater probability that a diversity of heritage practices and beliefs will be identified.

Initiation is central to the Matatiele's communities' heritage. In most cases in southern African, initiation takes place in rock shelters. Some of these shelters have paintings in them. Negotiating the use of these sites and the protection of paintings is imperative. This study shows that recognising the importance of initiation and relating it to the past cultures (in this case the San) is one way of protecting these sites by bringing forth the significance and value of the rock art. Traditional healers imbue value to the sites because they use the sites for spiritual reasons and the art itself is related to spirituality.

Although the financial sustainability of heritage centres is not guaranteed unless major marketing strategies are put in place, such projects can positively contribute to the promotion of heritage value and protection of heritage sites. In the case of all the rock art centres researched, monitoring of rock art sites helps to ensure sustained protection of the sites. One common benefit of heritage centres is that they serve as educational hubs. Involvement of schools at all levels, local community members, and tourists are forms of knowledge dissemination and educational programmes. Heritage centres therefore assist in addressing heritage values through the educational materials and displays. Responses of the communities of Matatiele emphasised the significance of a heritage centre as an educational hub. Teachers specifically stated the problem of not having practical resources for teaching about different aspects of heritage. A heritage centre will provide schools with outsourced cultural heritage materials.

Recommendations

Introducing a heritage centre in Matatiele is one dimension of heritage management. In order to ensure the viability and sustainability of the centre, I recommend that all stakeholders participate in its planning and implementation. Views of community members regarding their heritage should be incorporated into the heritage centre representations. Government and private sector involvement is also important in ensuring informed implementation of such heritage projects. In addition, methods of participation should be agreed upon by all parties involved.

In order to ensure an all-inclusive heritage management plan, particularly in the event that a heritage centre is established, display of heritage should include that of past communities and living communities, using museum-like exhibitions and digital presentations of heritage resources. Mobile exhibitions, for example, would be appropriate for those communities located in isolated areas (Mhando-Nyagila 2006; Byrne 2008).

School involvement could provide another form of community participation in heritage management. Educators in Matatiele expressed concern over limited educational resources in heritage studies, and an important way that schools can get involved is to help manage rock art sites and run the proposed heritage centre. Similar projects have succeeded elsewhere (Mawere, Sagiya, and Mubaya 2012, 12). Doing so here would help to ensure continuity and propagation of heritage values.

To address rock art management, outreach programmes that target herders, schools, traditional healers, and initiation teachers would be culturally appropriate, particularly in community meetings where different values are shared (c.f. King and Arthur 2014).

Note

1. Female researchers are limited as to what kind of questions they can ask about male initiation.

Acknowledgements

I thank MARA and RARI for allowing me to be part of the team at the University of the Witwatersrand. I am thankful to the South African National Research Institute for funding my research project. I am grateful to Dr Sam Challis and Dr Rachel King for supervising my master's research, and to the different communities of Matatiele especially ntate Puseletso

Lecheko and ntate Tsepo Lesholu for their unwavering support, and other stakeholders for taking part in this research. I thank Professor Peter Schmidt, Dr Catherine Namono, and Dr Ndukuyakhe Ndlovu for giving me the courage to produce this work.

Disclosure statement

No potential conflict of interest was reported by the author.

Suggested citation

Mokoena, Nthabiseng. 2017. 'Community Involvement and Heritage Management in Rural South Africa.' Special Series, African Perspectives on Community Engagement, guest-edited by Peter R. Schmidt. *Journal of Community Archaeology and Heritage* 4 (3): page 189–202.

References

Andah, Bassey. 1995. "Studying African Societies in Cultural Context." In *Making Alternative History: The Practice of Archaeology and History in Non-Western Settings*, edited by Peter R. Schmidt and Thomas C. Patterson, 149–181. Santa Fe, NM: SAR Press.

Atalay, Sonya L. 2007. "Global Application of Indigenous Archaeology: Community-Based Participatory Research in Turkey." *Journal of the World Archaeological Congress* 3 (3): 249–270.

Atalay, Sonya. 2010. "'We Don't Talk About Çatalhöyük, We Live It': Sustainable Archaeological Practice Through Community-Based Participatory Research." *World Archaeology* 42 (3): 418–429.

Atalay, Sonya. 2012. *Community-based Archaeology: Research With, By and For Indigenous and Local Communities*. Los Angeles: University of California Press.

Beaudry, Mary C. 2009. "Ethical Issues in Historical Archaeology." In *International Handbook of Historical Archaeology*, edited by David Gaimster and Teresita Majewski, 17–29. New York, NY: Springer Science LLC.

Bendremer, Jeffrey, and Kenneth A. Richman. 2006. "Human Subjects Review and Archaeology: A View from Indian Country." In *The Ethics of Archaeology: Philosophical Perspectives on Archaeological Practice*, edited by Chris Scarre and Geoffrey Scarre, 97–114. Cambridge: Cambridge University Press.

Biesele, Megan. 1993. *Women Like Meat: The Folklore and Foraging Ideology of the Kalahari Ju/'hoan*. Bloomington: Indiana University Press.

Byrne, Denis. 2008. "Heritage Conservation as Social Action." In The *Cultural Heritage Reader*, edited by G. Fairclough, R. Harrison, J. Jameson, and Schofield, 149–173. London: Routledge.

Challis, Sam. 2009. "The Impact of the Horse on the AmaTola 'Bushmen': New Identity in the Maloti-Drakensberg Mountains of Southern Africa, University of Oxford, 2008." *Azania, Archaeological Research in Africa* 44 (1): 156–157.

Challis, Sam. 2012. "Creolisation on the Nineteenth-Century Frontiers of Southern Africa: A Case Study of the AmaTola 'Bushmen' in the Maloti-Drakensberg." *Journal of Southern African Studies* 38 (2): 265–280.

Chirikure, Shadreck, Munyaradzi Manyanga, Webber Ndoro, and Gilbert Pwiti. 2010. "Unfulfilled Promises? Heritage Management and Community Participation at Some of Africa's Cultural Heritage Sites." *International Journal of Heritage Studies* 16 (1): 30–44.

Chirikure, Shadreck, and Gilbert Pwiti. 2008. "Community Involvement in Archaeology and Cultural Heritage Management: An Assessment from case Studies in Southern Africa and Elsewhere." *Current Anthropology* 49 (3): 467–485.

Colwell-Chanthaphonh, Chip, and T. J. Ferguson. 2008. *Collaboration in Archaeological Practice: Engaging Descendant Communities*. Lanham, MD: Altamira Press.

Derricourt, Robin M. 1977. *Prehistoric Man in the Ciskei and Transkei*. Cape Town: C. Struik Publishers.

Echo-Hawk, C. Roger. 2000. "Ancient History in the New World: Intergrating Oral Traditions and the Archaeological Record in Deep Time." *American Antiquity* 65 (2): 267–290.

Fontein, Joost. 2006. *The Silence of Great Zimbabwe: Contested Landscapes and the Power of Heritage*. Harare: Weaver Press and London.

Fouseki, Kalliopi. 2010. "Community Voices, Curatorial Choices: Community Consultation for the 1807 Exhibitions." *Museums and Society* 8 (3): 180–192.

Hall, Martin. 2005. "Situational Ethics and Engaged Practice: The Case of Archaeology in Africa." In *Embedding Ethics*, edited by Lynn Meskell and Peter Pels, 169–194. New York, NY: Berg.

Jolly, Pieter. 1986. "A First Generation Descendant of the Transkei San." *The South African Archaeological Bulletin* 41 (143): 6–9.

Jolly, Peter. 1996. "Interaction Between South-Eastern San and Southern Nguni and Sotho Communities, c.1400–c1880." *South African Historical Journal* 35: 30–61.

Jopela, Albino. 2011. "Traditional Custodianship: A Useful Framework for Heritage Management in Southern Africa?" *Conservation and Management of Archaeological Sites* 13 (2–3): 103–122.

Jopela, Albino, and Ditlef Fredriksen. 2015. "Public Archaeology, Knowledge Meetings and Heritage Ethics in Southern Africa: An Approach from Mozambique." *World Archaeology* 47 (2): 261–284.

King, Rachel. 2014. "Voluntary Barbarians of the Maloti-Drakensberg: The BaPhuthi Chiefdom, Cattle Raiding and Colonial Rule in Nineteenth-Century, Southern Africa." Unpublished PhD Thesis, University of Oxford.

King, Rachel, and Charles Arthur. 2014. "Development-led Archaeology and Ethics in Lesotho." *Azania: Archaeological Research in Africa* 49 (2): 166–183.

Lane, Paul. 2011. "Possibilities for a Postcolonial Archaeology in Sub-Saharan Africa: Indigenous and Usable Pasts." *World Archaeology* 43 (1): 7–25.

Lewis-Williams, J. David. 1981a. "The Thin red Line: Southern San Notions and rock Paintings of Supernatural Potency." *The South African Archaeological Bulletin* 36 (133): 5–13.

Lewis-Williams, J. David. 1981b. *Believing and Seeing: Symbolic Meanings in Southern San Rock Paintings*. London: Academic Press.

Lewis-Williams, J. David. 1986. "The Last Testament of the Southern San." *South African Archaeological Bulletin* 41 (143): 10–11.

Lewis-Williams, J. David, Geoffrey Blundell, William Challis, and J. Hampson. 2000. "Threads of Light: Re-examining a Motif in Southern African San Rock Art." *The South African Archaeological Bulletin* 55: 123–136.

Lynott, J. 1997. "Ethical Principles and Archaeological Practice: Development of an Ethics Policy." *American Antiquity* 62 (4): 589–599.

Mallen, Lara. 2011. "Metolong Cultural Resource Management, Phase 2. Rock Art Recording and Interpretation." Unpublished report for the Commissioner of the Water of the Government of Lesotho.

Manyanga, Munyaradzi. 1999. "The Antagonism of Living Realities: Archaeology and Religion the Case of Manyanga (Ntabazikamambo) National Monument." *Zimbabwea* 6: 10–14.

Maradze, J. 2003. "Back to the Old School? Revival of Traditional Management Systems in Zimbabwe." Papers from the 14th General Assembly and Scientific Symposium of ICOMOS, Victoria Falls. Accessed February 2006. http://www.international.icomos.org/victoriafalls2003

Marshall, Yvonne. 2002. "What is Community Archaeology?" *World Archaeology* 34 (2): 211–219.

Mawere, Munyaradzi, Munyaradzi Elton Sagiya, and Tapiwa Mubaya. 2012. "Conservation Conversations and Community Participation in the Management of Heritage Sites in Zimbabwe." *Greener Journal of Environment Management and Public Safety* 2 (3): 007–016.

Mazel, Aron D. 1982. "Principles for Conserving the Archaeological Resources of the Natal Drakensburg." *The South African Archaeological Bulletin* 37 (135): 7–15.

Mguni, Siyakha. 2015. *Termites of the Gods: San Cosmology in Southern African Rock Art*. Johannesburg: Wits University Press.

Mhando-Nyagila, J. 2006. "Museums and Community Involvement: A Case Study of Community Collaborative Initiatives–National Museum of Kenya." Conference Paper, INTERCOM.

Mitchell, Peter. 2002. *The Archaeology of Southern Africa*. Cambridge: Cambridge University Press.

Mokoena, Nthabiseng. 2012. Interpretation of Rock Paintings at the ARAL 258 Site in the Phuthiatsana Basin, Lesotho. Unpublished Honours Dissertation, University of the Witwatersrand.

Mokoena, Nthabiseng. 2015. "Community-Involved Heritage Management: The Case of Matatiele." Unpublished Master's Thesis, University of the Witwatersrand.

Ndlovu, Ndukuyakhe. 2009. "Access to Rock Art Sites: A Right or a Qualification?" *The South African Archaeological Bulletin* 64 (189): 61–68.

Ndoro, Webber. 2001. *Your Monuments Our Shrine: The Preservation of Great Zimbabwe*. Uppsala: Uppsala University.

Ndoro, Weber. 2003. "Traditional and Customary Heritage Systems: Nostalgia or Reality? The Implication of Managing Heritage Sites in Africa." *World Heritage Papers* 13: 81–84.

Pearce, David, Catherine Namono, and Lara Mallen. 2009. "Meaning Then, Meaning Now: Changes in the Interpretative Process in San Rock Art Studies." In *The Eland's People: New Perspectives in the Rock Art of the Maloti-Drakensberg Bushmen. Essays in Memory of Patricia Vinnicombe*, edited by Peter Mitchell and Ben Smith, 69–70. Johannesburg: Wits University Press.

Pwiti, Gilbert, and George Mvenge. 1996. "Archaeologists, Tourists and Rainmakers: Problems in the Management of Rock Art Sites in Zimbabwe: A Case Study of Domboshava National Monument." In *Aspects of African Archaeology: Papers from the 10th Congress of the Pan-African Association for Prehistory and Related Studies*, edited by Gilbert Pwiti and Robert Soper, 817–824. Harare: University of Zimbabwe Publications.

Pwiti, Gilbert, and Webber Ndoro. 1999. "The Legacy of Colonialism: Perceptions of the Cultural Heritage in Southern Africa with Special Reference to Zimbabwe." *African Archaeological Review* 16 (3): 143–153.

Pwiti, Gilbert, Ancila Nhamo, Seke Katsamudanga, and Alinah Segobye. 2007. "Makasva: Archaeological Heritage, Rainmaking and Healing in Southern Africa with Special Reference to Eastern Zimbabwe." *Zimbabwea* 9: 103–111.

Schmidt, Peter R. 1995. "Using Archaeology to Remake History in Africa." In *Making Alternative Histories: The Practice of Archaeology and History in Non-Western Settings*, edited by Peter R. Schmidt and Thomas C. Patterson, 119–148. Santa Fe, NM: School of American Research Press.

Schmidt, Peter R. 2009. *Postcolonial Archaeologies in Africa*. Santa Fe, NM: School of Advanced Research Press.

Schmidt, Peter R. 2014a. "Rediscovering Community Archaeology in Africa and Reframing Its Practice." *Journal of Community Archaeology and Heritage* 1 (1): 37–55.

Schmidt, Peter R. 2014b. "Hardcore Ethnography: Interrogating the Intersection of Disease, Poverty, Social Collapse, Human Rights, and Heritage." *Heritage and Society* 7 (2): 170–188.

Schmidt, Peter R., and Innocent Pikirayi. 2016. *Community Archaeology and Heritage in Africa: Decolonizing Practice*. New York, NY: Routledge.

Shepherd, Nick. 2002. "'When the Hand That Holds the Trowel Is Black' Disciplinary Practices of Self-Representation and the Issue of 'Native' Labour in Archaeology'." *Journal of Social Archaeology* 3 (3): 189–209.

Shepherd, Nick. 2003. "'When the Hand that Holds the Trowel is Black…': Disciplinary Practices of Self-Representation and the Issue of 'Native' Labour in Archaeology." *Journal in Social Archaeology* 3 (3): 334–352.

Shepherd, Nick. 2005. "Who is Doing Courses in Archaeology at South African Universities? And What Are They Studying?" *South African Archaeological Bulletin* 60 (182): 123–126.

Sheridan, Michael J., and Cecilia Nyamweru. 2008. *African Sacred Groves: Ecological Dynamics and Social Change*. Oxford: James Curry.

Siteleki, Mncedisi Jabu. 2014. "Plant Power and Land Use in the Maloti-Drakensberg: A Case Study in GIS and IKS in Matatiele, Eastern Cape, South Africa." Unpublished Honours Dissertation. Johannesburg: University of the Witwatersrand.

Smith, Benjamin. 2006. "Rock Art Tourism in Southern Africa: Problems, Possibilities, and Poverty Relief." In *Of the Past, for the Future: Integrating Archaeology and Conservation*, edited by Neville Agnew and Janet Bridgland, 322–330. Los Angeles, CA: Getty Conservation Institute.

Smith, Laurajane. 2006. *The Uses of Heritage*. Oxford: Routledge.

Smith, Laurajane, Anna Morgan, and Anita van der Meer. 2010. "Community-driven Research in Cultural Heritage Management: The Waanyi Women's History Project." *International Journal of Heritage Studies* 9 (1): 65–80.

Solomon, Ann. 1997. "San Rock Art Contemporary South Africa." In *The World Archaeology Congress Newsletter: Southern African Focus*, Guest edited by Sven Ouzman, 5: 1. Accessed 5 August 2017. http://worldarch.org/wac4/the-wac-newsletter-southern-african-focus/

Statistics South Africa. 2014. "Statistical Release P0302, Mid-Year Population Estimates." Accessed 5 August 2017. https://www.statssa.gov.za/publications/P0302/P03022014.pdf

Taruvinga, Pascal, and Webber Ndoro. 2003. "The Vandalism of the Domboshava Rock Painting Site, Zimbabwe: Some Reflections on Approaches to Heritage Management." *Conservation and Management of Archaeological Sites* 6 (1): 3–10.

Tully, Gemma. 2007. "Community Archaeology: General Methods and Standards of Practice." *Public Archaeology* 6 (3): 155–187.

Vinnicombe, Patricia. 1967. "Rock Painting Analysis." *South African Archaeological Bulletin* 22: 129–141.

Vinnicombe, Patricia. 1976. *People of the Eland: Rock Paintings of the Drakensberg as a Reflection of Their Life and Thought*. Pietermaritzburg: University of Natal Press.

Watson, Sheila. 2007. *Museums and Their Communities*. New York, NY: Routledge.

Understanding 'the community' before community archaeology: A case study from Sudan

Jane Humphris and Rebecca Bradshaw

ABSTRACT

Since 2014, UCL Qatar has undertaken a diverse programme of community engagement as part of an archaeometallurgical research project at the Royal City of Meroe, Sudan. We present initial analyses of anonymous questionnaires conducted as part of this programme. We designed the questionnaires to evaluate qualitatively residents' knowledge about, outlook on, and experience with local archaeological sites, to generate an understanding of the social fabric within which archaeology is situated. Additionally, we collected quantitative demographic data to assess critically the local community composition. Statistical analyses of the questionnaire have highlighted the heterogeneous nature of the local communities, and how their often-divergent knowledge, outlooks, and experiences with archaeology are influenced by numerous social, economic, historical, and political factors: an idealized audience for 'community archaeology' does not exist in our context. Nevertheless, community engagement, leading to community archaeology, should form an integral part of an archaeological research programme from inception to completion.

Introduction

The Royal City of Meroe (henceforth 'Meroe') is situated c. 200 km north of Khartoum on the east bank of the Nile in the Republic of the Sudan (Figure 1). Meroe is one of a number of spectacular and monumental archaeological sites in a region known as 'The Island of Meroe', which became a UNESCO World Heritage Site in 2011. The site was a royal capital of the Kingdom of Kush, which ruled vast territory from at least the early eighth century BCE to the fourth century CE. Meroe has long attracted attention from scholars visiting the region (e.g. Bruce 1790; Cailliaud and Jomard 1826; Shinnie 1967), and archaeological research projects continue to investigate details concerning the origins, development, and organization of Kush (see Török 2015 for the most recent consideration of Kushite history). The impressive architectural remains of Meroe's temples, palaces, and the so-called Royal Baths, as well as the associated pyramid burials, demonstrate the significance of the site as a key Kushite period centre of power. The landscape surrounding Meroe comprises a number of architecturally remarkable archaeological sites including Meroitic religious and administrative centres.

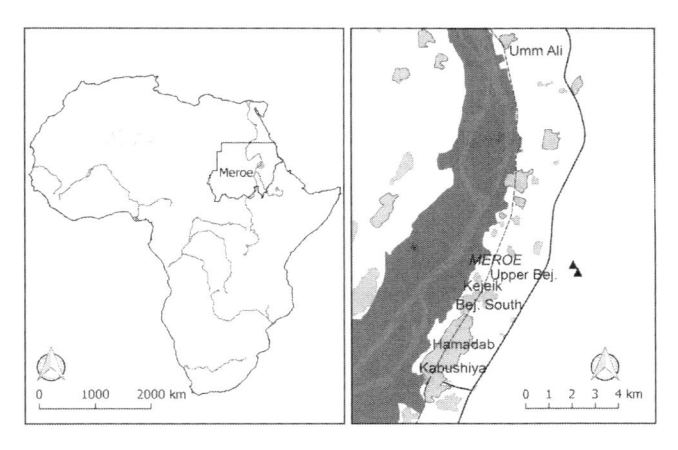

Figure 1. Map showing the location of Meroe in the Republic of the Sudan (left) and the locations of each village within which community engagements were conducted (shown in relation to Meroe, right). Map produced by Frank Stremke.

Meroe in its modern context

Like many archaeological sites along the Nile, Meroe is situated on the banks of the river and surrounded by modern villages. Today, as in the past, populations live within the Nile Valley to exploit the river water, and thus thousands of residents live and work near or next to the archaeological remains of Meroe. The site's physical location in a riverine residential locale fosters subtle but frequent(ly meaningful) interactions between 'people' and 'place': children play among the ruins, men pass through on their way to the fields, and local people sell souvenirs to tourists and offer camel rides around the pyramids. Festivals and gatherings are also held at the sites throughout the year. Since the early twentieth century, Sudanese and international teams have regularly employed a significant number of local people to work on archaeological excavations. Meroe and the surrounding sites are thus firmly embedded within social and economic aspects of local life.

Unlike other areas of Sudan, recent conflicts have not scarred this region, known as the Shendi Reach. It has not experienced large-scale population displacement or the loss of the archaeological past, such as has been the case along other stretches of the Nile during the development of hydroelectric dams (see Säve-Söderbergh 1987; Hopkins and Mehanna 2010 at the First Cataract; Hänsch 2012; Näser and Kleinitz 2012 at the Fourth Cataract). Nevertheless, an average of 57.6 per cent of Sudan's rural population live below the poverty line, and rural populations, such as those near Meroe, face perpetual challenges in accessing basic resources (World Bank 2011). Existing land and water sources are under severe pressure from the increasing number of people moving into the area (many of whom have been gradually pushed south by long-term factors such as desertification across the Sudanic belt), and the commoditization and long-term renting of land to private investors (Linke 2014; Umbadda 2014).

UCL Qatar at Meroe

Since 2012, University College London (UCL) Qatar-based researchers have been investigating ancient iron production associated with the Kingdom of Kush, the extensive remains of which are prominent in the Meroe landscape. At this writing, the team has spent 10 seasons excavating at Meroe and at the nearby Meroitic site of Domat al Hamadab. Sudanese archaeologists and Sudanese trainee-students form part of the multi-national team, which can reach up to 70 people including the local workforce.

The UCL Qatar research project attempts to 'decolonize' archaeological practice by implementing a long-term strategy to involve an increasing number of Sudanese specialists and non-specialists in developing research questions and implementing research programmes (a process sometimes referred to as 'indigenization', see Lane 2011). We aim for collaborative decision-making and broad public participation to create 'useable pasts' that contribute 'practical knowledge' to Sudanese society (Lane 2011). For the more immediate future, such a decolonizing process involves communication and discussions with members of local communities about our research objectives and results, as well as involving and training Sudanese students and members of other stakeholder professions. Around 80 per cent of the UCL Qatar community engagement team are consistently Sudanese, and during the most recent archaeological season, almost 50 per cent of the specialist excavation team were Sudanese.

We appreciate, of course, that to 'decolonize' also means addressing notions of knowledge pursuit – perhaps evolving the questions we ask of the archaeological record and challenging long-held, western-developed assumptions about the past (Edwards 2004). This also applies to questions of knowledge production, particularly in terms of the languages and spaces in which we choose to publish. Nevertheless, our commitment to decolonizing our archaeological practices is strong, recognizing that 'Archaeology on the African continent is a century-long practice, characterized largely by research approaches that do not consult and engage with local and indigenous communities' (Pikirayi and Schmidt 2016, 1). This is true in the case of Meroe: archaeological investigations here pre-date the twentieth century, yet comprehensive, long-term 'community archaeology' has been lacking.

General impressions based on informal conversations with local people in the early years of the project revealed a diversity of local outlooks towards the history of Meroe. Some people expressed pride in the achievements of 'their ancestors', while others spoke of a disassociation between themselves and the ancient inhabitants of Kush. Many were keen to receive 'more information' about the sites, and still more were interested in the potential economic benefits tourism could bring to the area.

After we recognized the diversity of opinions within the broader community, we decided to undertake a diagnostic study to generate a more comprehensive understanding of these opinions and investigate what steps would be necessary to develop community archaeology around Meroe before we tried to conceive locally relevant programmes.

Why 'community engagement'?

Debates concerning relevant terminology for the diverse approaches linking archaeology with non-professionals, including local communities, are discussed elsewhere in detail (e.g. Smith and Waterton 2009, 11–20; Belford 2014; Richardson and Almansa-Sánchez 2015). Here we use the term 'community engagement' to signify both our broad involvement with local communities, and the specific activities we undertake in six locations around Meroe. We use the term *engagement* to highlight the differences between our comparatively new work, compared to that of an active and long-term, sustainable community *archaeology* programme. As expressed by Museum of London Archaeology (MOLA), such programmes aim 'to stimulate enquiry and promote active discovery through partnership and participation, widening access to and appreciation of … heritage' (http://www.mola.org.uk/community-archaeology). Sustainability, defined by Belford (2014, 27) as 'the creation of a solid and focused local understanding of, and care for, the historic environment', is essential at the social, intellectual, and economic level and a key feature of well-established community archaeology programmes. Important too is the co-development of participatory or collaborative research designs, in which communities are equal partners in and co-producers of research projects (Schmidt 2016). While our engagement with local communities is based around interaction and archaeology, it does not, in our case, mean that non-archaeologists are involved in the *archaeological* decision-making process, beyond the fact that we provide information about the past to interested members of the community (which could, of course, be considered a first step – see Atalay 2012).

Our engagement, rather, attempts to collect data on what knowledge, outlooks, and experiences exist locally in relation to archaeology, and relate these to how 'the community' is constituted demographically. Thus, we may fully understand the audience with whom and for whom community archaeology strategies might be conceived, developed, and implemented effectively in the future. We argue that each community should be considered as distinctive, with its own demographic make-up, histories, and resulting outlooks, and perceived needs and priorities, in relation to the heritage around it. Our results indicate that in addition to intra-community diversity, significant inter-community diversity exists (see also Meskell 2005, 90; Straight et al. 2015, 394). This identifiable intra- and inter-community complexity creates significant challenges to developing appropriate and valuable community archaeology packages for different groups within 'the community'.

We thus see this community engagement as the critical first phase towards developing and integrating community archaeology into formal research, from start to finish. In British archaeology (and elsewhere), this would often be termed 'consultation', which has different formal and informal meanings worldwide. Space does not permit us to explore the global literature about consultation here, but our intent was to gain an intuitive understanding of the communities for whom (and with whom) we work – how they identify themselves (collectively or individually), their livelihoods and education, and what is important to them, in relation to the archaeology around them. We argue that in Sudan this phase is essential, because UCL Qatar archaeologists are often culturally, linguistically, and religiously different from those local communities.

'Community engagement' thus encompasses all of our community interactions, from meetings and tea drinking to attending weddings, funerals, and graduations; from student training to two-way community lectures (delivered for local people by the archaeologists and *vice versa*); from throwing festivals to multi-media output. Producing and delivering such activities requires and deserves significant time and dedication, particularly considering the absence of formalized and published engagement programmes so far in Sudan, the legacy of western archaeologists removing 'treasure' from archaeological sites, and of course the role of the British in colonizing Sudan for the first half of the twentieth century. At Meroe, we work in an Arabic-speaking Muslim context, one governed by conservative Islamic laws (*sharia*), the nuances of which were unknown to us when we arrived in Sudan. Sustained relationships of trust and multi-linear community engagements, therefore, serve as a basis for two-way learning and understanding.

The engagements described here comprised 11 community meetings designed to understand local views using quantitative and qualitative questionnaires and having open discussions. Here we present the framework used and initial analyses of some of these data. Even at this preliminary stage, we have begun to understand the complexities surrounding the concept of 'the community' (and thus future community archaeology and participatory projects), but also the potential for such work in this region of Sudan.

Methods

The locations

Most of the local excavation employees (mostly men but occasionally women), hired as part of the UCL Qatar archaeological team, live in two villages: Kejeik, situated on Meroe's south-western boundary and Upper Bejrawiya, just to the north-east (Figure 1). Our long-standing relationship with the local employees, plus UCL Qatar's residence in Hamadab (3 km due south of Meroe), made these three communities obvious choices for our engagement activities. In addition to employing a local workforce, social and economic relationships with other nearby areas have developed, leading us to include three additional villages in our programme. The team relies on the twice-weekly market held at the nearby town of Kabushiya, around 4.5 km south of Meroe, and, when travelling to Meroe from Hamadab each day, the team passes by the village of Bejrawiya South. Somewhat further afield is the large village of Jebel Umm Ali, chosen because it has been a past focus of UCL

Qatar archaeological research. 'Communities' are therefore defined by their residents' close ties of kinship and their interdependent political and economic relationships. We selected these six communities because they were where both the archaeological site and team have the most presence, and are thus likely to have the most impact. We held meetings in Kejeik, Hamadab, and Kabushiya in 2014 and in Jebel Umm Ali, Upper Bejrawiya, and Bejrawiya South in 2015.

The meetings

Each community meeting was tripartite in structure, and approximately 2.5–3 hours in length. The first section of each meeting was dedicated to conducting the questionnaire. Interviewees received information about the purpose and general content of the anonymous questionnaires before each interview, and were assured they could withdraw at any time. The UCL Ethics Research Committee approved the questionnaires and strategies prior to these being implemented in the field. At least five Sudanese team members spent an average of 90 minutes conducting these questionnaire-interviews (Figure 2), while non-Sudanese team members (such as the authors) handed out refreshments and talked with local people.

This was followed by a presentation, which introduced the UCL Qatar team, the research aims and objectives of the archaeological project, and its current results. The final section of each meeting was an open discussion, whereby both the audience and the archaeologists asked each other questions. The aim was to encourage informal dialogue which allowed salient topics to develop organically, and issues arose that were not anticipated by us or represented in the questionnaires, but were of crucial importance to the audience and, therefore, to archaeologists. This section in particular proved critical to the two-way learning process.

Following advice from Sudanese colleagues, to ensure maximum attendance we held meetings after evening prayers, and on separate days for men and women to ensure high female turnout (aside from Kabushiya, where this was not logistically possible). We spent much time advertising the date, time, and location of each meeting, via word of mouth and announcements at local mosques (kindly facilitated by the imams). We delivered questionnaires and presentations in Arabic to avoid continual translation during the meetings and to prevent confusion in delivery. In preparation (and to contextualize our reasoning), we used classroom lectures to train Sudanese students and colleagues in the theory and practice of community archaeology, using literature such as Bartoy (2012) and Little (2012) as reference material. This enabled them to effectively conduct the meetings, supported by non-Sudanese, non-Arabic-speaking team members. We also provided

Figure 2. Questionnaires being carried out by University of Khartoum students, Basil Kamal Bushra and Mohammed Nasreldein Babiker at a women's meeting. Provided by authors.

training to conduct questionnaires sensitively, particularly when interviewing members of the opposite sex. The concept of gender identity in Sudan, and the principles that structure how men and women interact in ways regarded as 'acceptable', are complex and beyond the scope of this paper (but see Boddy 1989). In addition to ensuring professional and effective meetings, this training allowed Sudanese students and heritage professionals to gain community engagement experience. All team members understood the reasons for the strategy and were able to communicate this formally and informally to local people.

The questionnaire

We developed the questionnaire with advice from Sudanese colleagues. The first half of the questionnaire collected demographic data that could be quantitatively analysed, including age group, *gabila* (pl. *gabaayil*, a social unit defined by paternal bloodline or family, often translated as 'tribe' or 'kinship group'), residence, livelihood(s), and educational experience. The second half of the questionnaire was a knowledge, outlook, and experience assessment, to understand each respondent's pre-existing relationship with archaeology and archaeologists. Questions included whether or not the respondent or their family had worked with archaeologists, before moving to questions such as 'what is 'archaeology?' and 'what do you know about the Kingdom of Kush?' Questions also investigated the channels through which archaeological and historical information is disseminated, and the aspirations respondents might have for the site. Of particular significance, for developing future community archaeology projects, were questions about outlook – such as whether the archaeological site brought benefits to the community, and if so, how. We deemed the residents' outlook as particularly important to help us avoid the simple assumption that all residents are predisposed to like, or be interested in archaeology.

The relationships between demographic data and knowledge, outlook and experience, were analysed statistically using the qualitative data analysis software NVivo (http://www.qsrinternational. com/nvivo-product). Many answers to the questions were 'bundled', i.e. made up of several strands, and the software provided data on the frequency of words and concepts as they emerged in the responses. Questions to which there was no answer from the respondents were marked 'undisclosed' and discounted from this round of analysis.

Over 200 participants completed the questionnaire, and the Arabic transcripts were later translated into English. We presented the original Arabic versions to the National Corporation for Antiquities and Museums in Sudan (NCAM), for their use in developing community archaeology programmes in the future.

Results

Tables 1–3 provide information about the numbers of attendees at each of the meetings and the total numbers of interviews conducted. We present below a selection of results from certain key questions. These results illustrate significant diversity of knowledge, outlooks, and experiences of archaeology in

Table 1. 2014 participants.

Location	Date	Men/women?	Number of attendees	Number of interviews
Hamadab	13 February 2014	Men	115	21
Hamadab	14 February 2014	Women	97	18
Kabushiya	26 February 2014	Mixed	60	13 men; 18 women
Kejeik	9 March 2014	Women	103	17
Kejeik	10 March 2014	Men	77	15
Total			Men: 222	Men: 49
			Women: 230	Women: 53
			Total: 452	Total: 102

Table 2. 2015 participants.

Location	Date	Men/women?	Number of attendees	Number of interviews
Upper Bej	24 November 2015	Women	70 women; 45 girls	30
Upper Bej	25 November 2015	Men	48 men; 45 boys	17
Bej. South	15 November 2015	Men	80 men; 40 boys	9
Bej. South	19 November 2015	Women	42 women; 35 girls	19
Umm Ali	1 December 2015	Men	57 men	19
Umm Ali	2 December 2015	Women	730 women; 23 girls	19
Total			Men and boys: 270	Men: 459
			Women and girls: 288	Women: 68
			Total: 558	Total: 115

Table 3. Total numbers of people who attended the meetings and the number of people interviewed in total.

	Men	Women	Total
Attended meetings	492	518	1,010
Interviewed	94	121	215

this relatively small area, and demonstrate that 'the community' is not a homogeneous unit, in terms of intra- or extra- group and village relationships.

Knowledge assessment: What is archaeology; what do you know about the Royal City of Meroe?

These questions aimed to evaluate existing knowledge about western-conceived notions of 'archaeology' and in particular about the archaeology of Meroe. When asked, 'what is 'archaeology?'', 20 per cent of the responses included the term 'history' and 12.5 per cent included the phrase 'old things' (Figure 3). Other frequent responses included the words 'civilization', 'heritage,' and 'science'. This indicated that, in general, people living in these villages know that the archaeological enterprise can include professionally investigating the past via material remains ('science', 'things'), and creating a chronological narrative sequence of events ('history'), one that centres on people ('civilization'). Given the extensive history of archaeology at Meroe, this was perhaps to be expected. What was surprising, however, given this history, was that a large number of respondents, 13.75 per cent, answered that they 'do not know' what archaeology is, and a further 14.17 per cent gave no answer to this question. We are uncertain why.

In answer to the question, 'What do you know about the Royal City of Meroe?' many respondents provided examples of the general functions and idiosyncratic elements of Meroe (76.26 per cent). Yet nearly one quarter did not know anything or gave a negative response to this question (Figure 3). On aggregate, we suggest that there was some recognition of Meroe's original function and of the site's

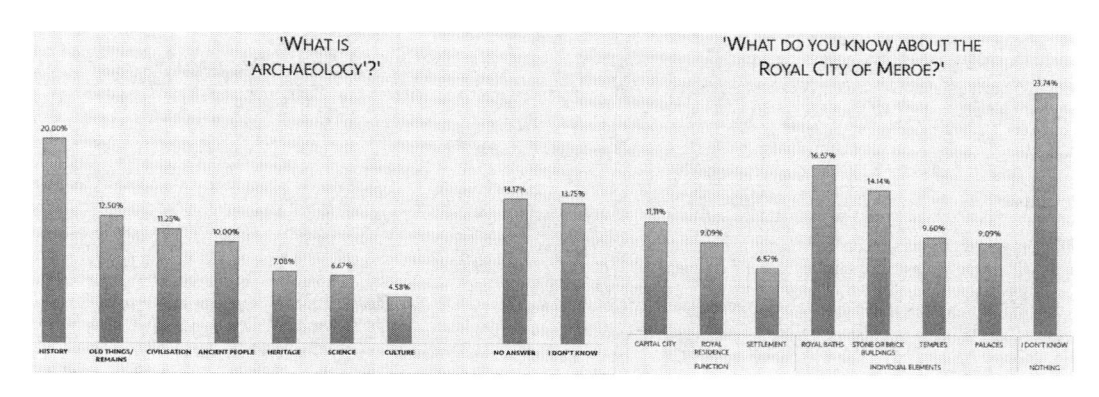

Figure 3. Examples of knowledge assessment responses. Provided by authors.

key buildings. However, knowledge levels vary (both within and across the six communities) and respondents currently have, at best, only the most basic knowledge of Meroe's role in Kushite civilization (the 'official history' of the site).

Outlook assessment: Does the archaeological site benefit your community, and if so, how; do you want to be involved in the archaeological activities of the area, and if so, how?

The majority of questionnaire respondents answered that 'yes', the archaeological site is beneficial to their community, and that they were keen to get involved in archaeological activities in the region (84 per cent and 83 per cent, respectively). Figure 4 represents the ways in which respondents provided their answers. When asked if the site benefits their community, 30.26 per cent noted that it provides 'historical information' or more simply 'history'; 23.68 per cent included the idea of the site generating tourism; 21.05 per cent mentioned job opportunities, and others mentioned 'the economy' and 'development'.

When asked, 'how would you like to be involved in archaeological activities?', a significant number (44.32 per cent) said they wanted to learn more – whether about the pyramids, local history, or about archaeologists themselves. Interacting with the archaeologists, either as colleagues, friends, or advisors, also made up a significant percentage of the responses.

Based on these responses, we propose that for the majority of respondents in these six communities, community members perceive the current main benefits of archaeology to be historical information and contributions to the local economy (via employment with the archaeological team, via infrastructural developments and/or via tourism). This suggests that our community archaeology efforts should focus on implementing educational programmes and stimulating channels for local economic development (many respondents noted that we partially do this already through archaeological employment, though they often noted pointedly that they, too, 'want jobs'.) Many might suggest that these are predictable conclusions, but we suggest that in Sudan and elsewhere across Africa, archaeologists often dismiss these messages, and do not seek to understand various dimensions of community needs (see similar critiques of archaeology in the Middle East from Starzman 2012). Indeed, our data further suggest the Sudanese experience of archaeology is much more complex than this, as we will describe below.

Experience assessment: What are archaeologists looking for?

Earlier approaches to the archaeological heritage of Sudan by foreign archaeologists add complexity to the relationships we are attempting to develop with these local communities. From 2012 to 2016, as described above, we made significant efforts to develop a transparent working model for interaction. People were continually invited to the sites to observe excavations; the team made numerous

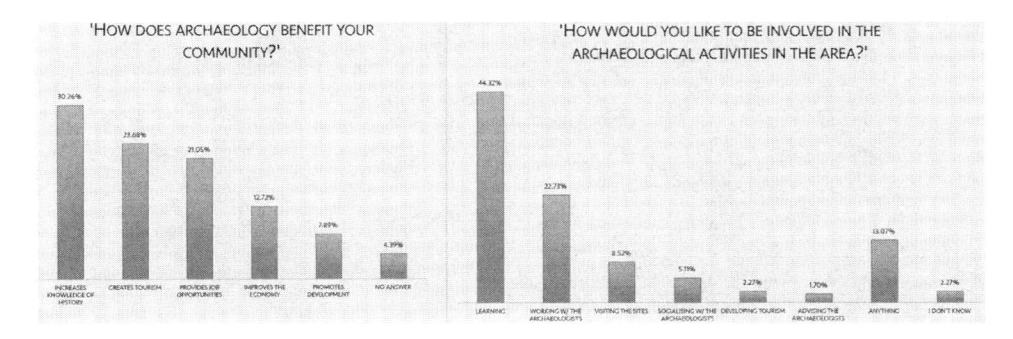

Figure 4. Examples of outlook assessment responses. Provided by authors.

formal and informal social visits, and advertised the dig house as permanently 'open' to visitors. However, we sometimes found a certain level of indifference in what archaeologists were actually doing. We attribute this, at least partly, to the history of archaeological research in Sudan, which has typically overlooked comprehensive, systematic engagement, or knowledge exchange with local communities. It was noticeable, for example, that in the questionnaires we conducted only six months after a major community engagement event (January 2015), 20.93 per cent of responses to the question 'what are archaeologists looking for?' still included the words, 'gold' and 'treasure.' Particularly troubling was that a total of almost 20 per cent (19.77 per cent) of respondents answered 'I don't know', 'They don't tell us, they take it away', or gave no answer.

These responses clearly suggest that more meetings and educational opportunities are necessary to reach mutual understandings of motivation. They also show that we must readily acknowledge the parallels our discipline has with other exploitative, extractive industries, and other structures in Sudan, and the prominent role westerners continue to play within them. This is particularly relevant around Meroe. The previous lack of systematic archaeological engagement has compounded the more general culture of top-down exploitation in Sudan. Overcoming such outlooks and creating new experiences is important, not just for site management and conservation issues (such as protection from looting and other forms of site destruction) but also to build mutual trust between archaeologists and the local communities, and dispel the notion that archaeologists benefit by depriving local people of cultural and economic resources.

Demographic assessment

One of the most salient concepts of collective identity in Sudan is that of *gabila*, and the majority of residents living around Meroe self-identify as belonging to the riverine agricultural Ja'aliyin, one of the largest *gabaayil* in the Nile Valley. In 2014, 96 per cent of questionnaire respondents identified as 'Ja'aliyin', as did 89 per cent of the 2015 respondents. However in 2015, as we gained understanding of the region's social complexity, we amended the questionnaire to include more questions on individual and collective identities (although we recognize the fluid and often momentary nature of identity). Respondents then began to identify themselves secondarily as belonging to seven smaller family-community branches of the Ja'aliyin *gabila*, such as the Sa'adab in the Bejrawiya area, and the Omerab in Jebel Umm Ali. The results also show that in 2015 we were able to attract a statistically relevant number of attendees from members of other, non-Ja'aliyin *gabaayil* living around Meroe: 4.5 per cent respondents identified as Manasir, and 3.6 per cent as Hassaniya.

Nevertheless, while residents in the newer settlement area of Upper Bejrawiya primarily self-identify as belonging to the pastoral Manasir or Hassaniya, they were still not well represented within either meeting attendees or questionnaire respondents. Contrary to our strategy to try and engage specifically with pastoralists, the questionnaires demonstrate that riverine Ja'aliyin came the (albeit short) distance from their villages to the Upper Bejrawiya meetings in much larger numbers than the Manasir or Hassaniya residents. Low pastoralist attendance, even at the meetings in or near their own residences, characterized all the meetings and reflects the local intra-group power dynamics in which the agricultural Ja'aliyin are the dominant group, with consequences for the development of inclusive community archaeology programmes. For these initial analyses, we evaluated the Manasir and Hassaniya's questionnaire responses alongside those of the Ja'aliyin, but future analyses will seek to tease out, explain, and address the differences between them.

In the open discussions, almost none of the respondents mentioned feeling biological or cultural attachments with the ancient Kushite inhabitants of Meroe, identifying instead as descendants of the Islamic Arab groups of the Peninsula whose gradual arrival and settlement in Sudan in the later medieval periods marks the 'golden age' of their history (see also Edwards 2004). This result is particularly noteworthy because it helps foreground the importance of identity and context, or perhaps more specifically 'identity *in* context'; perceptions of archaeology here are most likely to be different from perceptions of the Nubians in the north, who openly claim descent from the people of ancient Kush.

Moreover, in place of ancestral or patrimonial claims, most of the 84 per cent of respondents who agreed that the archaeological site 'is a benefit to our local community' cited purely economic reasons for their answer. Similarly, questionnaire data concerning the development of Meroe as a tourist destination show that respondents embrace it as a prospect: 65 per cent of responses clustered around the potential that tourism has for local economic gain, many noting that tourism development is long overdue. The economic pressures briefly outlined at the beginning of this paper explain, in part, the value placed on economic and infrastructural development in relation to the archaeological sites in the area. Indeed, these economic pressures are caused by such similar industries that it compounds the level of mistrust evident in the some questionnaire answers, specifically regarding what archaeologists are looking for and potentially benefitting from.

It is important to note that the approval obtained from the UCL Ethics Research Committee did not include administering questionnaires to minors (under-18 years old). This is a significant loss in terms of evaluating local perceptions of archaeology: Sudan, like the rest of the continent, has a very young demographic profile, wherein 53 per cent of the population is under 19. Nevertheless, we interviewed people from all other age groups (18–30, 31–45, 46–65, and 66+) in each village aside from Kabushiya and Upper Bejrawiya, where we interviewed neither female nor male respondents over the age of 66 (in general, this age group is less represented than the rest, which is unsurprising considering Sudan's young profile).

Respondent information is therefore not proportional across age groups, or between male and female respondents. However, some differences may be accounted for. For example, official data (as well as observations) show that Kabushiya is a small town with a large population of young adults and the social setting is more amenable for young people, including women, to attend events at night. In contrast, Jebel Umm Ali and Bejrawiya South are older, well-established but industry-less villages, with smaller populations of young people, but with women who have attained higher levels of education than elsewhere and who have more confidence about interacting with foreigners. This may explain why in Kabushiya the majority of male and female respondents were aged 18–45, whereas in Jebel Umm Ali and Bejrawiya South female respondents are mainly from the 46–66+ categories.

Education is also important to consider, and a particularly heterogeneous picture is evident within and between the six villages. In the case of Upper Bejrawiya, a higher proportion of males compared to females completed primary school, a slightly higher proportion of women than men completed secondary school, and while no men went to university, six women had completed university. In part, this is significant because in the Sudanese curriculum, pre-Islamic history is taught in depth only at secondary school, and only then for students who elect to pursue a humanities course. This means that, theoretically, only the students who complete(d) secondary school would have any significant knowledge about Kushite history from school. We were thus surprised that when asked, *how do you learn about archaeology?*, 22.82 per cent of respondents identified 'school' as their main source of knowledge. Perhaps less surprising was that the lowest number of answers mentioned 'archaeologists', but again our curiosity was sparked at the very low number of attributions to 'archaeological employees' such as the site guard, whose post has been held by members of one family since 1939. Although 19.92 per cent said they learn about the sites from 'local people', no one mentioned official or unofficial custodians of tradition or site information (nor were we ever directed to such an individual).

Future analyses should help us link these demographic variables more closely with responses. Nevertheless, the analyses begin to illustrate how the area's broader community is far more diverse than it first appears, and that answers are not always predictable. For now, perhaps the most important results are that the questionnaire respondents are predominantly self-identifying Ja'aliyin, and that, because we did not interview minors, it is Ja'aliyin *adults* that are the main demographic group we 'engaged' with at our meetings.

Discussion

Although uneven demographic representation of respondents prevents generalized conclusions across all six communities, the results clearly indicate that each community should be considered as distinctive, with its own demographic make-up, histories, outlooks, perceived needs, and priorities. This adds significant complexity to the challenges of developing appropriate community archaeology packages, and we fully anticipate this diversity to translate into differing needs and archaeology-related priorities (although precisely how is unknown). For example, although local aspirations could be partially fulfilled by developing a local tourism sector at Meroe, it (or other strategies) may not be sustainable if applied across all six villages – or perhaps even within a single village. With reference to 'packaging' community-specific archaeology, our preliminary results provide strong foundations for development. It is tempting to move forward by identifying the sections of the community who *we* might perceive to be most detached from archaeology, such as the groups of pastoralists, women, or even children, and use archaeology as a tool for intersubjective cohesion. But would this really create a *community* archaeology, or should we be aiming for community archaeolog*ies*? Until further analysis, we feel cautious about prioritizing the vision of one section of any heterogeneous community over another: contested notions of how to allocate resources have a long history of causing conflict both here and across the globe.

Progress

From 2014 to 2016, we made encouraging progress, notably in the increase in the overall number of meeting attendees. The number of women who attended the 2015 meetings and agreed to complete questionnaires increased, as did the number of kinship groups. Several reasons may account for these positive changes. For example, in 2015, a dedicated community engagement officer Bradshaw), was tasked with developing community relationships and organizing meetings. In 2014, the project director (Humphris) had undertaken this role, as an additional task while running the field research project. Thus, in 2014, there had been more limited time to meet and socialize with people, to develop two-way relationships, and to actively advertise the meetings. Additionally, in 2015 the deliberate involvement of pastoral Manasir and Hassaniya groups who live on the village outskirts in Upper Bejrawiya increased the diversity of kinship groups represented at the meetings.

Another development began in 2014 and flourished in 2015, namely the attendance of children at the community meetings (although not as interviewees). At first, we had envisioned our engagement with children to be in a more formal educational format. In part towards this goal, we had produced a five-day community iron smelting festival in 2015 (documented in a film freely available online in English and Arabic, Double and Humphris 2015). In the weeks preceding the festival, we canvassed local schools and arranged for primary and secondary schoolchildren to attend, meet the team, have interactive talks, and participate in a Q&A session. In the end, we hosted over 300 schoolchildren and 24 of their teachers. Although we initially discouraged children from attending our other, adult-focused community meetings, it became apparent that this approach was not socially appropriate for a number of reasons: in Sudan, children are usually included in all social events, especially those taking place in semi-domestic settings, as was the case with most of our meetings. Following further consultation with Sudanese colleagues, we began actively to encourage children to attend and learn with their parents. We, therefore, hope that through this extra-curricular learning, younger people can begin to benefit from our meetings and learn how people from different cultures may live and work together.

Lessons learned

Throughout the processes described here, we have learned several lessons. Language continues to be a challenge, with few of the non-Sudanese team members speaking fluent Arabic. This means we are dependent upon Sudanese students and colleagues to deliver the questionnaires and the presentations, and to translate and transcribe the open discussions as they progress; they are also responsible for translating all the questionnaires into English after each meeting. These are significant tasks, requiring the dedication of Sudanese team members with very strong English language skills, willing to work collaboratively to ensure the validity of the translations.

Organizing meetings also posed particular challenges, and relied on the good will of either existing or newly established contacts. The Hamadab Local Committee (the basic unit of state apparatus in rural villages, thus an important local 'gatekeeping' institution) as well as several other Ja'aliyin men and women kindly lent us their reception rooms (*saloons*) as venues for the meetings so that we could use their electricity. However, we notice that this affected the participation of Manasir and Hassaniya residents. Therefore in future, we wish to reduce our reliance upon PowerPoint (and thus electricity) as a means of visual display, so that meetings can be held in electricity-less Manasir and Hassaniya houses. Similarly, we noted that on the occasions where events were not deliberately gender segregated, women did not attend in large numbers. We were not unsurprised by this result, but we had been – and still are – encouraged by some community residents to hold joint meetings. To 'test' this, we attempted a number of joint meetings in autumn 2016. Our rationale was that if mixed meetings were successful (as we were assured by some community members that they would be), we would be able to provide a greater number of meetings in each location, and therefore more opportunities for people to attend. However, at the 2016 mixed meetings, again, the female turnout was noticeably low. In contrast, at the segregated events we had more female attendees than male, and the atmosphere was tangibly more relaxed. While it is of course not our default preference for segregation, we will thus continue to keep men's and women's meetings separate.

The importance of a continual, critical analysis and constant consideration of 'how our individual identities affect our work, how we can be changed personally by the work, and how our work can change other people' (McDavid 2007, 73) is essential, to develop new ideas and ways of meeting challenges and to ensure that work is conducted appropriately. Certainly the power of archaeologists to shape and create systems of knowledge and to raise and deploy significant sums of money in resource-scarce areas inevitably leads to their incorporation into power relations (whether these relations exist horizontally, across communities, or vertically, through national and transnational institutions). This requires considerable reflection on the possible impacts of our work (Little and Shackel 2014).

Conclusions

This diagnostic study, undertaken to investigate exactly what steps would need to be taken to develop community archaeology around Meroe, has provided important information from which we are developing our future community archaeology strategies. Questionnaire data show that the communities living around the UNESCO World Heritage Site of the Royal City of Meroe are heterogeneous, and that an idealized 'community' for 'community archaeology' does not exist in this context. This diagnostic study, and the engagements described here, helped to identify the complex diversity of the area. Our results demonstrate that there is an interested wider community, keen to learn more, contribute to, and benefit from the development of a tourism sector.

We believe that archaeology can be inclusive, mutually beneficial, and sustainable, and that community research (such as that described here) may help archaeological projects to meet this potential within the diverse contexts of Sudan. We aim to work alongside the National Museum in Khartoum and other relevant heritage organizations to embrace this possibility.

The transition from 'community engagement' to 'community archaeology' has already begun. In autumn 2016, we held nine community meetings across the same six villages. Each meeting featured an Arabic presentation about the history of the Kingdom of Kush and how people lived during this time, directly addressing the respondents' stated desire for more information about local history. An additional aim was to promote the sort of sustainability described by Belford (2014, 27). After an update on the project's results (and our team's future plans), we held discussion sessions, some of which ran for over two hours. As people discussed current and future plans, their growing knowledge and understanding of our scientific approach to archaeology was reflected in the types of questions they asked the team. These ranged from research-focused enquiries (such as the techniques we use to date archaeological materials) to questions about whether the Meroites used different types of iron ore. Questions extended to broader, 'heritage' concerns about the role of museums in Sudan, and how Sudan's antiquities are protected by international law. Around 300 people attended these meetings, which, we feel, represents solid progress towards developing a sustainable community archaeology effort.

These recent conversations confirm Atalay's (2012) detailed observations about the need to establish solid educational foundations before embarking on participatory practices. The work described here was the *first* step in developing a long-term programme of capacity building in the Meroe Region.

Ultimately we feel that community engagement and community archaeology should be context-specific. Even though international and cross-cultural critiques and comparisons can be useful, they often do not allow for the diversity of local social, economic, and political situations. Although we feel our first phase, 'community engagement' offers a good example, we also recommend that ideally the sorts of 'engagements' we described here be conducted parallel to other, more typical archaeological first-steps, such as landscape survey. In this way, the results of both archaeological survey and community survey can help to develop relevant and sustainable archaeological research.

Acknowledgements

We first presented this paper at the Society for Africanist Archaeologists (SAfA) conference of 2016 in a session convened by Innocent Pikirayi and Peter Schmidt, 'Success Stories about Community Archaeology and Heritage in Africa'. We are grateful to Innocent and Peter for their engaged comments on an earlier draft of this paper, and to the editors and reviewers of the *Journal of Community Archaeology and Heritage.* We thank the National Corporation for Antiquities and Museums in Sudan (NCAM), for allowing and supporting this research, and UCL (Beacon Bursary), UCL Qatar and QSAP (Qatar Sudan Archaeology Project) for providing funding which enabled this work or associated work to take place. Many of the UCL Qatar team working in Sudan have played an integral role in implementing the meetings, often late at night during periods of intensive archaeological research. We specifically thank Basil Kamal Bushra and Sayed Ahmed Mokhtar (both University of Khartoum), as well as Abdelhai Abdelsawi Fedlemula (NCAM). Ahmed Hamid Nassr of the University of al Nileen and Abdel Monim Ahmed Abdalla Babiker of the University of Shendi are also specifically thanked for their assistance and support. To all of the other team members who contributed by delivering and translating questionnaires, handing out drinks and biscuits during the meetings, assisting with the meeting setups and taking photographs, we owe you a huge thanks. Meetings would also not have been possible without non-team members such as the local women and imams, who so kindly advertised the meetings for us. We also thank Paul Belford and Stavroula Golfomitsou for offering comments on an earlier draft of this paper. We would like to finally thank all of the local community members who, some with amusement and some with curiosity, gave their time to attend the meetings and provide input through the discussions and questionnaires. We thank you for your trust and hope we can meet your expectations in the future.

Disclosure statement

No potential conflict of interest was reported by the author.

Suggested citation

Humphris, Jane and Rebecca Bradshaw. 2017. 'Understanding "the Community" before Community Archaeology: A Case Study from Sudan.' Special Series, African Perspectives on Community Engagement, guest-edited by Peter R. Schmidt. *Journal of Community Archaeology and Heritage* 4 (3): page 203–217.

References

Atalay, Sonya. 2012. *Community-Based Archaeology: Research With, By, and For Indigenous and Local Communities*. Berkeley: University of California Press.

Bartoy, Kevin M. 2012. "Teaching Through, Rather Than About. Education in the Context of Public Archaeology." In *The Oxford Handbook of Public Archaeology*, edited by Robin Skeates, John Carman, and Carol McDavid, 552–565. New York: Oxford University Press.

Belford, Paul. 2014. "Sustainability in Community Archaeology." *Online Journal in Public Archaeology* SV 1: 21–44.

Boddy, Janice. 1989. *Wombs and Alien Spirits: Women, Men and The Zār Cult In Northern Sudan*. Madison: New Directions In Anthropological Writing, University of Wisconsin Press.

Bruce, James. 1790. *Travels to Discover the Source of the Nile in the Years 1768, 1769, 1770, 1771, 1772, and 1773*. Edinburgh: G.G.J. and J. Robinson.

Cailliaud, Frédéric, and Edme-François Jomard. 1826. *Voyage À Méroé, Au Fleuve Blanc, Au-delà De Fâzoql Dans Le Midi Du Royaume De Sennâr, À Syouah Et Dans Cinq Autres Oasis, Fait Dans Les Années 1819, 1820, 1821 Et 1822*. Paris: Imprimerie Royale.

Double, Graham (Director), and Jane Humphris (Producer). 2015. "Ancient Iron, Experimental Archaeology in Sudan." film available in English and Arabic. https://www.youtube.com/watch?v=SPU8Uwa-jBQ (English) and https://www.youtube.com/watch?v=PBCrKLx0R0I (Arabic).

Edwards, David. 2004. "History, Archaeology and Nubian Identities in the Middle Nile." In *African Historical Archaeologies*, edited by Paul J. Lane and Andrew M. Reid, 33–59. New York: Kluwer Academic/Plenum Publishers.

Hänsch, Valerie. 2012. "Chronology of a Displacement: The Drowning of the Manāsīr People." *Meroitica* 26: 179–228.

Hopkins, Nicholas S., and Sohair R. Mehanna. 2010. *Nubian Encounters: The Story of the Nubian Ethnological Survey, 1961–1964*. Cairo: The American University in Cairo Press.

Lane, Paul. 2011. "Possibilities for a Postcolonial Archaeology in sub-Saharan Africa: Indigenous and Usable Pasts." *World Archaeology* 43 (1): 7–25.

Linke, Janka. 2014. "Oil, Water and Agriculture: Chinese Impact on Sudanese Land Use." In *Disrupting Territories: Land, Commodification and Conflict in Sudan*, edited by Jörg Gertel, Richard Rottenburg, and Sandra Calkins, 77–101. Rochester, NY: Boydell and Brewer.

Little, Barbara J. 2012. "Public Benefits of Public Archaeology." In *The Oxford Handbook of Public Archaeology*, edited by Robin Skeates, John Carman, and Carol McDavid, 395–409. New York: Oxford University Press.

Little, Barbara J., and Paul A. Shackel, eds. 2014. *Archaeology, Heritage, and Civil Engagement. Working Towards the Public Good*. Walnut Creek, CA: Left Coast Press.

McDavid, Carol. 2007. "Beyond Strategy and Good Intentions: Archaeology, Race and White Privilege." In *Archaeology as a Tool of Civic Engagement*, edited by Barbara J. Little and Paul A. Shackel, 67–88. Lanham: Altamira Press.

Meskell, Lynn. 2005. "Archaeological Ethnography: Conversations Around Kruger National Park." *Archaeologies* 1 (1): 81–100.

Näser, Claudia, and Cornelia Kleinitz, eds. 2012. "The Good, the Bad and the Ugly: A Case Study on the Politicisation of Archaeology and Its Consequences from Northern Sudan." *Meroitica* 26: 269–304.

Pikirayi, Innocent, and Peter Schmidt. 2016. "Introduction." In *Community Archaeology and Heritage in Africa: Decolonising Practice*, edited by Peter Schmidt and Innocent Pikirayi, 1–20. Oxon and New York: Routledge.

Richardson, Lorna-Jane, and Jaime Almansa-Sánchez. 2015. "Do You Even Know What Public Archaeology Is? Trends, Theory, Practice, Ethics." *World Archaeology* 47 (2): 194–211.

Säve-Söderbergh, Torgny. 1987. *Temples and Tombs of Ancient Nubia: The International Rescue Campaign at Abu Simbel, Philae, and Other Sites*. London: Thames and Hudson.

Schmidt, Peter. 2016. "Collaborative Archaeology and Heritage in Africa, Views From the Trench and Beyond." In *Community Archaeology and Heritage in Africa: Decolonising Practice*, edited by Peter Schmidt and Innocent Pikirayi, 70–90. Oxon: Routledge.

Shinnie, Peter. 1967. *Meroe: A Civilization of the Sudan*. London: Thames & Hudson.

Smith, Laurajane, and Emma Waterton. 2009. *Heritage, Communities and Archaeology*. London: Duckworth.

Starzman, Maria Theresia. 2012. "Archaeological Fieldwork in the Middle East: Academic Agendas, Labour Politics and Neo-Colonialism." In *European Archaeology Abroad: Global Settings, Comparative Perspectives*, edited by Sjoerd. J. van der Linde, Monique. H. van de Dries, Nathan Schlanger, and Corijanne. G. Slappendel, 401–415. Leiden: Sidestone Press.

Straight, Bilinda, Paul. J. Lane, Charles. E. Hilton, and Musa Letua. 2015. "It Was Maendeleo That Removed Them': Disturbing Burials and Reciprocal Knowledge Production in a Context of Collaborative Archaeology." *Journal of the Royal Anthropological Institute* 21: 391–418.

Török, László. 2015. *The Periods of Kushite History from the Tenth Century BC to the Fourth Century AD*. Studia Aegyptiaca Supplements 1. Budapest: Izisz Foundation.

Umbadda, Siddig. 2014. "Agricultural Investment Through Land Grabbing in Sudan." In *Disrupting Territories: Land, Commodification and Conflict in Sudan*, edited by Jörg Gertel, Richard Rottenburg, and Sandra Calkins, 31–51. Rochester, NY: Boydell and Brewer.

World Bank. 2011. "A poverty profile for the northern states of Sudan." The World Bank Poverty Reduction and Economic Management Unit, Africa Region: p. 2. http://siteresources.worldbank.org/INTAFRICA/Resources/257994-1348760177420/-2011.pdf.

Community cultural identity in nature-tourism gateway areas: Maun Village, Okavango Delta World Heritage Site, Botswana

Susan Osireditse Keitumetse ⓘ

Michelle Genevieve Pampiri

This paper focuses on our research in Maun village, near Okavango Delta, a World Heritage Site (OD-WHS), Botswana. We hoped to illuminate the presence and strength of 'dormant' community cultural identities, and to learn how they are constituted in cultural values and tied to landscapes that have become re-branded as nature-tourism areas. To unveil these 'dormant' cultural values, we conducted ethnographic interviews among the Maun village traditional leaders, Dikgosi (Chiefs), who are cultural custodians of communal heritage, to identify and re-acknowledge cultural and heritage values from communal memory. The aim was to create a balance between the nature tourism identity and the more fluid socio-cultural identities of people. Our results show that Maun village has communal cultural values that can complement the gateway tourism image. This work provides a model for other nature-tourism gateway communities who wish to salvage and safeguard the cultural heritage identities connected to their particular landscapes.

Introduction

Branded landscapes are common across the globe — 'wonders of the world', 'world heritage' and 'Ramsar sites', to mention a few. However, a brand's existence is often preceded by an indigenous understanding of landscape heritage borne from local communal identities that have evolved through time (Keitumetse 2011, 2014).

Maun village in Botswana is one such geographical location, and is currently popular as a tourism gateway into the inland Okavango Delta World Heritage Site (OD-WHS). The OD-WHS is protected under the United Nations Educational, Scientific, and Cultural Organisation's (U.N.E.S.C.O.) 1972 Convention Concerning the Protection of the World Cultural and Natural Heritage (UNESCO 1972) (the World Heritage Convention, or WHC). It is also protected under the Wetlands Bureau's 1971 Ramsar Convention (Ramsar Bureau 1971) on the sustainable utilization of wetlands. Maun falls within the border of the Ramsar site but outside the world heritage site border. The Ramsar convention on wetlands protection recognizes the cultural heritage of wetlands. Article 1 of the WHC also recognizes the 'combined works of nature and man'. The WHC further contains definitions of landscapes that acknowledge the relationship between people and landscapes as follows:

(1) *Clearly defined landscape* — deliberately made by people.

(2) *Organically evolved landscape* — starts off with social, economic, administrative and religious aspects, but later develops to associate solely with the natural environment. This can mean that the process of evolution ended and led to a relic (fossil). It can also mean that evolution is in progress, as evidenced by its active social role in contemporary society, and/or traditional way of life. The latter is true of the Maun community's relationship with the Okavango Delta.

(3) *Associative cultural landscape* — where powerful religious, artistic or cultural associations exist in addition to material culture. This category is characteristic of the OD-WHS and is also supported by the premises of the U.N.E.S.C.O. 2003 Convention on Safeguarding Intangible Cultural Heritage (UNESCO 2003; UNESCO n.d.).

Even though the above categories are all characteristic of Maun, the village's historic, traditional character and heritage values are absent within the relatively new tourism branding. Maun can therefore be referred to as a gateway locality that lacks the significant activities of a gateway community since the village's local people are currently not positioned to function as active hosts in a landscape that provides a profound experience for most visitors (McMahon 1999).

Before continuing we will clarify terms. We use 'dormant' to refer to cultural values tied to geophysical places where important cultural activities took place in the past. Our interviews unveiled these previous uses and their associated cultural values. We use the term 'forgotten' in a specific way, because of its meaning in Setswana (the language used in Maun), where 'forgetting' does not mean something is no longer valued, but rather that other priorities have taken over (temporarily or otherwise). This is the sentiment that the interviewees communicated to us as they 'remembered' certain places during the course of our interviews.

Using ethnographic methods, we set out to inventory and assess the cultural and heritage components of Maun village, to understand the village community's inborn cultural competencies that place them as portals to the site, and by extension salvage their sociocultural relationship to the landscape. We hope this inventoried heritage can supplement the overwhelming wilderness and wildlife tourism identity that now dominates the area. Our study population included the village traditional and cultural leadership known as *Dikgosi* (chiefs; singular, *Kgosi*), from various traditional centres known as *dikgotla* (wards; singular *kgotla*) that house the sociocultural and sociopolitical network of a traditional village in Botswana. In almost all cases, a chief invited ward elders (who serve as advisors on ward history) to assist during interviews.

Our research revealed that several components of intangible cultural heritage are attached to selected landscapes and historical features in Maun village and have, in the past, provided a sense of communal identity and belonging. As we will discuss later, leaders can now use these dormant and previously 'forgotten' cultural heritage values as leverage to participate in Okavango Delta high-end tourism.

First we will provide some theoretical, geographical and historical context. We will then describe our methods and explore what we learned from the interviews. We will close with some observations about ongoing and future work in Maun village.

Gateway status: pressures and transformations

Literature on the gateway concept illustrates a gradual transition from an understanding of 'gateway' as a concrete geographical space (Burghardt 1971) to 'gateway' as a contact community that defines experiences of a particular geographical area (cf. McMahon 1999; Frauman and Banks 2011). As a geophysical phenomenon, a 'gateway' is a place that is '... in command of the connections between the tributary area and the outside world' (Burghardt 1971, 269). Frauman and Banks (2011) define a gateway community as a communal encounter, whereby a community borders and serves as entry point to a nation's public lands and parks. Maun constitutes/represents both types of gateway. Whereas the literature illustrates that since prehistoric times gateway communities developed as a response to trade, where most influential communities chose strategic locations to control trade goods (Hirth 1978, 37), Maun became a village before the tourism commerce it experiences today. The origin of Maun is largely a result of eighteenth century regional sociopolitical turbulence (cf. Tlou 1971a; 1972; Chirenje 1977; Dikole 1978). Trade took place mainly through the bartering of environment-specific goods between ethnic groups living in the depths of the Okavango delta waters (e. g. Bayei and River San) and those within dry land areas like Maun village (such as Batawana, Hambukushu and Basubiya people).

A locality's gateway status can exert pressure on cultural spaces and features associated with both tangible heritage (archaeological, architectural), and/or intangible heritage (historic, symbolic values), because ethnic communities living in villages like Maun are pressured to conform to the tourism gateway status requirements. In this process, local and/or resident communities can lose direct connection to the landscape. In addition, commercial developments often demand land spaces for commercial activities, as is the case with tourism facilities in Maun. This, in turn, pressures the community to change how it uses culturally valuable land and spaces. With no strategy to retain the village's sociocultural character or benefit from the demands of commercial enterprise, communities become overwhelmed and help-less. Research interventions such as this one can provide options for community empowerment, as we will demonstrate.

Another transformation can be through legislation, such as that concerning modern landscape planning. For example, the government has declared Maun a physical planning area under its re-enacted 2013 Department of Town and Regional Planning Act (DTRP 2013),[2] which focuses on modern development planning, but does not incorporate historical value of landscapes.

Maun village: geographic context and cultural meanings

Maun is located in the Ngamiland district in northwest Botswana. The village of Maun has evolved since its establishment around 1915 to the tourism gateway village it is today, and currently has a population of 65,693 people including associ-ated localities (Statistics Botswana 2011). It is traversed by the Thamalakane river, that is filled by river channels that originate as far as the Angolan highlands, con-tinues through Maun and evolves into the Boteti river to the south, which in turn connects with the palaeo-lake of Makgadikgadi pans (Figure 1). This geographical phenomenon has shaped people–environment interaction for over 100,000 years (Robbins et al. 2000; Coulson et al. 2011), and the name *Thamalakane* (riddle/ puzzle) in itself bears testimony to local people's perception of their environment. By considering the river a puzzle, local and resident communities seem to have ques-tioned the presence of a water-filled river in a dry area environment, given that the Thamalakane river fills and flows through the village during winter time, when the rest of Botswana is dry and surrounded by scorched vegetation (see McCarthy et.al. 1998 and Wolski and Savenije 2006 for research on this geological process).

A brief history of Maun village

Although Maun history predates that of the Batawana ethnic group, and the village itself includes people from various ethnic groups (see Tlou 1971a; 1972; Chirenje 1977), the Ngamiland region and the Maun village are popularly known and traced through the settlement history of the Batawana. This ethnic group assumed domination and consequently political leadership over other ethnic groups in the Ngamiland area during eighteenth-century southern African political strife (Tlou 1971a; 1972; Chirenje 1977). The Batawana are an off-shoot of the Ngwato ethnic group currently found in the central district of Botswana, from whom they broke off around 1795 in an area of Shoshong village known as *pharolle* and/or *motse-o-dule* (a village has emerged). Together with other subjugated groups along the way, the Batawana set up territory in Ngamiland district, and subsequently established Maun village. The attestation of Maun as part of the Batawana ethnic group is as political as it is dependent on the knowledge producers, that is, those that documented historical events did so from the point of view of the dominant

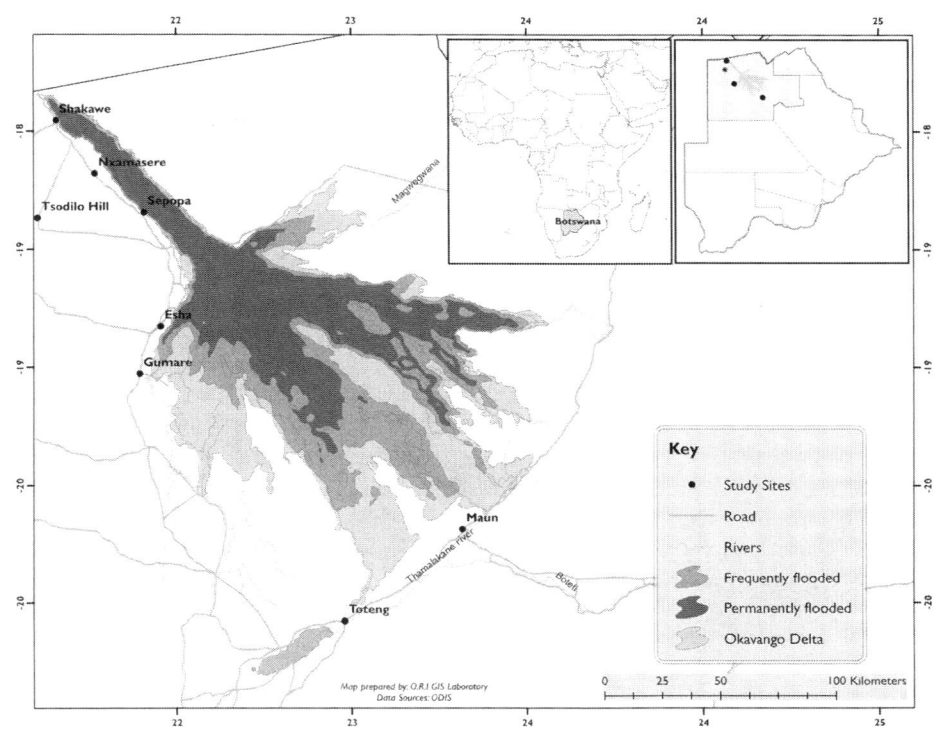

FIGURE 1   Map showing location of Botswana, Maun village and surrounding areas, features mentioned in text such as Thamalakane river. (Image courtesy of the Okavango Research Institute, A. Makati. ©Okavango Research Institute.)

Batawana. Other groups were appended to the Batawana ethnic group irrespective of their earlier territorial status, probably due to their lack of political status.

Linguistic heritage, however, points to a landscape identity dominated by different ethnic groups, including River San (Bushmen), Kgalagadi and Wayeyi (Peters 1972). Linguistically, the name 'Maun' is of Wayeyi ethnic group origin, pronounced /Mau/, referring to the tall reeds (*lethaka*) along the Thamalakane river (see Figure 1). Through time, immigrant settlers corrupted the pronunciation to 'Maun'. Our interviews indicated that inhabitants burned the river reeds along the Thamalakane river in the 1980s, seemingly to discourage thieves from taking refuge in them, hence ending the reeds' significance as the village's signature feature.

The ethnicities that make up Maun village community co-existed in surrounding areas in the past, under *Kgosi* (king) Letsholathebe I (1847–1874). They faced common enemies in land settlement and political power struggles before finally converging as Maun village around 1914–1915.

In the late 1800s Batawana faced various political conflicts with other African groups as well as British and Boer groups. Given these conflicts, several of the *Dikgosi* we interviewed referred to a place called *kwa-ga-Sethebe* (translated as 'a place of shield'), currently known as Toteng (meaning monument; see Figure 1).

As a result of other strife, Batawana abandoned Toteng in 1874, and it subsequently became populated by other ethnic groups.

For our purposes here, the main point is that our interviews (described below) revealed how, over time, place names tracked along with various historical political encounters. These place names both shaped and reflected the settlement dynamics that give Maun (which reached its centenary in 2015) its contemporary communal and geophysical identity.

Modern land-use planning and erasure of local cultural values in a village landscape

Cultural landscapes have natural and cultural values, often viewed as a mirror of communal cultures that created them (Mitchell et al. 2009). In spite of their value, cultural landscapes are gradually disappearing, consequently resulting in a loss of cultural heritage. Various activities (such as modern land-use planning to address socio-economic demands) can cause the disappearance of cultural landscapes (Rössler 2005). In the process, modern land use planners often fail to consider cultural aspects of land use when developing land policies.

Botswana has two legal tools that illustrate this problem because they influence the physical development planning of villages like Maun. These are the aforementioned DTRP Act 2013 (DTRP 2013) and the Development Control Code (DCC) 2013[3,4] (DCC 2013). Both operate under Botswana's Ministry of Lands and Housing, which supervises and monitors land planning and development in rural areas. Several articles of the DTRP Act of 2013 refer to community- and cultural heritage-related conservation activities. For instance, Article 16 section 18(1) requires the Minister responsible to consult with '… such persons or bodies of persons, including *Bogosi*, …' (DTRP 2013). Article 18, section 20 (2) instructs the planning authority that:

> The planning authority shall, by notice published in the *Gazette*, and in one newspaper circulating in the planning area, notify the public that there has been prepared in draft any such plan or proposals for the revision of any such plan, and of the place or places where the copies of such plan or proposals may be inspected by the public (DTRP 2013).

These articles, which appear to mandate consultation with local communities, are, in practice, incompatible with rural community members' literacy. As a result community members are not conversant with media publications associated with land planning as a development process. Neither do they have the professional capacity necessary to interrogate plans, development proposals or maps to gauge threats to their cultural resources. Much legislation elsewhere contains other forms of shortcomings (such as that illustrated by Ndlovu (2011) in South African Heritage Management). In addition, other sections of the DTRP Act 2013 recognize historic buildings, rather than communal memory, as 'significant' to planning — they prioritize architectural value over cultural symbols and meanings. In short, there are both knowledge (education) and value divides between Western-educated modern planners and non-literate local rural communities. Both divides leave vulnerable rural communities at the mercy of modern planners.

This situation in one African village is, of course, echoed in various global and national initiatives to protect cultural landscapes and other forms of 'intangible heritage' and 'traditional cultural properties' (Parker and King 1990; UNESCO 2003). It is outside our scope here to explore these global initiatives other than to note their relevance to the Maun context and the reality that poor public consultation and poor public understanding about land development is a common challenge to cultural sustainability worldwide (see Marcucci 2000 and Hammami 2012 for two widely disparate examples) where more often than not officially planned developments override cultural spaces and features in a rural village like Maun. Cultural features that we identified during our research that do not appear in official planning maps are discussed in sections below.

Identifying community cultural heritage in a commercial (tourism) landscape

Methods and changing directions

As noted earlier, we sourced the interview sample from the *dikgotla* (wards), headed by *Dikgosi*, traditional leaders of a community that shares sociopolitical and/or sociocultural lineage and history. All traditional villages in Botswana have a *kgotla* (ward) and a *kgosi* (chief). The village *dikgotla* are classified in the sociopolitical hierarchy by kinship ties and history of conquering and domination, whereby the conqueror becomes the ruler (not necessarily the first settler). In a traditional village like Maun, the *dikgotla* are then graded according to the ruler's kingship relations in line of descendancy and potential ruling. The other grading indicator is through allies (usually immigrants) in the struggle for dominance and control of sociopolitical systems.

Whereas it is common for some international scholars to define a *kgotla* as a traditional court system (Düsing 2002), the social dynamics of a *kgotla* overwhelm the political attributes that would lead to denoting it as a 'court' in an international legal sense. In our work, we use the more traditional term *kgotla* as the villagers refer to it. As such, it is as much a physical geographic space as it is a sociopolitical and sociocultural entity, because of its intangible characteristics, which we will explore later. Governed by a *kgosi*, the *kgotla* has evolved as a space where traditional leaders, village community, central government and district council ideas interact (cf. Düsing 2002).

Various factors infringe ethnic identities and a sense of communal belonging in Maun landscape (Nyathi-Ramahobo 2002), but we have considered the *dikgotla* as they currently appear on the landscape, as our interviewees discussed them. We chose to study the Maun wards that *Dikgosi* suggested — that is, because *they chose them*, and because they had cultural information to share about those wards. Interviews also revealed the historical origins of the *dikgotla* and in several cases the *kgotla* elders accompanying the chiefs provided additional information.

Dikgosi tended to be younger than the elders, so they often depended on them for historical guidance.

We initially aimed to use a structured questionnaire to interview a select number of *Dikgosi* from various *dikgotla*, based on Keitumetse's knowledge of traditional village leadership. However, after a few interviews it became clear that we needed more in-depth engagement, as the *Dikgosi* requested more time to narrate their settlement histories. During our first interviews, they realized the significance of the research to village heritage revival, which they perceived as forgotten and gradually overshadowed by the tourism identity. In light of this, we expanded the scope of our research to include both guiding questions and informal discussions on each *kgotla* history which, more often than not, culminated in spontaneous fieldwork visits to 'remembered' sites and features around the village.

In addition, we intended to interview all of the identified *Dikgosi*, but instead covered 79.2 per cent (19) because we knew, from prior cultural knowledge, which of the *dikgotla* had deeply entwined histories, and thus would have provided overlapping information had we interviewed them all. The key themes of the questionnaire were as follows:

- history of a *kgotla*;
- historical events of a particular *kgotla* and associated ethnic/tribal group;
- landscapes/features of cultural significance associated with the history of a *kgotla*;
- impact of modern development on a *kgotla*.

In addition to interviews, we used a Global Positioning System (GPS) to collect coordinates of the 'forgotten' cultural spaces and features in Maun where the *Dikgosi* could trace and reconstruct cultural activity. We later downloaded the GPS coordinates into map processing software, or a Geographical Information System (GIS) system, and overlaid this information on existing base maps to show location of identified sites, layout patterns, relationships with existing land use activities, and impact areas. We also drew on secondary sources such as legislative policies, district town and regional planning documents, and general archival literature to supplement these data.

What we learned

The history of Maun, and, thus, the arrangement of its *dikgotla*, are stratified socially and politically. At the top of the social and political hierarchy are those *dikgotla* that belong to the dominant or paramount chief, his/her uncles who are related by birth and sometimes marriage. In addition to this there are the dominant chief's loyalists and/or helpers, who may or may not be biologically related to the dominant chief. Following are the categories and some of the culturally important place names that emerged in our interviews.[1] It is clear that place names themselves have a direct relationship to *dikgotla* histories.

- Kgosing *kgotla*: This is commonly known as the 'main' ward. Its rulers (Batawana, who are the dominant leaders, or paramount) migrated to Ngamiland in around 1795 from east-central Botswana (Shoshong village) to a site known as *pharolle* or *motse-o-dule* (village has emerged). We also interviewed the dominant chiefs' uncles for the Mabudutsa and Meno wards because they share the same settlement history.

- Matomo, Lebodu, Mhapha and Mopako wards: These were made up of the paramount or dominant chief's men (*basimane ba kgotla*), and/or paramount chief's loyalists or social guards (*badisa kgotla*). They originate from various ethnicities and settlement histories. These wards protect and take care of the paramount known as *basimane-ba-kgotla* (ward men).
- Boyei/Sanyedi and Basarwa/Bushmen/San, Shorobe and Sexaxa wards: These wards belong to ethnic groups that are either indigenous to or early settlers of Maun and surrounding areas but became politically dominated by the paramountcy.
- Shageng, Shashe, Borolong, Kubung, Bombadi, Wenela and Sedie wards: These wards consist of ethnic groups that immigrated into the Batawana paramount or dominant rule in the twentieth century, bringing along various competencies and skills. Some focused on agriculture along the river. For example, Bombadi means 'farmer'. The *kgotla* was first allocated to a carpenter and agriculturalist who first settled in the Wenela *kgotla* along the Thamalakane river, and was later re-located to the Bombadi *kgotla* area. His group made gardens for vegetables to be sold to the village, and their settlement site eventually became the Bombadi ward. The ethnic groups in these wards have a cultural and political history distinct from the paramountcy, but became accepted as settler communities under it.
- Boseja, Sexaxa, Botshabelo, Moeti, Thitoyamokodi, Riverside and Disana wards: These wards emerged due to population and geophysical growth of the village. For example, the Boseja ward was established in the 1950s and was made up of immigrants of European descent, Mr Zakarius Wellio and (later) Andrew Wellio. They came originally from Scotland and owned the only boat used to cross the Thamalakane river. Boseja means 'across the river'. The Sexaxa ward is a historical retreat area for Yei and San communities of Gwexhai/Ghweikao origin. The word *sexaxa* describes a reed-like grass that acted as a barrier against cows crossing the Thamalakane River. Its presence served as an indicator of low water, where people could cross without fear of drowning.
- Botshabelo, Moeti wards: These wards emerged in response to environmental disasters which dislocated certain groups. Botshabelo translates as 'where one takes refuge', and Moeti translates as 'visitor'.

'Remembered' sites and 'dormant' cultural values in Maun: examples

We identified a total of 23 cultural landscapes, although it is outside the scope of this study to discuss them all in detail here. Some 'dormant' *dikgotla* of historical value are eroded by modern developments. For instance, the Mabudutsa ward (headed by *kgosi* Leatile Mogalakwe) is now just a single residential plot serving as office space, and is no longer populated by family residential plots. The sociopolitical settlement pattern is gone, and the residents were relocated to the new Disaneng ward to pave way for a bus and taxi rank. In another example, the Matomo *kglota* headed by *kgosana* (headman) Keoikantse Segole was affected by growth of commercial development in the village and is still under further threat of absolute disappearance. It is designated a suburban zone under the Maun Development plan, 1997–2021, and as such, its remaining residents are earmarked for possible relocation to pave the way for new developments compatible with modern planning. With holistic and inclusive physical landscape planning, however, these traditional wards could be incorporated as part of the village identity and be part of the village heritage trail development.

When questioned about the main significance of the 'remembered' cultural features and cultural landscapes, the *Dikgosi* pointed out that having a rich history was the most important factor in providing a sense of belonging to a location. Below we will highlight two examples of such histories: a monument (old granaries) and a site (a tree). These illustrate the rich history of some of the neglected and threatened village cultural heritage components.

Old granaries located at the paramount kgotla

Figure 2 shows grain storages that are a common feature in the paramount chief's yard, and are known as symbols of Maun *kgotla*. However, this study revealed that the cultural significance extends way beyond the physical and visible grain storages, now seen as monuments. In our interviews, the intangible/symbolic cultural significance of the features was narrated. The *Dikgosi* related the grain storages to a traditional system of annual communal ploughing sustained by communal cooperation and volunteerism to plough the fields, known as *masimo a kgosing*

FIGURE 2   Old granaries at the *Kgosing* (main) ward. Chief Charles Letsholathebe narrating history of granaries to Michelle Pampiri. (Photo provided by authors.)

(paramount chief's ploughing fields). Both social understanding and practical arrangement (that the fields were communal property) nurtured volunteerism — essentially activating free communal labour. Community members could tap into the grain storages during times of need, illustrating that these seemingly isolated features had intangible cultural significance within the village community. The monuments now provide opportunities for hands-on activities that can enable interaction between community and tourists (such as demonstrations on how such agricultural produce was handled).

Site of matsaudi (African mangosteen) tree along Thamalakane river

Another site with significant cultural meaning is along the Thamalakane riverfront, popularly identified through a seemingly isolated *matsaudi* (African mangosteen) tree (Figure 3). The area boasts recreational, traditional trade (bartering marketplace), and political cultural heritage values. The *Dikgosi* and elder members of the community shared intimate memories of the place as an island where socioeconomic interaction between communities from within the Okavango Delta swamps (e.g. Wayeyi community) and Maun village took place. Communities from the Okavango delta swamps travelled through the Thamalakane river system using *mekoro* (wooden boats) to barter for goods in the dryland area of Maun. This is confirmed in earlier ethnographic research among BaYei elders, describing their use of Mogomelo and Gomoti river channels about 120 km from Maun:

FIGURE 3 The site of *matsaudi* (African mangoose) tree along *Thamalakane* river, Maun village. (Photo provided by authors.)

All informants could themselves remember when dugout canoes (*mekoro*, singular *mokoro*) were the 'cars of the delta' and many spoke of long journeys, mostly in the era of their parents or their own childhoods (early to mid-twentieth century), to visit relatives, to hunt and fish, and to trade …Trips to Maun by *mokoro* to trade sorghum, brew beer, sell reeds and fish, buy goods in shops were common into the 1970s … (Bernard and Moetapele 2005, 266).

Interviews indicated that, in return, Maun residents exchanged goods that were abundant for them but rare for those residing deeper in the swamps. Examples of bartered goods brought by inland communities (mainly Wayeyi and River San) included dried wild animal meat, river reeds and other items. They exchanged them for goods not available in the delta, such as cans, bottles, safety pins, bracelets and so on, all associated with everyday use in a homestead.

Interviewees also indicated that there used to be long-stay camping at the site, in tents called *dixao* or *dixibi* (temporary houses), until all goods were bartered. The camping activity in particular illustrates that the tourism camping business now taking place in Maun has traditional roots, even among local communities. Because camping is one of the major tourist activities of Okavango Delta tourism, local communities could use this skill to tap into the tourism business.

Some *Dikgosi* and community elders also remembered the area around the tree as having hosted communal recreation activities, such as bathing/swimming, with virtual borders segregating the water along gender lines; that is, female/male bathing/swimming sections (*letsibogo-la-basadi* and *letsibogo-la-banna* respectively). At a political level, the *matsaudi* tree area is also associated with activities related to Botswana's independence, whereby the first President of the country, while visiting the Ngamiland region in 1966, made a historic first address to the Maun community at that location.

At the time of the study, modern developments (a primary school, sewerage lines' residential and commercial plot allocation, and others) had gradually reduced the tree area. However, the *Dikgosi* and elders believe that locals and tourists alike could use the space for cultural revival activities, such as a cultural market place.

Sharing interview results

In the end, the research evolved into a semi-participatory partnership between *Dikgosi* (representing their communal histories) and the university researchers. That is, as research progressed, the *Dikgosi* and other community members confirmed each other's narratives and suggested additional interviewees (processes known in social science research as 'triangulation' and 'snowballing'). *Dikgosi* also provided potential sources of new information about Maun village cultural heritage. Although some scholars have argued that a highly participatory research project would be one whereby '… community members would be involved in setting the terms of the research such as deciding questions to explore, information to collect, and how the information would be used' (Chung 2002, 41), what evolved here was somewhat different. We set research directions and developed initial interview questions, but made changes as needed in direct response to community input.

As it happened, in all cases, using both interviews and our knowledge of village people, the *Dikgosi*'s original versions were confirmed and added to, rather than disputed or discredited.

In order to cement the semi-participatory nature of the research, once we compiled the results, Keitumetse organized a seminar/workshop for all the interviewees and their associates to visit the Okavango Research Institute, University of Botswana. Here the attendees listened to preliminary results and corrected and supplemented it where necessary. We then incorporated their input into the final research report and all related publications (such as this one). The workshop took place on 11 September 2014 (Figure 4).

The seminar/workshop yielded fruitful results, and the *Dikgosi* pledged to tell us about more culturally important sites in future. In addition, most *Dikgosi* recognized the usefulness of the university as a partner in creating inventories of cultural heritage for reference and use by future generations. Several *Dikgosi* expressed this, enthusiastically, during the workshop, and Keitumetse still receives phone calls from participants to discuss the research. Their enthusiasm gave birth to a need to develop archival storage for Maun village cultural heritage of both published and nonpublished formats for use in various activities, such as the celebration of Maun village's centenary at the end of 2015.

Representatives of local government departments and media were also present at the seminar/workshop and covered the lecture in the local newspapers (e.g. Ketlogetswe 2014). The *Dikgosi* continue to engage with researchers in various forums through Keitumetse, who lives and works in the village. Although formal interviews

FIGURE 4 *Dikgosi* (chiefs) at a seminar discussing research results with the researchers at the Okavango Research Institute. (Photo provided by authors.)

are over, she continues (as a participant observer at community events) to engage community members in the cultural significance of landscapes and place names.

As already noted, the study's main objective was to identify forgotten cultural values attached to Maun landscapes and places, and to reconstruct a communal cultural identity of the village to enable direct community identity and participation in popular tourism in the future. The various *dikgotla* profiled yielded rich sociocultural histories, including the historical background of place names, as outlined earlier.

The categories are important because, now documented, they will influence future management of the village cultural heritage, which can now openly recognize all appropriate cultural categories. They provide an inventory to guide future heritage managers and stakeholders, and serve as a knowledge resource about how to articulate and/or express Maun village identity in its entirety, using communal cultural heritage. We will explore this more in the following.

Discussion, conclusion and recommendations

This section summarizes how identified or unearthed cultural values and landscapes can be incorporated into social and land development initiatives to benefit the Maun community.

Maun village dikgotla heritage devolution: from rich cultural landscapes to 'forgotten' cultural features

Our interviews revealed that the *kgotla* system continues to devolve from being an ethnic cultural landscape rich in communal identities (embedded in places, monuments and landscapes) to one in which cultural values are veiled, 'forgotten' or, in many cases, literally erased. Save for the *kgosing* 'main' ward, few *dikgotla* engage in consistent cultural activities necessary to sustain a *kgotla* as a living sociocultural forum. Even so, our interviews illustrated the continuing interconnectedness of ethnic groups in the cultural landscape that is now the cosmopolitan village of Maun.

The pressure to develop Maun village as a tourism gateway is taking its toll. As noted before, most of Mabudutsa ward has been replaced by the Maun bus rank, leaving the *Kgosi* with only an administrative office plot, and no people in his vicinity to preside over ward activities as was the case in the past. Although the bus rank supports socio-economic development, it has also transformed the network of social and cultural relationships that were rooted within a traditional *kgotla* landscape system. Other Maun *dikgotla* that are now only symbolic structures/features are located in Mopako, Matomo and Lebodu, as shown in Figure 5.

Communities (through the village leaders and elders we interviewed) recognize the value of both economic development and cultural preservation, but heretofore had only limited understanding of how to advocate cultural heritage as part of economic development. Keitumetse, who also currently sits in the North-West district Council's (NWDC) physical planning committee, is using her expertise to sensitize traditional leaders to dealing with government land policy structures, and thus help them to infuse development plans with 'dormant' cultural values. One such

FIGURE 5   Evolving *kgotla* changed into an isolated feature rather than a living sociocultural space. This is an example of a Maun *kgotla* that has been reduced to an isolated feature in the village, as land is consumed by modern and urban development compatible with the tourism gateway area. Maun *dikgotla* such as mopako, matomo, lebodu, mabudutsa have already been transformed into this status. (Photo provided by authors.)

engagement involves landscape (physical) planning to recognize and incorporate the unique character of Maun cultural heritage, such that it enhances the village's position as a tourism gateway village. With informed planning, the heritage of *dikgotla* can be used to diversify tourist experiences, but first it is necessary to arouse communities to advocate for themselves. This research has accomplished that first step. For example, during the workshop discussed above, *Dikgosi* indicated that, had they earlier understood the potential of using their cultural heritage for development, they would have approached the Mabudutsa ward relocation for the bus rank differently. We hope that applied research such as this can help them to advocate confidently for village development.

This has led to the necessary second-step of our applied research: capacity building. We will continue to respond to *Dikgosi*'s stated lack of knowledge about the legal tools discussed earlier. Both pieces of legislation include text that a community can, if fully informed, deploy to conserve/safeguard its heritage spaces, including language which recognizes heritage as an amenity rather than a resource[2] and which recognizes 'cultural memory' (intangible heritage by interviewees) and 'place' as opposed to only physical 'buildings'.[3]

In particular, the Development Control Code recognizes and gives priority to uses of open spaces, under which 'Historical, archaeological and cultural sites[4]' are listed as eligible for primary open space use (DCC 2013, 297). Here lies an opportunity for the Maun community to initiate conservation of cultural spaces, such as the historical barter trade spot marked by *matsaudi* tree (Figure 4). In this case, Maun could form cooperatives to create trade activities that echo past activities, which would enhance heritage tourism enterprises. Currently the Maun Development Plan (1997–2021) core area designates only a small portion of land as a cultural heritage space amongst several priority zones that exist in competition with cultural features identified by the study. Maun leadership could take advantage of the open space provision within the Development Control Code to safeguard their heritage spaces and use them for local development.

Although the Maun Development Plan has allocated a portion of space to what is termed 'historical/cultural precinct', this separate zoned area assigns community heritage to a separate, distant corner, away from village space. However, our research illustrates that spaces with cultural value are located randomly all over the village. Keitumetse, as part of her applied work, brought this particular example to the local planning authority's attention, who responded with interest. In her capacity as a member of the district's physical planning committee, she is now facilitating communications between the planning officials and the *Dikgosi* and, at the same time, counselling the *Dikgosi* about how they can be vocal on this and similar issues. Both parties have noted that these proactive efforts can provide a pathway for future cooperation. Although this example illustrates ill-informed planning by government departments, it also shows how doors can open with well researched, sensitive advocacy and capacity-building. Other ideas, yet to be developed, include forming a village foundation to coordinate activities, such as having village interpretation centres for cultural and natural heritage resources. One popular though narrow idea is to develop cultural villages as a tourism attraction in themselves (Saarinen et al. 2014).

Towards sustainable communities

In summary, our research objective was to understand and highlight how a skewed focus on areas and resources categorized as 'natural' can impede communities in tourism-rich areas from interacting directly with their own cultural heritage. Focusing on the village of Maun, we started by identifying stakeholders who were well versed in its cultural heritage, now overwhelmed by the pressures of being a gateway tourism village to the OD-WHS. For Maun locals to remain relevant in their village's development and participate directly in the new brand of tourism, they have to tap into inner resources — like cultural heritage. We identified 'dormant' cultural values in features and sites which had intangible but important cultural significance. We hope that this 'remembered' information about specific spaces and landscapes, and the 'dormant' values associated with them, will provide a way to reintegrate cultural values and meanings into contemporary consciousness, and by extension integrate them into newly branded tourism identities.

We have suggested several potential activities which could build on the values embedded in 'forgotten' places and landscapes, but we do not know if, or how, these ideas will become reality. Our goal is that this still on-going applied research project will benefit one village and provide a model for others that must intersect with the high-investment tourism industry. We believe that the type of cultural documentation described here can allow communities to participate meaningfully in tourism while using cultural and heritage resources to their advantage. Rather than being obscured by commercial tourism development, these communities can use cultural and heritage resources to safeguard their identities and as a comparative advantage to enhance their participation in modern tourism.

Acknowledgements

Our gratitude goes to Batawana Tribal Authority, in particular *Kgosi* Kealetile Moremi's office and *Kgosi* Charles Letsholathebe for putting us in touch with the various *Dikgosi* and village elders to interview. We thank all *Dikgosi* and elders that we interviewed for their time and patience in providing information and travelling around the Maun village surveying features and landscapes. Of particular mention are: O. Ledimo, R. Matlhare, R. Marumo, C. Lelatlhego, T. Lekang, K. G. Ramokwena, J. Sedumedi, M. Bendu, P.B Ledimo, P. Makwati, P. Shashe, R.K. Rabosigo, M. Moeti, M. Setlhare, M. Mhapha, B. Majatsie, K.R. Segole, M. Dithapo, L. Mogalakwe and elders T. Monwela and K. Diako. We would also like to thank the anonymous reviewers for their comments that enhanced the quality of the manuscript. Our gratitude also goes to the journal editors, Carol McDavid and Suzie Thomas, for their patient guidance in incorporating comments that improved the manuscript. We thank the University of Botswana (Okavango Research Institute), and the Government of Botswana's Ministry of Education Skills and Development for research funding.

Notes

1 Our research has both policy and research purposes. Thus it is important to include the names of leaders and place-names in publications.

2 Article 40, Part IV (4) (DTRP 2013).

3 Article 40, Part IV (4) (DCC 2013).

4 Part III, section 1.10 (DCC 2013)

ORCID

Susan Osireditse Keitumetse ⓘ http://orcid.org/0000-0001-8669-1049

References

Bernard, Ted, and Neo. Moetapele. 2005. "Dessication of the Gomoti River: Biophysical Process and Indigenous Resource Management in Northern Botswana." *Journal of Arid Environments* 63 (1): 256–283. doi:10.1016/j.jaridenv.2005.02.001.

Burghardt, Andrew F. 1971. "A Hypothesis about Gateway Cities." *Annals of the Association of American Geographers* 61 (2): 269–285.

Chirenje, Mutero J. 1977. *A History of Northern Botswana: 1850–1910*. London: Associated University Presses.

Chung, Kimberely. 2002. *Issues and Approaches in the Use of Integrated Methods.* In Michael Bamberger (ed), Integrating Quantitative and Qualitative Research in Development Projects, pp. 37–52. Washington DC: World Bank.

Coulson, Sheila, Staurset Sigrit, and Walker, Nick. 2011. "Ritualized Behaviour in the Middle Stone Age: Evidence from Rhino Cave, Tsodilo Hills, Botswana." *PaleoAnthropology* 42: 18–61.

Department of Town and Regional Planning Act, 2013 (DTRP 2013). *Ministry of Lands & Housing, Department of Town and Regional Planning.* Gaborone, Republic of Botswana: Government Printer.

Development Control Code 2013 (DCC 2013). *Ministry of Lands and Housing, Department of Town and Regional Planning.* Gaborone, Republic of Botswana: Government Printer.

Dikole, Walter. 1978. "Sekgoma Letsholathebe's Tawana Rule and its Check by the British Administration." Bachelor of Arts degree (History) diss., University of Botswana and Swaziland: University College Botswana.

Düsing, Sandra. 2002. *Traditional Leadership and Democratisation in Southern Africa: A Comparative Study of Botswana, Namibia, and Southern Africa.* London: LIT Verlag Munster.

Frauman, Eric, and Sarah Banks. 2011. "Gateway Community Resident Perceptions of Tourism Development: Incorporating Importance-performance Analysis into a Limits of Acceptable Change Framework." *Tourism Management* 32: 128–140.

Hammami, Feras. 2012. "Culture and Planning for Change and Continuity in Botswana." *Journal of Planning Education and Research* 32: 262–277.

Hirth, Kenneth G. 1978. "Interregional Trade and the Formation of Prehistoric Gateway Communities." *American Antiquity* 43 (1): 35–45.

Keitumetse, Susan O. 2011. "Sustainable Development and Cultural Heritage Management in Botswana: Towards Sustainable Communities." *Sustainable Development* 19: 49–59.

Keitumetse, Susan O. 2014. "Cultural Resources as Sustainability Enablers: Community-based Cultural Heritage Resources Management (COBACHREM) model." *Sustainability* 6 (1): 70–85.

Ketlogetswe, Ame. 2014. "Keitumetse Underscores Need for Sustained Cultural Heritage." *Botswana Daily News*, September 15, 2014. Accessed June 9, 2015. http://www.dailynews.gov.bw/news-details.php?nid = 14497.

Marcucci, Daniel J. 2000. "Landscape History as a Planning Tool." *Landscape and Urban Planning* 49: 67–81.

McCarthy, Terence S., A. Bloem, and P. A. Larkin. 1998. "Observations on the Hydrology and Geohydrology of the Okavango Delta." *South African Journal of Geology* 101 (2): 101–117.

McMahon, Edward T. 1999. "Gateway Communities." *Planning Commissioners' Journal* 34: 06–07.

Mitchell, Nora, Mechtild Rössler, and Pierre-Marie Tricaud. 2009. *World Heritage Cultural Landscapes – A Handbook for Conservation and Management.* Paris: UNESCO World Heritage Centre. Accessed June 5, 2015. Website: http://whc.unesco.org/documents/publi_wh_papers_26_en.pdf.

Ndlovu, Ndukuyakhe. 2011. "Legislation as an Instrument in South African Heritage Management: Is it Effective?" *Conservation and Management of Archaeological Sites* 13 (1): 31–57.

Nyati-Ramahobo, Lydia. 2002. "From a Phone Call to the High Court: Wayeyi Visibility and the Kamanakao Association's Campaign for Linguistic and Cultural Rights in Botswana." *Journal of Southern African Studies* 28 (4): 685–709.

Parker, Patricia L., and Thomas F. King. 1990. *Guidelines for Evaluating and Documenting Traditional Cultural Properties.* National Register Bulletin 38, edited by National Park Service. Washington, D.C.: US National Park Service.

Peters, Mark A. 1972. "Notes on Place Names of Ngamiland." *Botswana Notes and Records* 4: 219–233.

Ramsar Bureau. (1971). *Ramsar Convention on Wetlands.* Switzerland: Ramsar Bureau. Modified 26 October 2001. Accessed March 23, 2015. http://archive.ramsar.org/cda/en/ramsar-activities-wwds-cultural-heritage-of-20558/main/ramsar/1-63-78%5E20558_4000_0.

Robbins, Larry H., M. L. Murphy, George A. Brook, Andrew H. Ivester, Alec C. Campbell, Richard G. Klein, Richard G. Milo, Kathlyn M. Stewart, William S. Downey, and Nancy J. Stevens. 2000. "Archaeology, Palaeoenvironment and Chronology of the Tsodilo Hills, White Paintings Rock Shelter, Northwest Kalahari Desert, Botswana." *Journal of Archaeological Science* 27 (11): 1085–1113.

Rössler, M. 2005. *Cultural Heritage Landscapes – An Introduction.* Toronto: ICOMOS' International Scientific Committee on Cultural Landscape.

Saarinen, Jarkko, Naomi Moswete, Masego J. Monare. 2014. "Cultural Tourism: New Opportunities for Diversifying the Tourism Industry in Botswana." *Bulletin of Geography. Socio-economic Series* 26: 7–18.

Statistics Botswana. 2011. *Population of Towns and Villages and Associated Localities*. Gaborone, Republic of Botswana: Government Printing and Publishing Services.

Tlou, Thomas. 1971a. "Chief Sekgoma Letsholathebe II: Rebel or 20th Century Tswana Nationalist?" *Botswana Notes and Records* 3: 64–69.

Tlou, Thomas. 1972. "A Political History of Northwestern Botswana to 1906." PhD dissertation, University of Wisconsin.

UNESCO (United Nations Educational, Scientific, and Cultural Organization). n.d. "What is Intangible Cultural Heritage?" UNESCO web site: http://www.unesco.org/culture/ich/index.php?lg = en&pg = 00002.

UNESCO. 2003. United Nations Educational, Scientific and Cultural Organization (UNESCO) meeting, Paris, 29 September to 17th October 2003, 32nd session. Convention for the safeguarding of the intangible cultural heritage, adopted 17th October 2003. Paris: France.

Wolski, Piotr, and Hubertus Henricus Gerardus Savenije. 2006. "Dynamics of Floodplain-island Groundwater Flow in the Okavango Delta, Botswana." *Journal of Hydrology* 320 (3): 283–301.

Index